BLOOD ON HER HANDS

BLOOD ON HER HANDS

SOUTH AFRICA'S MOST NOTORIOUS FEMALE KILLERS

TANYA FARBER

Jonathan Ball Publishers
Johannesburg & Cape Town

All rights reserved.
No part of this publication may be reproduced or transmitted, in any form or by any means, without prior permission from the publisher or copyright holder.

© Text Tanya Farber, 2019
© Published edition Jonathan Ball Publishers, 2019

Published in South Africa in 2019 by
JONATHAN BALL PUBLISHERS
A division of Media24 (Pty) Ltd
PO Box 33977
Jeppestown
2043

ISBN 978-1-86842-926-4
ebook ISBN 978-1-86842-927-1

Every effort has been made to trace the copyright holders and to obtain their permission for the use of copyright material. The publishers apologise for any errors or omissions and would be grateful to be notified of any corrections that should be incorporated in future editions of this book.

Twitter: www.twitter.com/JonathanBallPub
Facebook: www.facebook.com/JonathanBallPublishers
Blog: http://jonathanball.bookslive.co.za/

Cover by publicide
Design and typesetting by Catherine Coetzer
Set in EB Garamond

This book is dedicated to my late parents, who understood and nurtured my love of writing, and to Jeremy, Sophia and Naomi, who have gently held my hand during the writing.

CONTENTS

INTRODUCTION		1
CHAPTER 1	DAISY DE MELKER	5
CHAPTER 2	MARLENE LEHNBERG	28
CHAPTER 3	CHARMAINE PHILLIPS	50
CHAPTER 4	JOEY HAARHOFF	73
CHAPTER 5	DINA RODRIGUES	103
CHAPTER 6	NAJWA PETERSEN	127
CHAPTER 7	CELIWE MBOKAZI	150
CHAPTER 8	CHANÉ VAN HEERDEN	173
CHAPTER 9	PHOENIX RACING CLOUD THERON	192
CHAPTER 10	INSIGHTS	213
ACKNOWLEDGEMENTS		237
NOTES		239
SOURCES		252

INTRODUCTION

✝✝

Meet Daisy de Melker, who 'lovingly' prepared a flask of strychnine-laced coffee for her son. She is very different from Najwa Petersen, who carefully planned a 'house robbery' to eliminate her musician husband. Chané van Heerden placed her victim's facial skin in the freezer for preservation, yet Phoenix Racing Cloud Theron wished to dispose of her mother's body before it was even cold. And Dina Rodrigues? She 'wouldn't harm a fly' – but then went and organised a hit on a baby.

Women are not paragons of virtue who cannot commit murder. Nor are they always insane when they do deliberately cause death. And the women with 'blood on their hands' are not homogeneous.

Ironically, the idea for this book came to life during the trial of a male murderer. For months, I had reported on the Henri van Breda trial in the High Court in Cape Town. The young man's parents and brother had been brutally axed to death in January 2015 at their luxury home outside Stellenbosch. His badly injured sister survived the ordeal but had no recollection of the attack.

There was a bottomless curiosity among readers about the trial, and obvious questions began to well up in my mind as to why this could be. Was it the family's wealth? The brutality of the attacks? The familial nature of it? Basically, what makes one murder trial more fascinating than another? Out of these questions came some uncomfortable answers. Whether we admit it or not, there's an insatiable hunger for tales of murder that sit outside the norm, and that's where female murderers come in.

Statistically, female murderers are major outliers, making up only five per cent of all killers. Also, they seldom match the more common masculine narratives of impulsive violence. With the careful planning that often goes into murders committed by women, we're drawn to their interior world in a way that we are not with their male counterparts. We find ourselves trying to fathom what they were thinking.

The result is that archetypes have proliferated over the centuries – black widows, femmes fatales, sexy assassins, creepy nurses, baby-faced butchers, to mention but a few. These archetypes dictate how we think or write about such women but leave little room for the minutiae of an individual's life, psyche and act of murder.

In the pages of this book I have, I hope, let each story speak for itself. Before going into the hard facts of each case, I've begun it with an up-close-and-personal imagining of the interior world of the murderer and what a day in her life and mind might have looked like; this has required a measure of poetic licence on my part.

INTRODUCTION

The final chapter gathers insights from local and international experts, analysis, data and other stories from across the globe that resonate with those from our own shores.

There are also many other South African women who are labelled 'murderers' but whom I've deliberately left out of this book. They include the woman who takes the law into her hands after years of savage abuse by her partner; or the single mother living in abject poverty in a shack who leaves her newborn baby at the bottom of a bin because she sees no way out of her situation; or the mother who kills her tik-addicted son because he is destroying everything in his path ...

The women in this book could not, in my opinion, blame their circumstances for what they did.

Tanya Farber
Cape Town
May 2019

CHAPTER 1

DAISY DE MELKER

✚

Germiston, 1932

One morning in late February, a middle-aged woman with a downturned mouth and deep blue eyes pulled back the covers of her bed with more vigour than usual.

Just to the left of her wardrobe was a chocolate-brown dress that she'd laid out on an armchair; placed neatly on top of it was a hat – almost brown but leaning more towards the colour of cream of mushroom soup. At 46, the woman had ceased to imagine herself in the glamorous slimline dresses drawn in fine detail on the sewing patterns sold in the shop down the road. For starters, they were tailored at the waist to such an extent that, on the rare occasions she had ventured to wear such a style, she felt as if she was in prison. That's not to say the brown summer dress and hat weren't some version of that style. They were just more – she paused to think of the word in her head – practical. The ideal outfit for the day that lay ahead.

Before putting on the dress, she made herself a strong cup of coffee and opened the window as wide as it would go. She remembered Robert, her late husband, always complaining that she liked to keep the house cool. If the roof could open, you would pull it back too, he used to tell her. Poor Robert. His glasses still sat on a small bookcase nearby. But the book he'd been reading, a detective novel, was just the perfect thickness to prop up the one side of the bed to even things out a little. She'd slipped it under one corner of the base and was delighted at how, for the first time since she'd witnessed violent convulsions on the mattress, the bed didn't feel as if it were tilting towards the South Pole. Come to think of it, it had always felt lopsided to her, even before the convulsions, even back in the day when the person on the other side was not Robert but her first husband, William – the one who'd bought the house in the first place and whose plumbing tools still sat in a metal box in the shed. Poor William.

She looked in the mirrored panel of her wardrobe, pulled the mushroom-soup hat over her head, and picked up her handbag. Walking down the narrow passage in a house that felt smaller every day, she glanced into the kitchen. She thought of how she'd rinsed her son Rhodes's blue coffee flask and stacked it on the drying rack the night before. There it still stood, next to the butter dish Robert had bought her at the department store. Or was it William who'd bought it? She couldn't recall.

She also glanced into her son's bedroom, off to the left, and felt her anger rise. After all she'd done for him! How she'd squandered her money on motorbikes for him and that trip to Europe! And now this:

the unmade bed, the plate that hadn't been taken to the kitchen, the perky cat sitting on the sill with no clue what a slovenly ... She stopped herself just short of swearing out loud. He was, after all, her flesh and blood. As had been the little twins. And her two other children. The dearly departed.

Leaving the house, she adjusted the collar on her dress. Not quite the picture on the sewing pattern, she told herself, but glamorous enough nonetheless. Hollywood will add the glitz later, she told herself, waving to someone's gardener as if she were a movie star on the red carpet and he an adoring fan. This added a bounce to her step, and as she made her way down the street, she thought of her son and the plan in her mind. The prospect made her walk with even more determination than before.

After a while, however, she could feel blisters developing on her feet. She was wearing a pair of velvet shoes, not quite the right size, that she'd bought just after William's untimely death.

Now she put her mind to the plan. Unusually, she had some distance to cover. Also unusually, she had no shopping list folded in her handbag; she would pass the butcher, the dairy and the greengrocer without so much as a sideways glance. Today, there was just one item she was after, and for that purpose she need only visit the chemist.

As she walked, she could feel the sun reddening her skin, but got some reprieve as soon as she boarded the first of two trams as she made her way into Johannesburg. It was a warm day, typical of February, with the temperature hovering around 25 °C. A few clouds were gathering for a possible afternoon thunderstorm that could burst just as quickly as it would end.

Daisy imagined herself taking a broad brush dipped in pale blue paint to the skyline, easily covering all that displeased her with one flick of the wrist. How hard could it be to remove all the things one detested from this world, she asked herself.

Earlier, on her way out of Germiston, she had noticed that even more factories had sprung up in the industrial area on the outskirts of the town, pumping out grey smoke. The factories weren't visible from her house; she could pretend to be living anywhere. But seeing them today had seemed to trap her inside the confines of a life too ordinary.

Later, after she got to Johannesburg and boarded another tram for the last leg of the journey, the conversations of fellow passengers automatically drew her in, but what she really craved was silence – the same thing she craved every day when her son returned from work, trampling heavily across the kitchen floor, with the large satchel on his back sometimes dragging a mug or two off the counter.

After catching one more tram, she finally arrived in Turffontein, not far from the racecourse, near her old home. Eager as she was to get to her destination, she first allowed herself the small indulgence of a 15-minute detour to visit the house at 22 Tully Street, which she had once called home. With a quickened step, she almost trotted down the road, the brown material of the dress now clinging to her legs as she moved. She turned the corner, and there it was – the double-storey, gabled house she had occupied with William.

The house, with its large bay windows, sunny *voorkamer* (front room), pressed-steel ceilings and wooden floors, had been built in 1903, by which time Turffontein was an established suburb thanks to its renowned racecourse, a Johannesburg landmark built in 1887. The racecourse had brought glamour, style and well-heeled crowds to the area, making Daisy feel cosmopolitan in a way her own mother could never have dreamed. The suburb was also the perfect place to bring up children.

As she stood there, she remembered Rhodes as a toddler, climbing up onto the window seat and staring out, with the ear of his fluffy bunny in his mouth. For a moment she felt a wave of tenderness, as if the intervening years had never happened and her life as a wife and mother still lay undiscovered in front of her …

The sharp bark of a dog brought her back to reality, and she turned in her velvet shoes and headed for the chemist.

Walking through its familiar ornate wooden doors, she felt almost dizzy with excitement. The smell of antiseptic and soap, the shelves stacked with plasters and painkillers, drugs to loosen the bowels or tighten them up, toxins, tonics, scissors, you name it … Almost aroused just by being there, she straightened her hat and walked towards the counter. There stood the pharmacist, Abraham Spilkin. As polite as ever, he told her how elegant she looked, and she beamed.

His tone made her feel like a lady who'd grown up in the dappled shade of an apricot tree on an expansive lawn with a governess at her side. Such thoughts brought stability to her mind, erasing the memories of being one of 11 children in a small town on the platteland. It was also a time when any opportunity 'up north' could suddenly lure parents and older siblings away.

'What can I get you today, madam?' Mr Spilkin asked.

Daisy quickly dropped the corners of her mouth, and said in a small, sad voice, 'I have a very sick cat in my care, I'm afraid. The poor thing can hardly move for wincing in pain.'

The chemist suggested she visit the vet to see what could be done for the poor creature, but Daisy clarified that the kindest thing she could do right now for an animal in a living hell was to put an end to its misery. The kindly Mr Spilkin offered to do the deed for her, in case the prospect was too traumatic for her.

'Thank you kindly for the most generous offer,' Daisy said, 'but I feel that the distance would be too far for the sickly animal to travel. Besides which, as a trained nurse, I'm more than capable of doing it myself, however much it's going to break my heart, and I know just the right dose to give.'

Mr Spilkin carefully prepared the package, then took from behind the counter the poisons register – a compulsory record of the sales and purchases of dangerous substances. Arsenic, after all, wasn't something to be trifled with. In England, the odourless, tasteless and colourless substance had gained notoriety as the poisoner's tool of choice: the so-called inheritor's powder had shown up in 237 cases in English courts between 1750 and 1914.

But this was clearly just about a sickly cat, and so Mr Spilkin passed Daisy the register. With a steady hand, she wrote, 'Mrs DL Sproat, 22 Tully Street, Turffontein'. This wasn't her legal name (by then she was Mrs De Melker), but she knew better than to betray herself in the register. Before Mr Spilkin could extend the conversation any further, she slipped her purchase into her handbag, thanked him, and quickly left.

The first thing she did when she arrived home was pull off the velvet shoes and soak her feet in a basin of warm, soapy water. The relief. The feeling instantly took her back to her nursing days in her early twenties. She had worked so diligently in a hospital in Johannesburg that she would forget about the tight-fitting shoes on her feet until her shift was over. Once home, just like now, she would let out a long but barely audible sigh of relief. It came back to her now – how she had decided one night, while staring at her toes in the murky water, that she would one day be married and leave the hard work of nursing behind her.

The cat, looking as spritely as ever, jumped off the windowsill and slunk past her. She could have sworn it knew what she was up to. After drying her feet with a fluffy cream-coloured towel, she climbed onto a chair in the kitchen with the package of arsenic held tightly in her hand. On the top shelf, just out of sight even as she stood on the chair, was an empty biscuit tin, the slightly rusted one with the navy-blue flowers along the lip. She felt for it, carefully slid it forward, and placed the tiny package directly behind it. There it would sit until five days later, when she prepared a flask of coffee for her son to take to work.

That trip to the chemist in her old stamping ground, where Mr Spilkin had served her at the varnished teak counter, would later seal Daisy's fate at the end of a hangman's noose.

The name Daisy de Melker would become synonymous with the cold-blooded modus operandi of a female serial killer. There have been few such women recorded across the globe, either before or after Daisy, which is strange when you consider the size of the world's population.

Would the telltale signs of such a personality have shown up in the early years of a child's life? Perhaps – unless they were buried under the noise and mayhem of a house teeming with children. How likely would it be that odd behaviour would attract the attention of parents trying to feed, raise and educate 11 children, as was the case in the household in which Daisy grew up?

The answer is 'not very', and if you were to scour Daisy's premarital life for any signs of psychiatric illness, the evidence plotted on a spectrum would only get as far as 'restlessness' and nowhere near 'psychopathy'. For the latter, she would have had to display signs such as cruelty to animals, fearlessness when breaking rules, violent outbursts, manipulating others, and lying and stealing just for the fun of it. Daisy's early life revealed no record of such traits. And yet, from the very day earmarked for her fairytale wedding, at the age of 21, the red flags of psychopathy begin to stand out.

Born to William and Fanny Hancorn-Smith in 1886 – the year Johannesburg itself was born – Daisy Louisa Hancorn-Smith spent her early life in the village of Seven Fountains, near Grahamstown, in today's Eastern Cape province. The village had been established in the 1700s as a resting place for ox-wagons making their way across this vast landscape. The Dutch had called the area the Zuurveld. In 1820, farms that had been abandoned by them were allocated to poor British settlers who had been recruited by their government to strengthen the English population on the frontier of the Cape Colony. The name 'Seven Fountains' came from the profusion of natural springs in the vicinity.

Though Daisy's family was not particularly poor, Seven Fountains never grew beyond its roots, and by the time Daisy was born, it was still a minuscule and undeveloped village surrounded by sparsely situated farmsteads. As is the case today, most of the local inhabitants were farmers.

In Daisy's time, the Methodist church was the heart of the Seven Fountains community. There are no records of whether Daisy's family sat in that church on the slow Sundays that linked one parochial week to the next, but what the records do show is that when Daisy was aged around eight, her father and two older brothers packed up and headed off to Bulawayo (in what was then Rhodesia), where land was being given to Britons for next to nothing. This journey, as well as the journey made by many others to Johannesburg on the hunt for gold, was commonly referred to as 'going north'.

Two years later, several other families from Seven Fountains made the same trip to Rhodesia, and Daisy was sent along with them on the seven-day journey to be delivered to her father and brothers. It is not known why she left her mother at such a tender age, but one record[1] speculates that this may have been for her safety. Tensions were brewing between the British and the Boer republics, and there was talk of war. Another record states that Daisy's mother had left the family by then and had married a man in Port Elizabeth, passing away shortly thereafter.[2] This would have been a major trauma for the young girl, and would also have necessitated her travelling 'up north' to join her father. Whatever the truth may be, her mother disappears from the record at this point.

In Bulawayo, she attended a farm school, and over the next two years two of her older married sisters also arrived in Rhodesia. Then, when she turned 13, she packed her bags once again, this time being sent off to board at the Good Hope Seminary in Cape Town, where she would wake up early each morning and get dressed in a prim black-and-white uniform and panama hat.

This notion of being shipped off for schooling elsewhere was not uncommon in those days. Many children left the homestead to attend school in more developed areas such as Cape Town. For Daisy, this was simply a part of life, and she remained at the Good Hope Seminary until she was 17. She had thus spent the better part of her teenage years in the company of fellow boarders rather than her own family.

In 1903, she returned to Rhodesia for a short spell, and then headed back to South Africa, this time to Durban, to enrol as a trainee nurse at the Berea Nursing Home. It was here that Daisy learned about medication, disease and the effects of different substances on the human body.

During her studies, she regularly travelled home to Rhodesia for holidays, and it was on one of these trips that Daisy met a young man named Bert Fuller, who worked in the native affairs department in the mining town of Broken Hill, in what was then Northern Rhodesia (today Kabwe in Zambia). Around the time of their whirlwind romance, Broken Hill was starting to flourish. In 1902, the discovery of lead and zinc deposits here had spurred the establishment of a fast-growing settlement. By 1906, the centrally located town was connected to the colony's fast-expanding railway system.

Bert and Daisy were likely among the many young people on the lookout for entertainment in a town that was on the brink of a major growth spurt. Any outing after dark meant calling on a *mlonda* (watchman), who would hold a paraffin lamp in one hand and an assegai in the other, in case a wild animal decided to pounce. The *mlonda* would wait until the social event ended before walking the partygoers back home.

Another part of life here was the *Anopheles* mosquito, and it was the bite of a mosquito that would change the fate of the besotted young couple. Daisy and Bert were to be married in late October 1907, but by the time the big day arrived, instead of donning his wedding suit and saying his 'I do's', poor Bert was prostrate in bed, overcome with a rapid pulse, high fever and extreme chills. The first day of their 'happily ever after' turned into a spectacle of death as Bert's life came to an excruciating end, with Daisy by his bedside.

The doctors said he'd died from blackwater fever, a complication of malaria that rapidly destroys the body's red blood cells, causes intense jaundice, and turns the urine a dark reddish-black colour (hence the name). Interestingly, the disease is thought to spring from an autoimmune reaction in some people when malaria and quinine come together in the body. In those days, quinine was given as a preventive against malaria, and civil servants like Bert were regularly given doses free of charge by the colonial government.

Given Daisy's unfolding history from that day onwards, it has been suggested – most interestingly by her own defence lawyer long after her trial – that it was she, and not the dreaded blackwater fever, that was the real cause of Bert's death. After all, many of the symptoms of the disease are not unlike those of poisoning: both arsenic and blackwater fever destroy red blood cells, cause havoc in the kidneys, and send chills through the body and blood into the urine. But, with little available evidence to back up this theory, it must remain confined to a dark corner of history.

What is certain, however, is that following Bert's death, Daisy got her first delicious taste of passive income. Not more than a couple of days before his end, Bert had signed a will bequeathing £100 (equivalent to about R100 000 today, at a time when the average salary was around £4 a week) to his wife-to-be, and after she had grieved at his bedside, the money promptly became hers.

She spent the next few months as a single woman, but then, at age 22, in Johannesburg, she happened upon one William Alfred (Alf) Cowle, a man 14 years her senior. A plumber, he plied his trade in a city that was developing so fast off the back of its booming mining industry that he was never short of work. Eighteen months after the death of her beloved fiancé, Daisy tied the knot with Alf and the blackwater tragedy was all but forgotten.

What happened over the next few years could be seen in two different ways, and therein lies the mystery of everything we think we know about Daisy de Melker. On the one hand, Daisy and Alf were an average couple living in Turffontein, enjoying the buzz of a growing city, making a good living from its need for services, and, eventually, bearing five children to share their lives in the gabled double-storey house on Tully Street.

On the other hand, all but one of those children succumbed to illness, and though death in childhood was far more common in those days than it is today, the circumstances surrounding the deaths of Daisy's children are chilling, as is the fact that they raised no suspicions. First, there were the twins. Born prematurely, as twins often are, they came out of their mother's womb slight and fragile. Entrusted to the care of a very young woman who clearly had mental-health issues, perhaps the little ones never had a fighting chance. But whether Daisy murdered them or they died from neglect, or they were simply too delicate for this world, is impossible to say. They both died in infancy, and the lack of historical data makes it impossible to know.

Child number three was ambitiously named Rhodes Cecil, after the British imperialist, businessman, mining magnate and politician who had died about a decade earlier. Born in 1911, Rhodes Cecil was a robust child, requiring far less attention than the twins had, and he soon became his mother's favourite. As much as she resented him when he got older, she doted on him as a young boy, and his childhood, as far as we know, was normal and stable, and probably not very different from those of his peers in the neighbourhood.

Then came Lester, born in 1913. There was nothing to suggest that the boy was unhealthy or frail, but at some point before his fifth birthday he was laid to rest under a hot sun, with Daisy standing by the grave in a broad-brimmed black hat. How tragic it had been, Daisy told her acquaintances and friends, that the little boy had developed an abscess on his liver for which there was no cure.

And then came the fifth and last child, who was named Alfred Eric. Perhaps because he was not as adored as his older brother Rhodes, or perhaps through the sheer coincidence of where diseases and mysterious ailments choose to strike, he too met an untimely death not long after his first birthday. When he was 15 months old, he was suddenly overcome with violent convulsions and taken upstairs to a room in the Tully Street house. There he writhed around on the bed for just a few minutes before all movement ceased.

The deaths of four out of five of Daisy's children did not attract much attention: no concerns were ever raised in the halls of gossip in her community, nor down at the police station. Daisy, instead, was viewed as a strong survivor who had endured the deaths of one fiancé and four children.

There is little documentation about family life in the Cowle home in the years that followed, but what is known is that they moved to a single-storey house in Germiston, where Alf worked as a plumber. Rhodes, having lost four siblings at a young age, might have been somewhat indulged by his parents. Daisy was utterly devoted to him and to her role as his mother. And life simply carried on – until 1923, when tragedy struck again.

One morning in January of that year, Daisy prepared some Epsom salts for her husband. There was nothing unusual about this – he had regular aches and pains, for which Epsom salts, a natural remedy, were just the ticket. But on 11 January, something strange unfolded: after taking the salts, Alf complained to Daisy that he felt even worse than before.

She immediately called a doctor, who came over to see what help could be administered. At that stage, Alf's symptoms were mild enough for the doctor to shrug them off, and he prescribed a bromide mixture. This prescription suggests that Alf was already showing signs of convulsions and muscle spasms; bromides, and particularly potassium bromide, were commonly used as a sedative and anticonvulsant in the early 20th century.

It was after the departure of the first doctor, however, that things really took a turn for the worse. Soon, the plumber was in agony, and Daisy, saying she was unable to cope on her own, called the neighbours to be with her. They decided that the opinion of a second doctor was in order, and rather urgently.

By the time the next doctor walked through the doors of the small white house, Alf had turned a decided shade of purple. Foam oozed from his mouth, his muscles were convulsing uncontrollably, and as the doctor tried to examine him, he recoiled in pain. Before the doctor could do anything, Alf died right there on the bed, his face contorted in agony.

If Daisy had fooled the first doctor, she had no such luck with the second, who had seen the symptoms in full force. He refused to sign the death certificate, as he suspected poisoning. All the signs pointed to strychnine. After ingesting strychnine, a person does not immediately start flailing around and turning purple. The symptoms come on more slowly, and at any rate, Daisy might very well first have given her husband a low dose. The symptoms of a low dose are consistent with what the first doctor had witnessed: agitation, fear, restlessness, muscle spasms and a tight jaw. With a higher dose, such as the one possibly administered by Daisy between the two visits from the physicians, the symptoms are far more extreme and present much more quickly. There are major convulsions, which injure the kidneys and liver. The arms and legs go rigid, and the back and neck arch. Finally, and quickly, the person can no longer breathe. Robbed of oxygen, they turn a shade of bluish-purple. Alf Cowle's symptoms certainly fitted the description.

At this stage, Daisy might have been in a bit of a panic. Would her plot be exposed? Would the doctor report his suspicions to the police, and would she hear an unwelcome knock at the door sometime soon? No. None of this came to pass. An autopsy was carried out on the badly damaged body of William Alfred Cowle, and the death certificate recorded the cause of death as 'chronic nephritis and cerebral haemorrhage'. The former is a disease of the kidneys and is characterised by nausea, vomiting, twitchy muscles and shortness of breath. Alf had experienced these symptoms, and the use of the word 'chronic' implied that the loss of his healthy kidney functioning had taken place over time. As for the cerebral haemorrhage, this simply meant he had bleeding inside the brain. The wording of the death certificate quickly put paid to any risk that foul play would be suspected on Daisy's part. It suggested a fatal episode resulting from a dread disease.

Daisy had watched her late husband's body being taken out on a stretcher. She'd seen the death certificate, which explained to the world how he'd died. All that remained in this three-act play was the cashing of a cheque to the tune of £1 795 (comparable to around R2 million today), which she'd inherited from the dearly departed.

For the next three years Daisy and Rhodes Cecil – who was no longer the sweet child she'd adored and was instead, as he entered his teens, becoming increasingly difficult – lived alone in the house she'd inherited. Then Daisy met Robert Sproat, another plumber, who at age 50 was ten years her senior.

Sproat, who had accrued considerable wealth through clever investments and financial planning, asked for Daisy's hand in marriage within months of meeting her. Strangely, the date they chose for the nuptials was the anniversary of Alf's death.

Daisy and Robert were married for almost two years, but by all accounts the household was not a happy one. The problem lay not with the married couple, but rather with the tension that quickly arose between Rhodes Cecil and his stepfather. It is alleged that Robert found his stepson to be spoilt, petulant and quick to anger, while Rhodes Cecil, for his part, was likely possessive of his mother. Having outlived all siblings and his father, he had had Daisy all to himself for several years, and now, in his teenage years, he did not take kindly to Robert's arrival.

Three months shy of Daisy and Robert's second anniversary, her second husband presented with symptoms uncannily similar to those of her first. Robert began vomiting and convulsing, and complained of severe pain. It was during this bout of illness that his brother, William, travelled from Pretoria to see him. While the sick man lay in his bed, Daisy convinced William over a cup of tea to get his brother to sign a new will that would leave everything to her. As it turned out, Robert survived the ordeal, during which his wife had acted as nurse. When he recovered, life as everyone knew it carried on for another month. All that had really changed was his will.

A few weeks later, on a Sunday in November 1927, Daisy prepared a tray of beer and brought it to her husband, who sat relaxing on the stoep on his one day off. Rhodes sat with his mother and stepfather, who sipped the refreshing drink. A few minutes later, Robert grabbed his abdomen in agony, stood up, and collapsed. The symptoms were similar to the attack of the previous month, but worse. Daisy once again summoned the neighbours and the doctor, flawlessly playing the role of the panic-stricken wife. She wedged herself firmly into a chair next to the bed of her dying husband – a bed to which he had now been strapped because of the violent convulsions washing over him.

Once again, the cause of death was recorded by the doctor as cerebral haemorrhage, and once again Daisy's bank account swelled. This time, she was left a whopping £4 000 (approximately R4.5 million today), plus a further £560 from Robert's pension fund.

Robert was buried next to Alf at the recently established Brixton Cemetery in Johannesburg. Family plots were common at Brixton, and so it was that two strangers who had never met one another, but who were joined in death by a past with Daisy, came to lie side by side.

With Robert now safely in the ground, Daisy had enough money to indulge her unemployed son's every material wish. This included setting off on a cruise to Europe together and even buying him a motorbike, which had to be shipped back to Johannesburg.

Some four years later, it was time to marry again. Seemingly with a penchant for plumbers, Daisy chose the widower Sidney Clarence de Melker, a plumber who had a daughter named Eileen, only two years younger than Rhodes Cecil. Loving and devoted, Sidney was everything Daisy had dreamed of: a kind stepfather, a man with a distinguished career as a Springbok rugby player and, like her two previous husbands, a reliable source of income. You might imagine that after marrying Daisy he too might not have been long for this world. But this is where a dramatic twist occurs: the next loved one marked for death was none other than Rhodes Cecil, by now aged 19, who had outlived four siblings, a father and a stepfather.

With the motive a little less clear, various theories have been advanced to explain the poisoning of Rhodes Cecil: one was that the lazy and pampered young man stood to inherit money of his own (willed to him by his father) on his 21st birthday – or at least he believed he did – and spoke of it often in Daisy's presence. He had also, by then, become a menace in the house, frequently hurling abuse at both his mother and his stepsister. Another theory was that he had witnessed the symptoms of the previous poisoning events, and Daisy was worried that as he grew older, he would realise what had unfolded.[3]

On 2 March 1932, Rhodes headed off to the only job he'd been able to hold down: carrying out minor repairs on cars and trucks. Slung across his body was the leather satchel in which he carried some neatly cut sandwiches and a blue Thermos of coffee that his mother had prepared for him.

During the first coffee break of the day, he generously offered his friend at work, James Webster, a swig of the still-warm coffee. It was strong, and James had only a little. Rhodes, however, poured himself a large mug of it and finished it all before the shift recommenced.

Very suddenly, both men began to feel decidedly ill – but both recovered. James felt better within a day, and Rhodes even went off to play rugby after work. The experienced Daisy apparently hadn't dosed the coffee with enough of the white powder purchased from Mr Spilkin. One theory is that Daisy was more familiar with the workings and dosages of strychnine than arsenic, or perhaps, on a subconscious level, she was wavering about whether to kill her only child. If the latter was the case, she soon recovered the courage of her convictions.

A few days later, Rhodes played his part in the by-now-familiar final act: the convulsing man in bed, the panic-stricken woman at his side, the neighbours and doctors called in to help, only to witness a patient foaming at the mouth, turning purple, and taking his last breath.

And, once again, the post mortem kept Daisy's secret: Rhodes had died, it was reported, of cerebral malaria, contracted when he'd worked in Swaziland, and which had lain dormant until then. Daisy once again received a sum of money, although in this case it was only £100, paid to her because of an indemnity form that Rhodes, at her request, had filled in during that same contract job in Swaziland.

Rhodes was interred beside his father and stepfather at Brixton Cemetery. It seems strange that nobody – or almost nobody – suspected Daisy to have had a hand in the remarkably similar deaths of her loved ones. Was it because the unsophisticated medical diagnoses and post mortems of the time lacked the rigour and technology we have today? Or was Daisy's skill in the performing arts so spectacular that nobody thought to question events, despite the glaring coincidences? It might have been a combination of both.

William Sproat, Daisy's former brother-in-law, was the first to realise that something was amiss. His suspicions had been raised five years earlier, when he'd travelled from Pretoria to visit his ailing brother, and had been convinced by his sister-in-law to talk the very ill Robert into altering his will. And when his brother died suddenly just a month later, he'd taken it upon himself to keep an eye on what Daisy did next.

When Rhodes died, William Sproat wasted no time in taking his suspicions to the police, who, upon hearing the various stories from across so many years suddenly stitched together, knew they had grounds to investigate further.

The only forensic evidence left to test William Sproat's hypothesis was buried in the family plot at Brixton Cemetery, and the only way to revisit this was to exhume the corpses of the three men. And so the digging began: if William Alfred Cowle, Robert Sproat and Rhodes Cecil Cowle had all been lowered into the ground under the teary eyes of Daisy de Melker, history was being reversed. Neat mounds of soil slowly formed at the gravesides as, one by one, the authorities dug deep and hauled out the three large, dark coffins.

First to go under the microscope was the relatively fresh corpse of young Rhodes. Just six weeks dead, the body was in a fine state, all things considered. This was perhaps not surprising: the powers of preservation of arsenic were well established. As far back as 1838 (almost fifty years before Daisy was even born), a letter to the editor of the medical journal *The Lancet* had noted that while it was very convenient to preserve bodies for dissection with arsenic, it presented a fatal risk to the dissector, who could possibly inhale some of the powder in the course of his work. The letter was written by John Snow, an esteemed English physician who became known as 'the father of epidemiology' and who was a pioneer in the use of anaesthesia.[4]

'Arsenic poisoning', the examiners pencilled in, followed by a question mark, in their preliminary report. The state forensic pathologist then examined the corpse more closely, and voilà! Arsenic was found in Rhodes's spine, hair and viscera.

The bodies of William and Robert, who had lain in the ground for far longer, were badly decomposed. Unlike Rhodes, their bodies had not been preserved by arsenic. But, on close examination of their spines, what was found? Traces of strychnine – just as deadly if administered in the right amount, and just as readily available for Daisy to purchase. Additionally, their bones were tinged with pink – a clear sign of the presence of strychnine. Because strychnine is colourless and odourless, chemists would dye it pink (and, less frequently, green) to make it more visible to the human eye and thus prevent accidents, since its main use was in pest control in cities.

The fourth body to be put under a microscope was a living one – that of Rhodes's colleague James Webster, with whom Rhodes had shared the laced coffee. Sure enough, cuttings of his fingernails and hair showed clear traces of arsenic poisoning, and when the police asked him to recall what he had consumed that day, he took no time to mention the blue flask from which Rhodes had poured him some coffee. The police went to the De Melker household, retrieved the blue flask, and tested it for traces of arsenic. The test came back positive.

With any doubt as to the validity of William Sproat's suspicions of murder now removed, the police came knocking on the door of Daisy de Melker. She was arrested, charged with the three murders, and immediately transported to the Women's Jail at the Fort prison complex (nowadays Constitution Hill) in Braamfontein.

When Daisy's trial began on 17 October 1932, the then High Court of the Witwatersrand was transformed into a public spectacle. There was great demand for seats in court, and each day a queue snaked down the road outside the court, with some people selling their seats in the public gallery for a fine sum of money. Daisy de Melker had become a household name – an icon to some, a curiosity to others, and a macabre subject of morbid fascination to many. Catching a glimpse of her in person in the dock in a courtroom was a great thrill. This was, after all, the Union of South Africa's first serial killer, and a female one at that.

Finally, when one local newspaper managed to procure a studio photograph of Daisy, it wasn't so much the quenching of the public's thirst for details that became important. It was, instead, the moment at which Abraham Spilkin, standing behind his teak counter at his chemist's shop in Turffontein, opened his copy of *The Star* newspaper – and the penny dropped. The Daisy de Melker on trial for killing two husbands and a son was the same Mrs Sproat who'd come about her ailing cat, and who'd carefully signed the poisons register. He immediately folded the paper, asked an assistant to serve the customers in his absence, and headed down to the local police station.

The Crown (as the State was known until South Africa left the Commonwealth) called 60 witnesses to the stand as they built their case that Daisy was a cold-blooded murderer. The defence, for its part, called only a few witnesses. But, of all those who testified for either side, it was the testimony of Spilkin that had the spectators spellbound. As he described in detail how Daisy had spoken of her sickly cat before purchasing a small package of arsenic, any traces of reasonable doubt that Daisy had murdered her son began to fade.

In the cases of William and Robert, Daisy's guilt was harder to prove. The traces of strychnine found in the bodies of the two men certainly provided forensic evidence that they had been murdered. But, to prove beyond reasonable doubt that Daisy was behind the murders would require circumstantial evidence too. In the case of her son, the tell-tale signs in the blue flask, the purchase of arsenic at Spilkin's pharmacy, and the illness of James Webster were enough to wipe out any reasonable doubt. With William and Robert, although it was relatively obvious that she was behind their murders, it could not be proven beyond reasonable doubt.

And so it was that the murder of her own son proved to be Daisy de Melker's undoing. According to eyewitness accounts, she appeared utterly shocked upon hearing the words, 'You have been found guilty of the murder of your son, Rhodes Cecil Cowle.'[5] When asked if she wished to say something before hearing her sentence read out, she stated, 'I am not guilty of poisoning my son.'[6] Then came the words that sent a shiver across the courtroom: 'You will be taken from here to a place of execution where you will hang by the neck until you are dead. And may God have mercy on your soul.'[7]

With that, she was whisked away to her cell in the Women's Jail one last time to collect her few belongings. She was taken to Pretoria Central to await the hangman's noose.

On the morning of 30 December, one month and five days after her trial came to its sensational conclusion, Daisy de Melker was led by a warder down the passage to the death chamber. There, just as the judge had decreed, she was hanged by the neck, struggled for a moments, and then went limp.

Sidney de Melker, Daisy's only husband to survive marriage to her, placed two white violets on her coffin.

Right up until his own death, 22 years later, he maintained her innocence.

CHAPTER 2

MARLENE LEHNBERG

╪

Cape Town, 1974

Eighteen years old and preoccupied with her looks, Marlene Lehnberg decided that morning that even her big umbrella wasn't enough protection from what the rain might do to her hair. Just before leaving the boarding house, she took a plastic shopping bag from the kitchen and, using the glass of the eye-level oven as a mirror, secured it firmly around her hair. Tucking each last strand under the plastic, she checked one last time to make sure her make-up purse was inside her bag. On a day like this, there was no way she was going to do her make-up at home and take the risk of walking into the office with mascara running down her cheeks.

When she stepped onto the bus, the umbrella, the shopping bag and her raincoat sent a mini-deluge of water onto the floor, causing the driver to shake his head resignedly as he looked down at the puddles.

'I'm so sorry,' she said, smiling.

'That's okay,' came the reply. 'I'm used to the Cape Town rain.'

Marlene sat on the bus alone, propping the wet umbrella on the seat next to her to discourage other passengers from sitting there. The window was so fogged that she could barely see what street they were on. Using her index finger, she wrote 'Christiaan' on the glass, then quickly drew a heart around the name before the letters started melting away, running down into the frame of the window.

As more passengers boarded the bus at every stop, Marlene became increasingly ashamed of the wet umbrella on the seat next to her. Her cheeks flushed as she thought of what her mother would say: 'That isn't very Christian of you, Marlene. We must always think of other people.'

The mere thought of her mother at once made her angry, but also filled her with the delight of mischief. Ever since she could remember, her parents had carefully stitched together a world in which you could feel shame at any given moment – about your clothing, the words that came out of your mouth, the shows you wanted to hear on the radio … Every aspect of life became a tributary winding its way down into one big river of shame. The weeks were measured by Sundays in church, morning prayers, saying grace at the dinner table before a single morsel of food could be eaten.

But now she had a secret. And nobody could take that away from her. Not her mother. Not her father. Not the dominee. A bolt of delight shot through her body, and she used a hand to cover the smile spreading across her face.

When the bus came to a halt outside the hospital, she wasn't quite ready to leave its warm interior, but she knew that dithering could mean missing her stop. She got up and opened the umbrella with a jerk as she stepped into the rain. The umbrella seemed too big for her slender frame and she held it tightly over her head, so low that she looked like a black beetle scurrying across the car park to the front entrance of the hospital.

'Name, please?' the security guard said, looking down at his clipboard.

'Don't you recognise me?' Marlene laughed, a slightly accusing tone in her voice. Then she remembered: the shopping bag on her head. She carefully peeled it back, revealing the flattened strands of hair underneath it. 'And now?' she asked, running her fingers through her hair to bring some bounce back.

'Miss Marlene!' he finally said, and made a notation on the clipboard.

'That's right,' she said. Closing the umbrella, she wound the thin black strap around it and pushed the press stud in as hard as it would go until she heard a click. Then she leaned in behind the reception desk and stood the umbrella upright against the wall. 'I'm leaving it here for the day, okay?' she announced.

The security guard suddenly looked nervous, his eyes pleading with her to remove it.

'The baas doesn't like finding things here behind the desk. Last week somebody left a suitcase for somebody else and I pushed it under the counter and he asked me if I'd stolen it.'

With an irritated sigh, Marlene said, 'Ag, nee. I'm just going to leave it here. If that man has a problem, you can tell him to come to the orthopaedic workshop where Miss Marlene in reception will tell him how to watch his mouth.'

She walked off, clickety-clacking across the linoleum passage to the bathroom. With no make-up on, and hair that was last spotted alive in the reflection of an oven door, she hoped nobody would see her. Especially not Christiaan.

Inside the bathroom, she cursed the poor lighting. She thought of her pink dressing table at the boarding house – the stool at the perfect height, the lamp placed just so, the four fluffy toys leaning on the mirror. Today, instead, she had a cold vanity slab and the smell of disinfectant, one flickering bulb in a toilet stall behind her and one dim yellow light above the soap dispenser.

Her father had always said that a woman who wore blush was 'asking for trouble'. Today, just to spite him, she added a little more of everything – including the sweet perfume that Christiaan had bought her. Even just the smell as she opened the little orange bottle made her dizzy with excitement. It was going to be a good day. Rain, after all, is a romantic thing … once you've made a plan with your make-up.

When Marlene emerged from the bathroom, she was a different creature altogether. The make-up was like an elixir that instantly restored her self-esteem. She held her head high, making her way along the passages until she was seated behind the reception desk in the orthopaedic workshop of the Red Cross War Memorial Children's Hospital in Rondebosch. She pulled the large, dark-blue appointment diary towards her, and started stacking up the patient files to pass the time.

The vast majority of patients she met on a daily basis were children, but on the odd occasion an adult who needed an artificial limb and who could not be serviced by one of the other tertiary government hospitals would be sent to the workshop. That was how Marthinus Choegoe became a patient at Red Cross, and that was how his fate was sealed.

Shortly after meeting Marthinus, Marlene earmarked him for a grisly task. This was the man for the job, she told herself, the man who could help execute the plan that kept her awake at night, got her up in the morning, and spirited her through the weekends when Christiaan was off limits. 'I need to be with my family,' he would say every other Friday afternoon, as they clutched each other on the leather back seat of his old Mercedes-Benz. And, with that, he would plant one last kiss on her forehead, a kiss that danced strangely between paternal love and the final act of a sex drama.

'Good morning,' Marthinus stuttered, looking down at the ground where his single leg stood pinned to the floor like the narrow base of a lamp. Under his frayed clothing, his scrawny frame was slumped as if to apologise for its very existence.

'Speak up,' Marlene said, quickly clapping her hands. 'I can't hear you when you mumble.'

Marthinus cleared his throat. 'I say, good morning.'

'Have you been here before?' she asked him.

He shook his head.

'Do you know how to write?'

'My name, yes,' he said.

'Okay, come and stand here by me at the desk and I'll write the information for you,' she said, rifling through a set of stacked filing trays and pulling out a form. Picking up a pen, she asked without looking up, 'Name and age?'

'Marthinus Choegoe, 33,' the man said, his eyes downcast.

'Reason for visit?'

He looked confused.

'Why are you here?' Marlene said, an edge of impatience in her youthful voice.

'My leg,' he said, looking down again.

'Are you here to be measured for a new leg by the technician?'

He nodded.

'And what happened to your leg? How did you lose it?' she asked, pulling her fingers through her fringe one last time to make sure the rain hadn't won.

'Car accident,' he said. 'The doctor had to cut it off afterwards.'

Marlene picked up the office phone, dialled an internal number, and wrapped her fingers around the coils of the cord. 'Mr Van der Linde?' she said into the mouthpiece, enjoying the façade of the formal mode of address while knowing what would follow later. 'I have a Mr Marthinus Choegoe here ready to see you. He's come for the fitting of an artificial leg.'

'Bring him through,' Christiaan's voice said in her ear. The sound of it made her feel calm and out of control all at once.

She walked the patient into Christiaan's office and introduced Marthinus to the technician, her boss – to whom she then gave a smile so subtle that only an illicit lover would have picked it up. As she closed the door behind them and resumed her seat behind the desk, the moment of conception came: a thought was created and its cells began to multiply. Over the next few months they would grow inside her like an embryo. *That is the man*, she said to herself. *That is the man who is going to help me do what needs to be done.*

As the sound of the rain slowly tapered off outside the window, she began copying down Marthinus's details on a separate piece of paper.

✠

At any moment of the day or night, across the world, there are people engaging in sexual acts, many of them with someone other than their partner. While you're reading this, there are two creatures not far from where you live checking into a hotel to make use of nothing but the mattress (and maybe the complimentary hand cream). Tonight, as you brush your teeth, there will be someone within a ten-kilometre radius awkwardly climbing into the back seat of a car before misting up the windows with heavy breathing. To say it's common is an understatement. But when the man is 45 and married, and the woman barely 18, there are clearly other dynamics at play.

In the case of Marlene Lehnberg and Christiaan van der Linde, the setting of their first encounter and growing attraction was a place of true virtue – one of the few dedicated children's hospitals in the southern hemisphere. The Red Cross War Memorial Children's Hospital is so vast that it looks more like a military compound than a place of tiny beds and fluffy toys. It was here that Marlene finally cast off the shackles of her puritanical upbringing, and proudly took up her post as a receptionist in the hospital's orthopaedic workshop.

But the childhood she'd experienced meant she was not prepared for the working world 'out there' beyond the confines of her ultra-conservative household.

Her father, Arthur, had left school before completing matric, and when he married Marlene's mother, Mavis, they endured several years of financial hardship. Unable to afford accommodation of their own, they moved into the garage at Arthur's parents' house. It was here where they began their family, eventually having five children. Marlene was two years old by the time her father found gainful employment, and the family finally moved from the garage to a smallholding near the

Cape Flats. A few years later, they sold this and bought a house in the suburb of Plumstead.

Despite the outward appearance of being a young daughter in a close-knit family, Marlene's childhood was devoid of affection and was filled instead with harsh judgement. She was, according to the record, an unplanned child whose birth had upset her father so much that he formed no bond with her at all – withdrawing any form of affection and showering it instead on her sister Vivian. While she was slightly closer to her mother, theirs was also not a strong and affectionate relationship.

At school, she emerged as an outstanding scholar, but her social and cultural education was sorely lacking. She was a loner, and after a day of solitude at school, she would return to a family home that was also isolated from social connections.

At a time when television had not begun to drop its cultural confetti over the *verkrampte* (conservative) world of South Africa's white suburbs, Marlene was not even allowed to visit the cinema – or the bioscope, as it was quaintly called. After all, her parents must have thought, what type of moral decay might she be exposed to through seeing the images on the screen? Dancing was also strictly forbidden, as was the wearing of any make-up. By her early teenage years, the isolation had become too much for Marlene, and she immersed herself in a local church, joining the choir and assisting at the Sunday school. Her family was ultra-conservative but were not churchgoers, and perhaps this connection to the church was Marlene's way of trying to develop a social life.

Despite her achievements at school, she was even forbidden to attend the end-of-year prize-giving, and left school at age 16 after completing only her Standard 8 (Grade 10).

Immediately thereafter, she took up her post at the hospital. At sweet 16, she should still have been doing her learning in a classroom. But the 'education' that Marlene began within the grey walls of the children's hospital was of a different nature altogether. Some said her attraction to Christiaan van der Linde was a direct result of the vacuum left by an intensely strict and unloving father. Marlene's brain had, from a very young age, been wired for a very limited repertoire: guilt, shame, the absence of pleasure ...

After all those years of being kept under virtual lock and key, she walked gingerly up to the security guard at the Red Cross War Memorial Children's Hospital and began her first day at a job for which she had had little emotional preparation.

Marlene's attraction to Christiaan was allegedly instantaneous. It was likely a strange concoction of ingredients that led a teenage subordinate into the arms of her middle-aged, married boss, a family man with two sons and a daughter. Given her father's cold and Calvinist approach to life, perhaps she was drawn to Christiaan through a yearning for a caring paternal figure. Perhaps his work as chief technician fitting artificial limbs for amputees made him seem like the perfect saviour – a strong man fixing broken people. Marlene had felt her heart 'beating faster' from the very moment he uttered that first and formulaic word: 'Welcome!' She would later tell a journalist, 'He struck me as something special. He impressed me tremendously.'[1]

For the first year of their working together, the two had a close but platonic friendship. It is possible – perhaps even likely – that feelings were already stirring, but given her upbringing, she would have been acutely aware of the sanctity of marriage. Given his position, he would have been conscious of the implications of making sexual advances towards an employee – and a teenager at that. She would receive the patients at reception, he would fix them up with artificial limbs. She would do the filing, he would take the measurements.

Then, at some point, the implicit and silent agreement not to act on any inappropriate feelings was broken. It is not known who crossed the line, but the moment arrived when it was clear that the sexual instinct had overwhelmed the sense of right and wrong – and Marlene Lehnberg, at age 17, began an affair with Christiaan van der Linde, her 47-year-old boss.

Soon, sneaking off together became a regular occurrence during the working day or at night when the workshop closed. Later, Christiaan would deny any scope for willpower in the situation. 'A determined, intelligent woman in love is difficult to contain,'[2] he said. Perhaps what he also meant was that it was difficult to contain what was happening in his own trousers. After living cloistered like a nun, Marlene had discovered the joys of infatuation and her own sexuality. Perhaps she also saw him as a one-way ticket out of an overprotective family.

As the affair gathered momentum, Marlene and Christiaan settled into a routine. Their two favourite haunts became Rondebosch Common and the Paarden Eiland industrial area. The common is a large and mainly featureless piece of land that, apart from a few clumps of trees and a romantic view of Table Mountain, hardly offers the hidden spots that an affair might require, but perhaps the proximity to the passing traffic upped the thrill factor for Marlene. More importantly, it was conveniently situated within walking distance of the hospital: the two could thus leave the workshop separately and meet up a few minutes later in the wild grass.

Their second-favourite spot, Paarden Eiland, is even more perplexing as the setting for an illicit affair. Located on the edge of Cape Town's docks, Paarden Eiland consists mainly of warehouses and factories, so it's difficult to say why the lovers chose it as their backdrop. Perhaps it was the counterpoint to what the common offered (and lacked): it was far from the workshop, it was the last place anyone might recognise them, and there were many walls behind which to hide.

By 1974, Marlene's adoration of Christiaan had turned to obsession. She was 18 years old by then, and firmly believed that they would be together forever. This was despite the fact that he had made his intentions clear: he adored her, but he wouldn't leave his wife, Susanna, and their three children.

According to newspaper reports from the time, in early 1974 Christiaan attempted to bring the affair to an abrupt halt. Whether on the exposed greenery of the Rondebosch Common, or behind the blank walls of the warehouses of Paarden Eiland, or through the frosted glass of the workshop where they worked, the two had likely been spotted together once too often. Or perhaps someone at the hospital had begun to notice the suspicious departures every day by two people who had no reason to leave the premises. Whichever way it happened, Marlene was told by her older lover that someone had been making anonymous phone calls to his house, warning Susanna that her husband wasn't just fixing artificial limbs during his working day. Suspecting they were being watched, he wished to provide no proof for a wife whose suspicions were now as strong as Marlene's desires.

With Christiaan as the object of her obsession, Marlene had begun to see Susanna as a barrier to her own 'forever after'. In July 1974, perhaps believing her own words or perhaps to manipulate him, she announced to Christiaan that she was leaving Cape Town. An implied ultimatum now hung over the relationship from Marlene's side: leave your wife or lose me forever. If this was a veiled threat intended to force his hand, it didn't work: Christiaan didn't leave his wife, and Marlene didn't leave the city. The affair, however, continued, even when the lovers had heated arguments about the prospect (or not) of a future together.

In the spring of 1974, Marlene went straight to the source of her misery. If she couldn't convince Christiaan to leave Susanna, perhaps she could convince Susanna to give up the grand prize to the teenager with the wavy tresses and flared pants. When the phone rang in the Van der Lindes' home that September afternoon, it wasn't the anonymous caller delivering messages about heavy panting in a car in Paarden Eiland. It was the panter herself, a single-minded Marlene on a mission.

'Christiaan and I are very much in love,' she told Susanna. 'We're seeing each other every night.'[3]

Susanna simply put the phone down.

Marlene, now desperate, began plotting her next move: she would try negotiation. She invited Susanna to meet her. A deal of this nature could, after all, only be drafted face to face.

The two met in the northern suburb of Bellville in October of that year, not far from Susanna's house in Gladstone Street. Marlene began by stating her case, but Susanna immediately nixed any notion of divorce, and said she would settle into the role of betrayed wife but she was not going to let go of the father of her three children.

'I don't mind playing second fiddle, as long as you don't mind doing likewise,'[4] she allegedly told Marlene.

So Susanna couldn't be removed through negotiation. There was, to Marlene's mind, only one method remaining – and Marthinus

Choegoe, the one-legged accident survivor, became her pawn. Doing her own little bit of investigative work, Marlene discovered that the unemployed and down-at-heel Marthinus was a regular at a shop called Solly's Trading Store, not far from his house in Retreat, a working-class suburb on the Cape Flats for people classified as coloured. Using Solly's as a delivery address, she wrote Marthinus a note, inviting him to contact her if he wanted to 'earn good money'.[5]

Within days, Marlene saw the figure of Marthinus silhouetted in the doorway. Sensing that her plan was coming to fruition, she drew a one-rand note from her bag and gave it to him. 'Meet me at the Rondebosch Town Hall at seven this evening,' she told him. It is not clear if this tiny sum of money (even for those days) was meant for transport or simply to create the impression that she had the 'means' to get what she wanted. But, either way, the two of them met at the allocated place and time as planned.

To sweeten the deal, Marlene brought along a bottle of gin in a brown paper bag. She got straight to the point and told Marthinus the job she had in mind for him. 'I'd like you to murder someone for me,' she said. 'A woman.'

Marthinus was, not surprisingly, appalled. 'But I'll be sent to the gallows, Miss Marlene,'[6] he said. He had never injured another person before, though he had once been caught in possession of a dangerous weapon and had appeared in court. Marlene had found this out and now used it to flatter him, saying he was just the sort of person she was looking for – 'someone who can handle a dangerous weapon'.[7]

Despite Marlene's drawing him into her plan as an accomplice, he made his way to the Van der Linde home planning to warn Susanna that she was in peril. But when she opened the door, he lost his nerve and asked for money. She refused and Marthinus simply hobbled away.

Another week would pass before Marlene attempted, one more time, to lure the amputee into her plot. By this time, Susanna van der Linde had shifted in the prospective murderer's mind from an anonymous victim whose death spelled money to a living, breathing woman.

Marlene had no such compunction, however. Desperate to get Marthinus to commit the act, she promised to expedite the production of his prosthetic leg, and threw in a small transistor radio for good measure.

And so Marthinus made his way to the house in Gladstone Street in Bellville once again. In Marlene's mind, Susanna would soon be lying in a pool of blood and then in a coffin. But, instead, Marthinus arrived at the place fixed for the murder ... and simply walked past.

Marlene wasn't going to give up, however, and Marthinus was soon handed another sealed envelope at Solly's Trading Store. 'Use a knife if you have to, but make sure the job is done,'[8] the note inside read. A short while later came an instruction for Marthinus to phone Marlene at the workshop.

He went to a nearby 'tickey box' (public phone) and dropped a silver five-cent coin into the slot.

'Good afternoon, orthopaedic workshop, Marlene speaking, how may I help you?'

On hearing the muttering Marthinus on the other end of the line, Marlene's heart began to race: another opportunity to coax him into the darkness of her plan. This time, she went all out and offered him a car – a grand prize she could never have afforded.

Still he refused.

Now she became desperate.

'I'll have sex with you – *after* you've killed her,' she said. There was, after all, no reason why, once the deed was done, she'd have to keep her side of the bargain. If she didn't, who was Marthinus going to complain to – the police?

There was a stunned silence, and she heard Marthinus swallow.

The next time Marlene Lehnberg ran her tongue along an envelope to seal it, it wasn't Solly's Trading Store she would write on the front. This letter, dated October 1974, was addressed to the hospital manager. 'Notice of Resignation' read the subject line.

A few days later, driving her white Ford Anglia, she pulled up in front of Marthinus's humble home in Retreat. It's hard to imagine the conversation that unfolded in that car, in South Africa, in 1974, between a white teenage woman and a one-legged man of colour with a hammer in his possession. They talked about the house in Bellville where a killing would take place.

Except, once again, it didn't.

Marlene stopped the car in front of the house in Gladstone Street, discharged Marthinus and the hammer, and quickly drove away. But Susanna, peeking through a window from behind a lace curtain, spotted a familiar figure. She'd seen the man loitering in the neighbourhood before – asking for money, hanging around, acting suspiciously. She called the police, who wasted no time in rushing over. At that time in South Africa, a 'non-European' man in a white suburb would instantly be suspected of having ulterior motives if he was there without a legitimate reason, such as delivering a parcel or working in someone's garden.

Marthinus was picked up just two blocks away and dragged off to the station, where his worst nightmare unfolded. The police did not hold back, and Marthinus was eventually sent back onto the streets with swollen eyes, bruises, other injuries and a clear warning never to return.

With not the slightest regard for Marthinus's condition, Marlene now began to look elsewhere for an accomplice. This time, it was twentysomething engineering student Robert Newman, who lived in the same boarding house as her. She knew he owned a Llama pistol, and asked if she could borrow it – as one might a tape measure or stapler. When he said no, she confronted him: would he carry out the murder for her, then?

Unlike the downtrodden Marthinus, who'd been dragged down to a place where choice and agency were nonexistent, the young engineering student knew a foul plan when he heard one. And his answer was as straightforward as could be. 'No,' he said.

Some days later, he came home to find the pistol missing from his room. Prime suspect: Marlene Lehnberg. And no guessing what she hoped to do with it.

At 8.30 am on 4 November, Marlene drove to Marthinus's Retreat home with the lethal weapon concealed in her car. Under the pretext of going to Bellville to say a last goodbye to Christiaan – she was moving to Johannesburg for good, she told Marthinus – she persuaded him to accompany her. It was only once they were on the road that she handed him the gun and told him what was expected of him.

Around 9 am, the Anglia pulled up once more in front of the house that had now been marked for several months as a place of murder. Inside, a single occupant was clearing away the breakfast dishes after the children had left for school, while her husband was (presumably) looking over at the empty reception desk in the orthopaedic workshop several kilometres away. She wouldn't be alone for much longer, though. Soon, the door would open and in would come her killer – the last person to see Susanna van der Linde gasp for air as the life left her body.

Who exactly was the killer? Was it Christiaan's lover herself, having finally realised that the only person she could rely on to remove the obstacle to her happiness was herself? Or was it the hapless one-legged man who didn't really have it in him to kill but who, by this point, had been manipulated and coaxed into committing homicide? It depends whom you ask.

In Marlene's version, she was the mastermind who hired an assassin and drove the getaway car. According to her, it was she who went up to the house and rang the doorbell – Marthinus had already been warned not to show his face in the neighbourhood again, so why tempt fate by forcing him to be the frontman? She claimed that as soon as the door opened, she jumped into her Anglia and sped off.

According to Marthinus, however, Marlene made no such dash back to the car after ringing the bell. Instead, she stayed on the scene as he too now appeared in the doorway. As soon as Susanna clapped eyes on him, she shouted that she was going to call the police.

According to him, what followed was like a scene from a horror film: as Susanna tried to flee, Marlene violently tripped her, then pistol-whipped her to the point of semi-consciousness. Marlene ordered Marthinus to strangle Susanna, but in the heat of the moment, also looked wildly around the room for a weapon, soon spotting a pair of scissors on the sideboard. She passed them to Marthinus, who plunged the blades into Susanna's chest several times – three, he said, though forensic pathologists later discerned six wounds to the chest area.

Was it such a frenzy that he erased some of those moments from his memory, or was it Marlene herself who inflicted the additional three wounds, so intent was she on murdering Susanna that she matched Marthinus's stabs until Susanna's chest was a relief map of hatred and jealousy?

A neighbour, a Mrs Marais, would later testify that the white Anglia stood empty outside the house for several minutes. This corroborated Marthinus's version that Marlene wasn't simply the mastermind and driver of the getaway vehicle but was indeed inside the house when the gruesome scissors murder took place.

When Marthinus was driven back to his house after the murder, he was covered in green dye from a gas pistol that Marlene had grabbed inside the house and used on him. He was, quite literally, a marked man and was dropped at home in a dishevelled state.

Why did she do this? Like most things about Marlene, it's difficult to say. But, it's likely that it was her way of saying, 'I've painted you as the criminal you are. If you go the police now, they will pin this crime on you alone.'

One can only imagine the sorry spectacle of this pathetic man who for so long had been reluctant to commit the heinous act of murder, now standing on one leg, unlocking the door of his small house, and looking at himself in the mirror of his bathroom: covered in green dye, blood on his hands, a soon-to-be-wanted man. And, in those moments while he was trying to scrub away the colours of crime, Marlene drove off in her Anglia up the N1 highway, bound for Johannesburg. In Beaufort West, some 450 km from Cape Town, she picked up two speeding tickets.

Back in Cape Town, Christiaan, as was his habit, called his wife from the office during the course of the morning to say hi. But there was no response, and none to the subsequent calls he made either. Growing increasingly concerned, and mindful of the one-legged man who had been seen loitering around their street, he called their daughter, Zelda, who worked at Tygerberg Hospital, and asked her to check up on her mother during her lunch break.

Around noon, as Marlene's little car ate up the distance on the national highway, Zelda drove over to the house in Gladstone Street, possibly expecting that when she got there, her mother would open the door and apologise for not answering the phone – she'd been out shopping all morning, perhaps, or tending to some roses in the garden. When her knocking produced no response, she peered through a front window and saw her mother lying lifeless on the bloody floor. There was no mistaking it: she had been murdered.

The prime suspect was, not surprisingly, a 'crippled coloured man' often seen in the area.[9] For the first week after the murder, he couldn't be located.

Bizarrely, the teenager who'd worked closely with the victim's spouse and had frequently been spotted with him away from their work premises wasn't a suspect, but she was nonetheless a person of interest – someone who could help the police with their inquiries. Called in for questioning after the police arrived at her uncle's house in Bryanston, where she was hiding out, she admitted to being Christiaan's lover but denied having any association with the crippled man. Asked about her attempts to get Robert Newman to shoot Susanna dead with his pistol, she claimed it had been said as a joke.

Later that day, however, after a few hours of questioning by the police, Marlene suddenly admitted to having hired Marthinus as the assassin and transporting him to the Van der Linde house.

She was arrested and charged with murder, but still insisted she didn't carry out the actual murder. She gave the police Marthinus's address, and a police van was dispatched to his house in Retreat. Marthinus, too, was arrested and charged with murder.

The trial began about three months later, in March 1975, in a courtroom packed to capacity. Proceedings lasted only seven days, but during that time the state called more than thirty witnesses to testify against the 19-year-old killer and her accomplice. At one point, the judge said, 'I have presided over many cases but have never heard evidence as strange and bizarre as this one.'[10]

When the guilty verdict came through for both Marthinus and Marlene, a cold shiver ran through the courtroom, as many knew what would happen next. South Africa was still 15 years away from ending the death penalty, and so Marlene Lehnberg and Marthinus Choegoe were sentenced to hang by the neck from the gallows.

Except that they didn't. Two months later, the case was reopened on appeal. Marthinus was sentenced to 15 years, and served 11 before being paroled. In 1992, five years after his release, while driving along the N7 highway near Nuwerus in the then Cape Province he was involved in another car accident. This one took his life.

As for Marlene, the fantasy life of romance for which she was prepared to kill was nothing like the one she ended up living. She was sentenced to 20 years for the murder, but, like Marthinus, was paroled after serving 11. Behind bars at Pollsmoor Prison, the bright student who had shown so much promise in her school days re-emerged. She studied music, computer programming and finance, and completed a degree in psychology. You can't help wondering if, in doing so, she gained any insight into why she had done what she did.

Almost 2 000 km away, Susanna was buried on her parents' farm in the Magaliesberg. Christiaan moved to nearby Krugersdorp so that he could visit her grave. In a series of interviews he granted to the media, the complex nature of his and Marlene's attraction was made clear. 'Men have had mistresses since time immemorial and will continue to have them. Many of these relationships flower into something really beautiful, as happened to me and Marlene, whom I called Sweetie,' he said. 'Her love for me drove her to kill my wife – but how does that make me evil?'[11]

Throughout the trial, Christiaan had sworn to visit Marlene in prison for the rest of his life, but in the months after her conviction, the flush of his attraction to her faded, and the reality hit home that his wife and the mother of his children had been brutally murdered. He never saw Marlene again.

Years later, he spoke of the 'torment' of being caught between a stable, loving wife and a seductive teenager with no sense of right or wrong. 'My dear wife is dead. I sincerely wish to God that I had never set eyes on Marlene Lehnberg,'[12] he said. Lonely and living in obscurity, he died in 1983.

On her release from prison in 1986, Marlene declined the option of changing her name so that she could start afresh. Her next relationship, which lasted nine years after her release, was with a former fellow prisoner, Jennifer Westfal. Following this and a few more failed attempts at a partnership, she never had another long-term relationship.

But what is most interesting about her post-prison life is that she never made use of her degree in psychology. Instead, she opened a beauty salon in Johannesburg and joined a modelling agency. She was always impeccably groomed, with big 1980s-style hair and the not-so-subtle shades of lipstick popular during that era. Perhaps this was all a reaction to an upbringing that saw lipstick as the paintbrush of the devil.

In her later years, when middle age had faded her once-bright appearance, it also took its toll on her health. By the time she was in her fifties, the delicate bones of her slim figure had turned on her, losing mass and becoming brittle. And to add to the pain and disfigurement of osteoporosis came a diagnosis of breast cancer.

In 2015, in the weeks leading up to her 60th birthday, the beautiful Marlene, whose wavy hair once reached down her back and who wore flared pants as if the fashion was made for her, weighed a sickly 38 kg. Five days shy of her birthday, she once again took a woman's life.

This time, that life was her own.

CHAPTER 3
CHARMAINE PHILLIPS
╪

Kroonstad, 2006

Charmaine Phillips lifted the small mirror, with its strawberry-pink handle, to her face. Turning her head slightly to the right, she examined the strands of hair on that side to make sure they were tucked neatly behind her ear. There was a single hair that seemed to have a life of its own. She tried to smooth it down, but it jumped back up like a crinkled streamer the morning after a party. She tried again. Still it defied her.

Drawing the mirror closer, like a camera lens zooming into the microscopic world of follicles and the grey-white skin of scalp, she dug her thumb and index finger into the spot where the hair was rooted to the head and gave a short, sharp yank.

Satisfied, she turned her head the other way and found nothing out of place.

Finally, stretching an arm out in front of her, she looked at the whole picture of herself: a woman in her forties, living outside prison walls.

A wave of sadness washed over her as the past flooded her thoughts, until the sound of a car arriving brought her back to the present. She fastened her jacket buttons, carefully pulling out the floral collar of her blouse and flattening it neatly over the black Crimplene, and adjusted the small gold-plated cross that hung around her neck. Giving herself one last look, she put the mirror face-down on the table.

It was a Friday, as good a day as any for a funeral, and although the owner of the hair salon where she worked had fixated on the weather and predicted incessantly what a warm day it would be, the universe had other plans. She walked across the road and climbed into the car under a cold sky. Johannesburg's autumn was stretching its dry and brittle hands over the tree-lined streets.

Charmaine knew that a thousand hugs from well-wishers wouldn't warm her against the thought of her son's ashes in that small box. Also, she knew there would be a clutch of journalists present, holding notepads where the handkerchiefs of grief should be. Her mouth, she told herself, must stay firmly shut.

As the car turned several corners and she lurched lightly from left to right in her seat, she felt slightly dizzy. During the years in prison, her life had fitted into a succession of parallel lines, right angles, regimens, clocks and schedules as straight as an arrow. Even 18 months after her release, the outside world seemed somewhat chaotic. For a brief moment, the cars rushing past the window mesmerised her. And, in that moment, there was no funeral about to take place. There was no child she had to mourn for a second time. No hand dipping into the cold water of the past. And no blame.

The car came to a halt and she was jerked back to reality.

'Charmaine?' a voice was saying. 'Charmaine, are you okay?'

Drawing in a deep breath, she said, 'Yes. Are we here?'

'I'm afraid so,' said Christopher. 'It's time.'

Christopher worked at the hair salon too, and had become a friend. She felt grateful not just for the lift, but also for the gentle support. He climbed out of the car, opened the door, and held out his hand to help her onto the pavement. On legs of iron she walked, leaning heavily on Christopher.

The jacaranda trees were bare now, and the grey-brown church was etched against the cloudless sky. When she entered, heads turned. Breathing shallowly, trying to ignore the eyes on her, she walked down the aisle to the front of the church where the priest stood waiting behind an altar bearing a small box, on either side of which sat small green foam bricks into which some daisies had been inserted.

Once she and Christopher were seated, the priest cleared his throat. 'We're here to honour a young man whose life was taken from him far too young for those left behind, but at just the right time for our Lord and Saviour Jesus. He was only 23 years old …'

The words cut into Charmaine's heart as if someone had taken a knife and carved into it the date of Pietertjie's birth.

'I never met Pieter, but Charmaine told me how loved and wonderful he was. He had a lot of hang-ups but his heart was always with Jesus.'[1]

Sensing movement among the assembled throng of journalists, the priest changed his tone of voice to one of chiding: 'I ask members of the press to refrain from making notes during the ceremony. I also urge them please to leave Charmaine, Pieter's grieving mother, in peace on this very sad occasion. Her situation is such that she is not allowed to engage with the press, so please do not waste your time or hers.'

She dipped her head, grateful for the priest's care but embarrassed by the attention, especially the veiled reference to her parole conditions. As the priest returned to his eulogy, Charmaine thought about the first time she'd said goodbye to her son – a baby of six months, then a man of 21, and now a box of ashes and the symbol of all that pained her.

She remembered that day in 1983, when he was only six months old, as if the sun had only just set on it. She thought back to how, early that morning, as the police were closing in on her and Pietertjie's father, she'd hurriedly dressed him in a small white babygrow and a bib with tiny blue bears, tied in a bow on his soft nape. It was a spring morning, with jasmine and Banks' roses spreading their scents through the Johannesburg air that rushed in through the open windows of the car. But, on high alert for the sound of police cars, Charmaine and Pieter senior barely noticed the heady smells around them.

As they pulled up outside a block of flats in Loveday Street in Braamfontein, she noticed she'd done the press studs on Pietertjie's babygrow incorrectly. She slid a thumbnail under one to start over again, but Pieter stopped her.

'Take him inside, take him inside,' he said, anxiously, looking in the rearview mirror.

Wrapping Pietertjie in a soft blanket, she got out of the car. She climbed the stairs to the apartment, cuddling her precious baby a little tighter with each flight.

'Adam, Isabella! Adam, Isabella!' she shout-whispered, tapping on the door furiously while holding the baby in one arm.

Her sister-in-law opened the door, a bewildered look on her face, but instinctively stretched out her arms when Charmaine thrust the baby forward. She opened her mouth to ask Charmaine what was going on, but stopped short when she saw Charmaine turn on her heels and rush down the stairs again.

When Charmaine jumped back into the car a few moments later, she felt as if someone had scooped out the inside of her being.

She sobbed quietly and Pieter knew to simply keep quiet as he pressed his foot on the accelerator.

It was 9.31 am, and as Pieter tuned in to the radio, the news bulletin had already begun. Hearing her own name on the radio was like an out-of-body experience. She didn't feel like a fugitive. She felt like a grieving mother. She closed her eyes and imagined Isabella and Adam unwrapping the blanket and seeing the small note peeping out of their nephew's babygrow. She had no idea how she'd brought herself to write those words just an hour before: 'Pietertjie's clothes are at the Johannesburg Station. Please fetch them there.'[2]

When Charmaine Phillips met Pieter Grundlingh, it was a match made in hell. She was a teenager of 19 with enough emotional baggage to last four lifetimes. He was a troublemaker, constantly on the wrong side of the law.

From the moment she was born, Charmaine lived in a world of misery. Her mother was an alcoholic, while her father, who was a schizophrenic, was permanently high on dagga. This only made his psychotic symptoms worse. Her dysfunctional parents already had her three older siblings in their care. Then, around the time of her seventh birthday, the twins came along – raising the emotional temperature in the house even higher. At that point, the authorities removed Charmaine and her siblings and placed them all in foster care. According to the records, Charmaine was, during this period, severely beaten for bedwetting – yet another trauma that affected her well-being.

All the children were eventually returned to the care of their parents, and one more sibling would follow, bringing the total number of people in the household to nine. Over those years, her mother's alcoholism would lead to bouts of anger and depression, and Charmaine would often witness her mother attempting to cut her wrists in the bathroom. Her father was no comfort. Kicked out of the house by her mother after she suspected he was molesting some of the children, he was eventually taken away to a mental institution but would reappear from time to time and stay with them.

Before Charmaine became a teenager, her mother took the children to a new home in Greytown, in what was then Natal. There they lived on welfare, and her mother turned to sex work to make ends meet. Because of this, Charmaine – not yet ten – became privy to her mother's sexual activities, as she used the family home as her base for clients. Not long after this, Charmaine and her siblings were removed by the authorities once again and placed in an orphanage in Durban. Her mother became a memory that loomed large. A few years later, she heard that her mother had been murdered by an angry boyfriend who smashed a bottle over her head.

Over the next two years, Charmaine – by this time an adolescent – was moved between the orphanage and various foster homes. One day, she left a cake and a note of thanks at the most recent home, and headed off on her own once and for all. In her pocket was some money she had stolen and a plan for a new life. She was barely 14 years old by then, but was soon living on the streets earning a living as a sex worker.

By the time the doll-faced teenager met Pieter Grundlingh three years later, she'd been a sex worker, stayed on a boat in Durban harbour with a Lebanese sailor, and fallen pregnant. The sailor abandoned her, and Charmaine moved into a home for unmarried mothers in Port Elizabeth, where she gave birth to a baby boy and called him Ricky-Lee. While he was put into foster care, she was sent off to a school in Cape Town. This, the authorities hoped, would be her chance to break the cycle of dysfunction into which she had been born.

But that was not how it played out. The authority and structure of a school environment were too foreign to her after years living and working on the street, and she lasted just three hours before exiting through the gates – never to return.

She returned to Port Elizabeth in the hope of being near Ricky-Lee, and soon picked up where she had left off. She would later write to a judge, 'I discovered that selling my empty, heartless body was just as popular in Port Elizabeth as it was in Durban.'

While the records do not state how, she convinced the authorities that Ricky-Lee could be returned to her care. Just as she had done in Durban, she shacked up with a sailor, a Greek by the name of Gavril Skubridis. While he was away at sea, she would ply her trade as a sex worker, often robbing her clients as the need arose. Gavril, however, appeared as some sort of 'saviour' from the life she was living. He had allegedly organised for her and Ricky-Lee to travel to Greece with him where they could begin a new life. A date was set. When Gavril returned from his latest voyage, the three of them would head off together, with Charmaine finally leaving behind the wretched life she had lived. Another version of events,[3] however, has it that the marriage was impulsive and short-lived, that Ricky-Lee was permanently removed from her care, and that Gavril left the country before they could secure a divorce.

Whatever version is true, she never saw him again and soon resumed her old life. One day, while she was standing in the harbour, she heard someone call her name. She turned around, and behind her was an ex-boyfriend who'd been part of her life on the streets, hustling together and sharing several hair-raising experiences. Time had taken a toll on his features, and she wondered if he thought the same of her. Before long, they decided to smoke some dagga together, but neither had any, and so they began to ask around.

It was on this mission, scouting around to get high, that Charmaine's future as a killer was mapped out. As she and the ex-boyfriend moved across the harbour, they came across a man whose eyes immediately drew her in. She was only 17 at the time, and she guessed correctly that he was in his early thirties. Even in their first encounter, she could feel it: he represented everything she had come to associate with glamour and excitement.

The man was Pieter Grundlingh, and when he offered to take her on a joyride to Johannesburg for two weeks, she had no hesitation.

Pieter had grown up in the town of Ermelo, about two hours' drive east of Johannesburg. There is no record of any delinquency during his early life, and according to his family, with whom he lived in this farming region of the then Eastern Transvaal, it was a stint in jail that had turned him into a violent man. His past, however, remains elusive, as does the reason he ended up in jail if he was the sweet man his family purported him to be. On the day he and Charmaine Phillips met, he had just been granted bail after being arrested on a weapons charge, and was looking for the next best thing.

It didn't take long before the two were pursuing a common interest in drugs, alcohol and earning a dishonest living. They became inseparable, although the passion of their relationship was matched by its turmoil. Although there is no record of how long Ricky-Lee stayed with his mother and her new and much older partner, he was soon placed in foster care once again. He was eventually adopted by an Irish couple who took him back to Ireland. Charmaine never saw him again.

What was it that bonded Charmaine and Pieter? Perhaps they were simply two dark souls thrown together in a world where life was cheap – a world where they valued themselves as little as the hapless victims who crossed their path. Or perhaps it was a relief finally for each to be in the company of someone who made no pretence of having empathy for others. Or perhaps they were just thrill-seekers.

Whatever lay beneath it, they brought out the worst in one another. With Pieter at her side, Charmaine discovered a far easier way to make money than selling her body – and that was down the barrel of a gun. They would hold up people at gunpoint, make off with the money, live on it until it ran out, and then rob someone else. This became their daily bread, and as traumatised as their many victims may have been, at no point did the pair injure anyone physically.

Charmaine gave birth to Pietertjie on Christmas Eve 1982, when she was 18. On 15 June 1983, in the North Coast town of Umdloti, the two ran out of money and were looking for their next victim to rob. Umdloti was hardly a thriving metropolis where one could commit a crime and escape undetected; rather, it was a small place of around 3 000 people. At this time of year, in the middle of winter, the influx of the tourist season was still six months away.

The previous night, they had slept in the car on the beach and were now grumpy, hungover and looking to get stoned. The best hunting ground, they agreed, would be the Smugglers Inn on Point Road in Durban, some 25 minutes' drive away. 'Smuggies', as the regular clientele called the bar, had earned a reputation as a place where sex workers and sailors rubbed shoulders with rich city kids out on a jol. Attached to the two-storey Alexandra Hotel through the 1970s and 1980s, it was a popular watering hole and dance spot.

This was how 39-year-old Gerald Meyer washed up there. Even in June, this part of the world can be hot and humid, and Gerald had been surfing during the day. In his faded blue shorts and slip-slops, he'd walked alone up to the bar and ordered himself a beer, then settled in to watch a recorded rugby match on the screen above the bar counter. And that's where Pieter Grundlingh met him, chatting while he waited for the drinks he'd ordered. When the drinks arrived, Pieter invited Gerald to join him, his partner and their baby at their table. The three of them sat chatting, with Pietertjie asleep in an old pram next to the table. As the evening wore on, and Gerald relaxed with a few beers in his belly, Pieter asked him if he wanted to smoke a joint with them and go for a bit of a drive. Up for some spontaneous fun, and with no reason to doubt them, Gerald climbed into the back of the car and wound down the window while Charmaine rolled a joint.

Some 20 minutes later, Gerald noticed that the car had turned off the main road. Unaware of the imminent danger, and complaining that Pietertjie's crying was annoying him, he asked Pieter where they were headed. Pieter said they were just looking for somewhere to smoke another joint without being caught by the police.

Pieter guided the car into a dark and isolated area surrounded by cane fields, and stopped. He invited Gerald out of the car to smoke, but

Gerald, possibly sensing something amiss, declined. Before he knew it, his door was pulled open and he was dragged out of the car. Terrified, he suddenly realised what was happening: the couple was frisking him, stripping him of his keys and money. A gun was pointed in his face and, in fruitless defence, he put his hands up over his cheeks. Under an uncaring sky, he was shot at point-blank range and died instantly.

Unlike other killers who shoot a random stranger for their resources, Charmaine and Pieter had been close enough to see the humanity in their victim. They'd spent an evening together and come to know at least some of the details of his personal life.

For three days after the first murder, they lay low. Gerald was reported missing and his body was found, but no connection was made to his chance encounter with a couple and their baby in a bar. On the fourth day, they headed out again in search of more twisted adventure. The man they had befriended was now nothing more than a dead body lying in the morgue. They left Umdloti and headed for Richards Bay, about 150 km away. There, with the seats pushed back and Pietertjie crying intermittently, they spent another uncomfortable night in the car. The next day, Pieter tracked down an old friend who agreed that the family could crash in his spare room for a few nights.

Using the money they'd stolen from Gerald Meyer, Charmaine and Pieter stocked up on milk, nappies, booze and dagga, and stayed out of sight for a few days. Then, on Saturday night, Pieter went out on his own for a drink at a local pub. He wasn't gone for long, and when he returned, it was with a six-pack and a companion.

'I've offered Vernon a lift to Empangeni,' Pieter explained to Charmaine, introducing her to the younger man. Vernon Swart, 28 years old and with no reason to mistrust the couple, joined them in their temporary home, ready to drink a beer and shoot the breeze.

Like Gerald before him, Vernon climbed into the car a while later with no suspicion of anything being amiss. Feeling lucky to have found himself a lift, he settled into his seat, ready for the drive with the couple and their baby. As they pulled off, more beers were cracked open and the music began to play.

An hour later, as they drove through the small town of Melmoth, Pieter suddenly pulled off onto the side of the road and parked among some wattle trees. Before Vernon could ask the reason for the pit stop, they'd dragged him out of the car and tied him to a tree. The rope was cutting into his skin, but there was no chance of anyone driving by to help. Vernon, shivering, realised he was in serious trouble, and no sooner had this dawned on him than a single shot rang out, the bullet entering his head and killing him instantly.

Pieter frisked the dead man, relieving him of his wallet, which contained R270 and some photographs, before jumping back into the car with Charmaine and driving back to Richards Bay. They slept that night at the friend's house, and in the morning gathered up their meagre belongings and headed back to Durban. There, they checked into a hotel using cash from Vernon's wallet and remained holed up there for one day.

With two dead bodies behind them, they knew the best thing to do was to keep moving. Over the next few days, keeping a low profile and living off the money they'd stolen, they moved from town to town, never staying longer than 24 hours in any single place.

A week later they reached Ermelo. This was Pieter's old stamping ground, the place he had grown up. Here, in a bar, a familiar pattern reinstated itself: Pieter introduced himself to a man in his early thirties named Barend Greyvenstein, who was unwinding with a beer, and the two got chatting. This time, Pieter was without Charmaine at the bar, but when he joined her and Pietertjie in the car, he told Charmaine that they would be giving Barend a lift to Kinross, about an hour's drive away. He was in no rush to get there, Barend told his new friends, so he wasn't at all put out when they made a stop in Secunda, about twenty kilometres short of their destination, to have a braai with some old pals of Pieter's.

While watching a game of rugby on television, Barend made the fatal mistake of joking that he would bet all the money in his bank account – some R800 – on his favourite side. Pieter soon jumped up and said it was time to leave. He, Charmaine and Barend quickly said their goodbyes and climbed into the car, with Pietertjie asleep in Charmaine's arms. But, instead of rejoining the road to Kinross, Pieter veered off towards a dam. There, in a darkened area, the couple pulled Barend from the car, robbed him of his bank card and pocket knife, and demanded his PIN number. He gave it to them, and less than a minute later, they shot him in the head with a single bullet and left his dead body next to the dam.

From here, they drove only another kilometre before stopping outside the house of another family that Pieter knew. They knocked on the door but there was no response. Pieter kept knocking, however, until eventually someone opened up. It was a domestic worker, who told them that the family was away. But, using his knowledge of the family, he was able to convince the domestic worker that he knew them well, that they were good friends, and that he and his partner and baby needed a place to sleep for the night.

When the sun came up the next morning, they set off on a five-hour trip that would end in Bloemfontein and would include drawing all the money from Barend's account. It was here, on the outskirts of the city, that they picked up their fourth and final victim. By then, on the tail end of their killing spree, the couple had dispensed with the ritual of sharing drinks and driving down deserted roads under cover of darkness. Or perhaps because Martin Mofosi was a black man in Bloemfontein in the 1980s, sitting at a bar and pretending to be friends was simply not an option. Instead, they intercepted him walking down a road that linked the white section of the city to an outlying township. Martin, who was 25, had a long way to go and was grateful for the offer of a lift. He climbed into the car with the couple and their baby, and they asked him if he had any dagga they could share before taking him home. As with the others, however, the couple had no intention of delivering Martin to his house. Instead, they drove to a deserted spot, dragged him out of the car, robbed him of his few possessions and money, and shot him at point-blank range.

A trail of four dead bodies and a clear modus operandi led the police to a single conclusion: these were the victims of the same person or people. The killing spree had lasted, thus far, 16 days. Investigators worked round the clock to figure out who the killers might be, and though there were no eyewitnesses to the actual murders, there were enough people who had seen the couple clearly before they headed off with each victim.

A few days later, Charmaine and Pieter saw their own faces on the weekly television show *Police File*, accompanied by a plea for anyone with information about the fugitives to come forward. A massive manhunt was launched. During the three-week nationwide search, a hungry media pursued the story behind the murderous couple. For the intrigued public, Charmaine and Pieter took centre stage, while the victims and their horrific last moments quickly faded into obscurity. For the victims' families, it was a living hell as journalists gave little attention to Gerald Meyer, Vernon Swart, Barend Greyvenstein and Martin Mofosi.

The manhunt was followed by the media like a live-action television series, and 'season one' ended a month later when Charmaine and Pieter, having successfully made it through a Johannesburg roadblock to dump their baby with relatives, were finally ensnared by the authorities near Vereeniging, while riding a stolen red Kawasaki motorcycle.

After the drama of the manhunt and arrest, it was now up to the criminal justice system to deal with Charmaine and Pieter. 'Season two', the trial, began in October 1983 in the Pietermaritzburg Supreme Court. With reporters' pens poised and the public gallery packed to capacity, the process began.

Pieter had the support of his mother, Christina, 66 at the time, who was in court every day following the trial word for word and looking at her son in the way only a mother can. She would sit there silently, with tears streaming down her face, as if holding in one gargantuan sob.

Charmaine was, in contrast, a curiosity that local journalists took pleasure in describing to their spellbound readers. With a father she hadn't seen for years, and a mother long since murdered, she enjoyed no such family support in the courtroom. Described as everything from an attractive waif[4] to a wildcat hissing in court,[5] the peroxided teen was infinitely more interesting to the public than was her older male accomplice. And she played the part to perfection. On one occasion, she turned towards a photographer as if to engage him in intimate conversation, but as he drew near, she spat directly in his face. She would suddenly hiss like a cat and use foul language at the slightest provocation, and was consistently reprimanded by the judge for her behaviour.

Three weeks into the case, the judge decided that Charmaine should be sent for psychiatric observation. During this three-month hiatus, analysis and predictions flew around the press and in conversations around braais throughout the country. But when the case resumed in early 1984, Charmaine's mental health was deemed of no significance. She was fit to stand trial.

What the period of psychiatric observation had afforded her, however, was a chance to buy a gift for Pietertjie, who was now 18 months old. For the evaluation, she had been transported under heavy guard to Pretoria. In her hand, sweaty from fear and anxiety, she clutched a R50 note given to her by her advocate to buy food at the facility where she was to be evaluated.

In those days, R50 could have bought her meals far superior to the sludge she was served in jail, but instead she had asked if she could use the money to buy a gift for her son. Flanked by policemen, and with her hands firmly cuffed, she had chosen a small fluffy bear, and had fantasised non-stop about the moment when she would give it to him and hold him tight. But the universe had other plans. Charmaine stood in the holding cells below the courtroom as Pietertjie was led in by a social worker, and held the teddy bear out to the little boy. But, instead of taking it, he clung even more tightly to the social worker and quickly turned away from the stranger who called herself his mother.

Throughout the trial, the nature of the relationship between Pieter and Charmaine provoked curiosity. Was Charmaine, with her button nose, blue eyes and blonde 'flicks', every bit the cold-blooded perpetrator acting in wilful unison with her murderous partner? Or was she another victim drawn into his web of violence, an innocent who had been spotted right away by the older man as ripe for the plucking? It was the mysterious layers beneath these questions and the possible dynamics that dominated the trial in the summer of 1984.

The pair tried to dupe the criminal justice system, or at least to keep it guessing, by both claiming to have been the main perpetrator. In written statements, Pieter took full responsibility for the murder spree. But Charmaine also insisted that she alone had shot the men to death, citing their supposed provocations for her decisions: 'He got fresh with me' became a common refrain.

The judge wasn't fooled, however, and saw through her ploy: she was simply trying to save her lover from the noose, he said, knowing that she, being under 21 years of age, could not be executed. And in the end, none of it mattered anyway: the two had acted together to brutally rob four unsuspecting men of their lives.

On judgment day, as the judge uttered the words 'staggeringly wicked' to describe the couple, it was the spectre of the hangman's noose that dangled in the public's mind. In that moment, it was Pieter Grundlingh and not his teen lover who was in the spotlight. Pieter was sentenced to death, while Charmaine received four life sentences. She had, said the judge, escaped the death sentence 'by the narrowest of margins'.[6] Both Pieter's death sentence and Charmaine's narrow escape from the gallows sent a shockwave through the country.

The gallows at Pretoria Central were busy during the 1980s. Over a thousand people were hanged, many of them political prisoners who had resisted apartheid. It was a white man's world, and almost every neck that convulsed against the rope in that cold room was black. In one year, for example, over a hundred people were hanged, but only three of them were white. Those on death row would receive a 'notice of execution', and would then spend their last seven nights before the allocated date incarcerated in a section known as 'the pot'. This was a small section of the notorious prison, so called because the warders would watch the prisoners stewing in their own fear as they faced the prospect of execution.

Pieter Grundlingh, like other prisoners, was given the option of seeing three people on the eve of his execution. He asked if he could see Ivor Human, the detective who had investigated the killing spree and had, strangely, invited Pieter to have dinner at his family home the night before his sentencing more than a year earlier. Ivor caught a flight from Durban to Pretoria and made his way to the prison. There he found Pieter surprisingly calm, with an unlit cigarette in his hand. Pieter asked Ivor if he minded him smoking, and Ivor said he should go ahead. Pieter asked after the family he had met at the dinner, told Ivor how he had found Jesus, and, finally, handed him a carefully written confession in which he took 'sole responsibility' for the killings. Ivor believed it was an attempt somehow to protect Charmaine from whatever fate awaited her in prison.

The next day, a cold July morning in 1985, after spending more than a year on death row, Pieter Grundlingh climbed the 52 steps up from 'the pot' to the notorious death chamber, where seven nooses hung from the ceiling above a trapdoor. He and the few others scheduled to die that morning stood still in a straight line on the trapdoor as their faces were covered with hoods and knotted ropes were placed around their necks.

Moments later, when the convulsions had stopped and the room went quiet, the prison warders in the room below cut Pieter free from the rope, placed his and the other men's bodies on metal gurneys, and carried on with their day. Later, the bodies were washed and prepared for burial.

Pieter's remains were buried in an unmarked grave in the veld west of Pretoria, among what the state calls 'paupers and condemned prisoners' in the Zandfontein Cemetery. Charmaine, having been spared the same fate, now had to adapt to prison life. With her survival instinct as strong as ever, she spent the first six years working her way up the hierarchy of the gang system that dictates who gets what privileges. Despite her being much younger than many of the other inmates, her feisty nature fast-tracked her to the top. Living on the streets from age 14 had spawned a toughness in her that worked in her favour, but her behaviour also landed her in solitary confinement more times than anyone could count.

It was only when she found religion, in her seventh year behind bars, that the tide began to turn. She also began to make a name for herself as a competent hairdresser. As her skills improved, her deft cutting, dyeing and curling became a currency in which she could trade. Warders would later comment not only on the brilliant wash-and-cuts they received from her, for less than R10 a time, but also on the type of person she was: quiet, filled with sadness, doing her time with dignity, more ordinary than they'd expected, peaceful maybe ...[7]

She also, during the years in prison, became a keen artist and sculptor.

Arno van der Walt, a retired banker who had time and money on his hands, was running a small part-time framing business. He heard from someone in the art world that Charmaine Phillips was doing pencil sketches, oil paintings and sculptures. Someone came to his house to show him a drawing she had done, and his interest was piqued. He wanted to meet her.

He travelled to the prison, and a friendship was immediately ignited. Arno became Charmaine's mentor and agent, securing commissions for her artworks beyond the prison walls. 'I saw her not as a killer, but instead as a vulnerable woman reaching out,'[8] he told a reporter.

But despite these pursuits, there was one thought that dominated her mind during her two decades behind bars: what had happened to Pietertjie, whom she'd dumped at her in-laws on that fateful morning when the police finally cornered her. Her attachment to a son she had mothered for six months was – according to those who got to know her behind bars – an obsession of which she spoke incessantly.

For years, she was haunted by that last encounter in the holding cell when he had rejected the teddy bear. She wondered what sort of person he had grown into.

But what chance did Pietertjie, the baby born into a world of violence and driven around by his murderous parents day and night, really have? Just like his mother years before, he was an angry and nomadic child, moving from one foster home to the next with little sense of the value of his own life. The media would later make much of how Pietertjie was cut from the same cloth as his mother and father, and many argued there was no other possible path for him after his early childhood and the turmoil that followed his dad's hanging and his mother's incarceration.

By age 12, he was already involved in criminal activities. When he turned 18, he was imprisoned for housebreaking, theft and possession of drugs and stolen goods. He was released, but at 21 he was back behind bars for possession of stolen goods. This time, he was sentenced to 18 months in prison.

Charmaine's connection to him, despite all those years of separation, was unchanged. During his troubled youth, he had not visited her in prison, but no sooner had he arrived in chains at Leeuwkop Prison in Johannesburg than he requested a transfer to Kroonstad in the Free State so he could be near his mother. This was eventually granted. He was sent to Kroonstad Medium B Prison for juvenile offenders, not far from the Kroonstad women's prison. Every second Wednesday, prisoners were allowed a short visit with another prisoner, and so Pietertjie would see his mother on those occasions. She, for her part, gave him whatever money she had earned while incarcerated.

Pietertjie served nine months of his 18-month sentence, and was then paroled. Within a month of his release, a rumour spread that Charmaine herself would soon be a free woman. She and 16 others, all serving life sentences, had applied to the parole board. Both behind the prison walls and in the outside world, Charmaine still had a kind of celebrity status. When the news finally broke that she was marked for freedom, every journalist in town hoped to capture the moment she stepped out from behind the walls and began her new life.

✜

It was Friday, 20 August 2004, and several journalists had travelled to Kroonstad Prison, where they sat clutching their coffee cups and chatting, waiting for Charmaine's release. Some had travelled several hours by car to capture the moment. But Charmaine was a no-show, and a warder broke the news to those gathered outside: she had slipped quietly from the prison at one minute past midnight. Her new life had already begun.

Diewie van Zyl, a hair-salon owner in Kroonstad, had given her a job. As Diewie told journalists still on the hunt for the story, 'We're giving her a chance but ultimately we're employing her because she's a talented hairstylist. We've seen the work she's done on warders in the town and there's no question – she's the best.'[9]

This new life of freedom and employment would not be without its limitations. Her parole conditions were such that she could be away from her house or place of work only for four hours per day, and was not to touch any alcohol or drugs. To break those conditions would mean a return to prison to resume her four life sentences. She was required to participate in local community-service projects, and though these conditions would be reviewed half a year later, some form of parole would persist for the rest of her life.

State-sanctioned freedom was one thing, as was a second chance from an employer who valued her skills. Forgiveness from the families of those murdered in cold blood was another, however. Shortly before her release at age 41, Charmaine – starting afresh after nearly twenty years behind bars – wrote a letter to the victims' families in which she said, 'I wish to apologise. I am sorry and regret the loss, grief and the harm we afflicted [sic] upon you and your deceased loved ones.'[10]

For Leon Greyvenstein, brother of Barend who was shot in the head after giving out his PIN number, this was yet another case of Charmaine Phillips being thrust into the public eye while his brother and the three other victims remained in the anonymous shadows of their own deaths.

'She killed four people and she must spend her life behind bars,'[11] he told the media upon hearing that she had been freed.

For two years following her release, Charmaine finally got to bond with her son. Pietertjie, however, had his own shattered life to deal with. Perpetually in trouble with the law, he became a prostitute and contracted HIV.

A commissioned sketch she had done in prison silently told the story of her and Pietertjie's relationship: a young woman holds a baby in her arms. The baby has the wings of an angel. Tears run down the woman's cheeks. At the bottom is written, 'My Little Angel of Comfort'.

One afternoon in March 2006, Charmaine got the call: Pietertjie had died, alone and in his sleep, at his home in Vrededorp.

The following year, Charmaine Phillips tied the knot in Kroonstad with Hennie Rabie, a man described by locals as the antithesis of the boys and men of her youth.

Still remaining silent about her past, present or future, she slipped into obscurity, or what some might call a life of normality – and remains the enigma she has always been.

CHAPTER 4

JOEY HAARHOFF

✝✝

Pretoria, 1988

Francina Johanna Hermina Haarhoff, or Joey as she was known, wasn't the first woman to look in the mirror above the basin at 227 Malherbe Street, Pretoria. Nor was she the first woman to fall in love with Cornelius Gerhardus (Gert) van Rooyen, the man she could hear stirring his coffee in the kitchen. It was just a few weeks into their relationship, and she felt as if she knew every part of his morning ritual, from the delicate trimming of his moustache to the low humming of a tune just before he'd say, 'I'll put in my own sugar, thanks.'

'Okay,' she would say affectionately, as if hearing it for the first time. At age 48, she had all but given up on the idea of finding love again. But suddenly, there it was, in the form of a well-dressed man four years her senior who was also not looking forward to growing old alone.

Coffee in hand, he would walk across the lawn in front of the single-storey house that was painted in a shade of apricot Joey had chosen. He would check if the newspaper had been delivered, thrown over the low concrete wall near the black metal gate. Collecting the paper, he would put it and his coffee on the wire-mesh outdoor table before bending down and dipping one hand into the shallow end of the small swimming pool. Straightening up, he'd rub his hands together, then give them a shake.

'Spring is here, bokkie,' she would call to him out of the bathroom window. 'I can smell the jasmine.'

He would give a half-smile, pick up the paper and cup of coffee, and carry on towards the house.

There is a very clever way to put on frosted-blue eyeshadow. Her mother had told her how, and she was right. She had mastered the trick during her first marriage: it was all about the eyebrows. The trick was to draw them on as if using a compass. Even as the years were spreading grey over her hair, the eyebrow pencil was dark brown with the slightest touch of auburn. Getting the two eyebrows to look identical was also part of the trick. With that done, she slowly ran the small brush along the square of eyeshadow powder, gave it a slight puff to remove any excess particles, and began to apply it.

She did her make-up this way on any given day, but today, really, was something special. She and Gert would be travelling all the way to Randburg in Johannesburg. She could already smell the toasted cheese-and-tomato sandwich that he would buy for her on the way out of Pretoria as they began the journey to the big city. Not that Pretoria itself was small, mind you. She wondered what it would be like if they lived in a small dorpie like some of her cousins did. Would people recognise Gert? Would they whisper behind their hands to each other, 'There's the man who just got out of jail.'

He had served his time, and now he was serving God, she told herself, and though Pretoria was certainly smaller than Johannesburg, it was large enough for a man with a criminal record to blend into the crowd. Not just that: he was now back on his feet running a construction company. 'It's very respectable work,' she would tell him, straightening his tie.

He was also a lay preacher at her church, which he had recently joined. She had been immediately attracted to his distinguished-looking face. After the service, having heard he had a construction company, she made up a question to ask him (about the way the church was built) just to be near him. As their eyes locked, a connection was established.

Over the next few weeks, things had moved rapidly. He'd poured out his heart to her about his three years in jail; he had been sentenced to four years but had been released on good behaviour. She immediately felt proud of him, and ever since then, took any opportunity she could to tell him how respectable he was.

She loved that word. Respectable. Those people who had put him behind bars obviously had no idea what a God-fearing man he was. She sometimes wished she could go back to Pretoria Central Prison and show the warders a photograph of the man Gert had become. The picture she had in mind had been taken just a few weeks earlier, at a small photographic studio on the outskirts of Pretoria. It wasn't a special occasion. It was simply her way of saying that the relationship was serious and that framed portraits on a mantelpiece would make that very clear to anyone asking questions.

Joey had spared no effort in preparing for the visit to the photographic studio, and had even bought a special outfit at Greatermans: a black Crimplene skirt, and a white blouse with sleeves that sat just above the elbow. The neckline, trimmed in black, was square – a shape that Bokkie said showed her off as the elegant woman she was.

Then she'd helped Gert choose his own outfit, a moment she knew would be special to him. No longer a prisoner, now a proud man of strength. She'd picked out a black suit with an ornate button on the breast pocket, and a well-cut white shirt. But, really, the most beautiful part was the tie: black and copper stripes. Just before they made their way to the cashier, she leaned over a wooden counter near the front of the store and picked out a tie clip. 'This will really complete your outfit,' she said.

He quickly chose an accessory for her too: a black disc on a long thin black rope that she could place around her neck.

Now, in the car, she put her hand on his leg, thinking back to that first encounter at the church. In the week that followed, she had done some investigative work. In 1954, when he was 16 years old, he had been sent to a reformatory after he had stolen a car. Four years later, he was caught stealing clothing and motor spares and couldn't seem to get his life on track. He 'settled down' with a woman named Aletta, and they had six children. For a time, all had been calm, but then, in 1979, he'd abducted two young girls, aged 10 and 13, and taken them to Hartbeesport Dam. There, he'd physically assaulted them, instructed them to strip naked, and forced them to perform sexual acts. He'd released them in Pretoria the following day, and had been arrested shortly afterwards.

She kept the information to herself. Others, she knew, would judge him – just like his previous wife, who had left him because of it. She found it secretly exciting, the way he'd wielded power like that, and besides, she knew how children sometimes just asked for it. Her mind went back to her own daughter, Amor, and how her behaviour had made it necessary to punish her. She could still hear the girl – now a woman in her late twenties – sobbing in her bed. She could also remember the girl's sullen face after her father went into her room twice a week and shut the door behind him.

But she had put all that behind her. She recalled when she and Gert arrived at the photographic studio. Gert had been a regular client of Marthinus's before his time in jail, and when Joey rang the bell, she wondered if the photographer's attitude towards Gert would have changed. But, as soon as the door swung open, it was as if the three years of Gert's absence had been erased from history. Over the next two hours, they struck a variety of poses that would tell the world who they were – a homely but respectable couple, upholding the principles of religion, family and country.

When they collected the prints a few days later, she laughed and said her favourite picture held a secret you could only see if you looked closely enough: Gert, dapper as dapper could be, had a kink in his tie just by the pin.

'Our little secret,' she said, stroking his back.

Now, a few weeks later, it was spring in Pretoria, and Joey felt a rush of excitement. As she finished applying the frosted-blue eyeshadow, and a layer of pearly pink lipstick, she gave herself one last look in the mirror. A special occasion, she said to herself, making sure one last time that the overnight curlers had done their job.

Hearing Bokkie's footsteps at the kitchen door, she turned and walked down the passage to meet him there. 'Are you ready?' she asked.

'I'm ready,' he said. 'Have you found the right place for us to go?'

She nodded. 'It's a place called Cresta Shopping Centre. There are lots of primary schools in the area, according to the map.'

✢

That morning, in a small house on the corner of Queens Avenue and Beatrice Street in Windsor Park, Johannesburg, 14-year-old Tracy-Lee Scott-Crossley was woken by the alarm clock. Monday morning. School. Ugh. She pulled the covers round her shoulders, but as she moved across the no-man's land between slumber and wakefulness, she coughed and then remembered: today she could stay at home. She was sick; she had a mild lung infection and an eye infection, the doctor had told her mother on Saturday after briefly examining Tracy-Lee.

Her mom, Noreen, came in and, smiling, stroked Tracy-Lee's face. She was worried about her daughter, who'd been experiencing blackouts recently, and who, she suspected, might have epilepsy. With no father in the house, she and her only daughter were very close, more like friends than mother and daughter. 'Nunu, do you want to come with me to work?' she asked.

'Thanks, Mom, but I think I'll just stay home in bed, if that's okay? If I'm feeling better later, I might walk down to Cresta.'

With that, her mother gave her hand a quick squeeze and then left, locking the front door behind her.

A few hours later, feeling much more cheerful, but bored in bed, Tracy-Lee asked her elder brother, Mark, to accompany her to Cresta Shopping Centre, a walk she and her mother often did together. When he declined, saying he had things to do, she set off on her own.

Was it Joey who spotted the girl first? With her short blonde hair, wise eyes that seemed older than the rest of her physique, and a baggy shirt over a pair of jeans, Tracy-Lee walked the familiar route. But, at some point that morning, a car slowly cruised up beside her. Joey rolled the window down, smiled at the young girl who had no reason to mistrust her, and motioned for her to come towards the car so she could ask her something.

Behind that smile and the appearance of a dependable 'tannie' (auntie) was a past that had left indelible scars on Joey's own daughter. As an adult, Amor was haunted by memories of being punched in the stomach when she was still young enough to be sleeping in a cot. Joey would wind Amor so badly that the young girl thought she was dying, and would drag her around by the hair and pull her ears so hard that the skin at the back would tear. Amor was constantly covered in bruises on her arms and legs, but none of her teachers, nor anyone in the community, saw fit to investigate what was happening in the house where she lived with her parents and brothers.

Then there was the emotional abuse, the constant put-downs – telling her that she was worth nothing and would amount to nothing. Joey would tell Amor she wished she was dead. Worse yet, while Joey abused Amor physically and emotionally, she allowed Amor's father to violate their daughter sexually on a regular basis.

Amor's father was in the military, and on Wednesdays and Sundays he was allowed to leave work early for regular sports events. On those days, when Amor returned home, her dad would be waiting for her and would call her into the bedroom where he would 'do things he shouldn't be doing, things that weren't right'.[1]

Joey was aware of what went on, and did nothing. She let her husband have his way with their young daughter. One day, Amor's grandmother came back to the house to fetch something she had forgotten there earlier. And it was then that she saw it, through the kitchen window: Amor's father sexually abusing his daughter. But, when she told Joey the shocking news, Joey said she already knew what was happening, and as before did nothing about it.

So, when Joey prowled the streets around Randburg with Gert on that day in 1988, she was hardly the sweet woman who had been turned into a monster by her lover. Instead, she played her role of trustworthy stranger to perfection.

Noreen later said that Joey must have said something very convincing to lure her daughter into the car, as Tracy-Lee had been hyper-aware of 'stranger danger'. In fact, just a few days before her disappearance, she'd fallen out with her friends when they'd said that going to a disco was a normal and safe thing to do, whereas Tracy-Lee had felt it was dangerous and that anything could happen there. Noreen thought it likely that Gert and Joey had said something along the lines of, 'Your mother has been in an accident. Get in and we'll take you to her.'[2]

It is not clear whether the couple abducted her in the parking lot at Cresta, or outside her house. Eyewitnesses claimed to have seen her getting into a VW Beetle at the shopping mall, but Noreen insisted that Tracy-Lee had made it home before she was abducted: she'd left work at 2.40 pm to check up on her daughter, and had arrived home less than half an hour later to find her daughter absent but the items she'd purchased at Cresta on her bed next to a textbook – pens and pencils, a pair of stockings and a packet of Whispers.

Those were the last signs of life.

In the days after Tracy-Lee's disappearance Noreen's personal tragedy became a cold fear that spread over the city. The idea of a child disappearing from the suburbs shocked every parent in Johannesburg. Those in other parts of the country knew about it, and no doubt shuddered to imagine their own children being scooped off the streets. But this was a once-off tragedy, a Johannesburg story, they told themselves.

Then, in December of that year, some 500 km away in what was then the province of Natal, 11-year-old Fiona Harvey set off from her house in the suburb of Clarendon in Pietermaritzburg. She was a petite girl with sparkling eyes, an impish smile and feathery short blonde hair. Her mother had sent her out to a local shop to buy some milk. It was just a few days before Christmas and her mother had much baking and other preparations to do.

Fiona lived in a world where children moved freely through the streets with little adult supervision: Clarendon was a small, close-knit community, and, according to other parents, kids could always be seen riding their bikes to each other's houses and walking unaccompanied to and from school. Fiona lived with her family in a typical Maritzburg house – wooden floors throughout, a lush garden wrapping around the front and back, a few steps leading up to the front door, and almost no security measures.

Her school, Clarendon Primary, had large open sports fields, and was surrounded by green hills. On that day, 22 December, Fiona walked right past the office of the principal, Digby Rhodes, who was at the school preparing for the academic year ahead. She knew the roads well, and was expected home from the shop, which was less than a kilometre away, within 20 minutes.

Except, 20 minutes turned into an hour, and then the hours piled up with no sign of the girl with the carton of milk. Her frantic family alerted everyone they could, and soon everyone in the community was searching for her, making their way up and down the streets of the suburb. The primary school soon became the headquarters of their efforts, the family home a nest of panic.

At the time, what had happened to Fiona was a complete mystery. Later, when the whole drama came to a head, eyewitness reports emerged that Gert van Rooyen had been seen in the area in a white Ford Bantam bakkie branded with the name and logo of his construction company. There were no mentions of Joey Haarhoff, and nobody knew for sure if she was with him in Pietermaritzburg, but the assumption was that Joey must have been waiting in the wings, if not in the bakkie, putting on her best show as an affable tannie.

Information also later surfaced that, at some time during the spate of abductions, Joey had phoned a children's home in Pretoria and, in her sweetest voice, had offered to take in young girls for the holidays and at weekends. The offer was declined but, undeterred, Joey and Gert applied to become foster parents. Their applications were rejected, and so the search for a supply of young girls had continued on the city streets.

On 7 June 1989, almost six months after Fiona's disappearance, 12-year-old Joan Horn went for a walk with two friends in Pretoria West, where she lived with her family. Just like Fiona Harvey, Joan lived in a world where young friends had always walked around safely – between each other's homes, to the shops, to school. On this particular day, a car had pulled up alongside Joan and her two friends. A middle-aged woman had rolled down the window and gently offered Joan R20 if she would hop in the car and show her where a certain shop was located. Joan, keen to earn some pocket money, left her friends and drove off with the woman. Joan's mother, Ansie, had expected her home as on any other day, but she never arrived.

As the Horn family's torment began, there was some hope that her two young friends would be able to provide some fruitful leads, but they had said everything that they could: Joan had driven off with an older woman in the hope of earning some pocket money.

A month later, with the other three families still living with the heartbreak of a missing child, Durban teenager Janet Delport, 16 at the time, was found wandering around a shopping mall in a state of disorientation. She immediately became the investigators' biggest hope as a source of information. She was treated by a doctor and then taken to the police station and given all the time she needed to recall what had transpired. Unfortunately, she could remember almost nothing of the incident, except that a blonde woman had approached her at the mall. Perhaps over the days that followed something would trigger her memory. Perhaps, as the shock abated, a faint image would come to mind, they thought.

But nothing ever came, and the authorities eventually moved on.

For Joey Haarhoff, a fetcher on the prowl for new victims, this had been a failed attempt. She now changed tack and began to prey on her own family and social circle.

Joey's sister, Babs Wessels, was the mother of five daughters. She lived directly opposite the public swimming pool in Kempton Park, a flat and featureless area not far from Johannesburg's biggest airport. Joey made the fifty-kilometre journey to visit Babs on a regular basis, and after she met Gert in 1988, he would join her. With Joey as the bridge, the paedophile found himself in a social milieu in which people took care of each other's children, with mothers and fathers, aunts and uncles becoming almost interchangeable in the lives of the young ones.

It's impossible to say if Joey's trips to visit her sister were part of some sort of master plan, or if what had once been innocuous sisterly visits took a sinister turn once Joey was coupled with Gert. Either way, the familiarity between the adults and children laid the ground for the next abductions, while the public pool, full of kids in bathing suits, became a convenient source of prey.

One day, Gert was hanging around at the public pool in Kempton Park. There, splashing around in the water with her friends, was Yolanda Wessels, Joey's niece. With Yolanda was her close friend and classmate, Odette Boucher, 11 years old. They got out of the pool and were standing on the side. Odette's older sister Natasha was also there with her friends. The older girls pointed out a 'handsome young man'[3] swimming in the pool. He later got out of the water and walked towards an older man. With the older girls commenting on the younger man's looks, Odette then boasted that she knew them, and just to prove it, went up to them and started chatting.

The younger man, a random stranger, hardly said anything before wandering off. But the older man was Gert van Rooyen, and within the social context, nobody thought anything of the encounter: Gert was simply seen as Yolanda's new 'uncle', and Odette was Yolanda's friend.

But that was probably the moment that he set his sights on Odette.

A few weeks later, on the afternoon of Friday 22 September 1989, Odette and her friend from Laerskool Kreft, 12-year-old Anne-Marie Wapenaar, decided to have a swim at Odette's house after school. The public pool was always much more fun, a place where everyone socialised in summer, but on this day they felt like being just the two of them in the pool at the house. They told Linette, Odette's mother, that they were going to Anne-Marie's flat a few blocks away to fetch her bathing costume, a route they often took.

So safe was their world that Linette thought nothing of it when they set off, and also had no concerns when they took a little longer than expected. They had probably just found something else that was fun to do at Anne-Marie's place.

When Odette's father arrived home after 3.30 pm, however, and found his daughter wasn't there, he became worried. It being a Friday, school had come out early, which meant that the girls had been gone for quite some time. Linette went with Odette's younger brother to Anne-Marie's flat to look for the girls, almost certain that they would find them there. But, on arrival, they discovered the girls had never been there. With panic slowly setting in, they drove all over Bonaero Park, a nearby suburb where many of their friends lived.

Still, there was no sign of the girls.

As they turned back into their street after searching, they thought they would now hear the sounds of the girls swimming and giggling in the water. Perhaps they had come home in the interim. But, as they walked through the house and into the back garden where the swimming pool was ... silence.

At 5.40 pm, after two hours of increasingly frantic searching, Linette went to the police station to report the girls missing. She was told, as was the rule in those days, that a person could not be reported missing, and a case opened, until two days had passed since they were last seen.

Over the weekend, the stress and anxiety of both the families and the broader community grew. On the Monday, a police report could finally be registered. Search parties were organised, there were moments of hope, prayer too, and then ... nothing.

What happened on that short walk from Odette's house towards Anne-Marie's flat where they never turned up? Unlike the previous victims, to whom Joey and Gert were total strangers, Odette and Anne-Marie probably recognised them as Yolanda's tannie and oom (uncle), and felt safe speaking to them when approached.

A week after their disappearance, Anne-Marie's mother, Kobie, received a letter in the post, ostensibly from her daughter. She and Odette had joined some boys and run away to Durban, the note said.

On the one hand, the letter gave a sliver of hope that the girls were still alive. On the other hand, it simply increased the families' anxiety since, although in Anne-Marie's handwriting, it appeared to have been written under duress.

A week later, another letter turned up, this time written by Odette and making the same claim. Curiously, it had been written and posted on the same day as Anne-Marie's – the day after the girls had disappeared. The reason for its arriving a week later never came to light.

After that, there was nothing.

Then came the next victim, Yolanda Wessels, and it is her story that takes us into the darkest chamber of Joey's heart. This was her flesh and blood, her own niece, and she handed her to the monstrous Gert.

With her dark eyes, short hair and a cheeky smile, Yolanda was a *laatlammetjie* (late arrival) who had four elder sisters and came from a loving family. Like everyone else in the community in Kempton Park, she walked around the neighbourhood with her friends but always returned home, where she was nurtured and protected by her parents.

On 3 November 1989, as she walked home from school, she was thinking about her missing friends. Odette and Anne-Marie still had not been found, and the devastated community was on high alert, issuing warnings to parents, drumming it into children's heads not to speak to strangers, and keeping a sharp eye on every one of them as they moved between home, school, shops, the public swimming pool ... So, when a car pulled up next to her, and it wasn't a stranger inside but her smiling, grey-haired aunt, she thought nothing of it. She opened the door, greeted Joey and her new oom, and slid in.

That was how Yolanda Wessels became the sixth face on the 'missing girls' posters that haunted every parent as 1989 came to an end. Drawn to the story by fascination and fear in equal measure, the public gaze fixated on what type of evil could possibly be lurking behind the disappearance of the girls, whose names were now known by heart to many people. It was a fear that soaked through the veil of suburban society.

The December holidays began, bringing summer rains and festive-season tinsel and tunes – but no trace of the six missing girls. For each of the families, the Christmas stretch was an endless cycle of emotional torture that began every morning the second they opened their eyes. For the families of Tracy-Lee, Fiona and Joan, it was the second such December holiday. For those of the three friends Anne-Marie, Odette and Yolanda, the reality began to set in: the girls might never come home.

Christmas. Boxing Day. Unbought gifts for a missing child. Preparation for the first day of school. No pressed uniform and packed lunchbox. No labelling of stationery or covering of books.

January 1990. A new year. A new decade. A new victim ...

On 11 January, Joey stood in Church Square in Pretoria, scanning the area. Joan Booysen, a petite 16-year-old, was making a call from a public telephone. Joan's family had moved far away from her school during the holidays, and she was still getting used to the new schedule of catching two different buses to get there. On that morning, she had missed one bus and was trying to get hold of her mother.

Joey, approaching Joan on the pretext of offering her a job, asked if she could help. Joan explained her transport issues, and Joey – in what became her notorious blonde wig – offered the young woman a lift. It was just the two of them in the car.

Joey said to Joan that she must first go past her house in Capital Park to tell her husband that she was making the drive to the school, and so she headed straight for 227 Malherbe Street. There, she asked Joan to wait in the car, but re-emerged from the house a few moments later to say that her husband wasn't home. 'He won't be long,' she told the young woman. 'Come into the house, we'll wait for him inside.'[4]

A curious backstory is that the previous year, Joan had had to do a project for school that focused on crime. She'd chosen to look at the case of the six missing girls, and had meticulously cut out the pictures of Tracy-Lee, Fiona, the other Joan, Anne-Marie, Odette and Yolanda. The project had made her keenly aware of stranger danger, as had her mother's constant injunctions never to get into the car of someone she didn't know – let alone enter their house.

Perhaps because it was so unthinkable that the face of evil might be a female with all the outward traits of a nurturer, Joan ignored all the warning signs of which she thought she was aware. As the schoolgirl sipped a glass of Tropika, Joey offered her a tour of the house.

Joan walked with Joey down a passage, and suddenly a man appeared from one of the rooms. He pointed a gun in her face and she tried to kick him, but then Joey wrestled her down and forced a handful of pills down her throat. Frogmarched down the passage, Joan's blood ran cold when she saw a photograph of one of the girls from a missing-persons poster and a schoolbag in one of the rooms. And then it hit her: this is the house of horrors. This is the end.

As the sleeping pills made her drowsy, Gert cut her school top off her body and molested her. He and Joey then locked her up in a cupboard and left the house, assuming that the girl would pass out from the pills.

But she didn't.

The adrenaline produced by terror and the effects of the chemicals on her brain fought in opposite directions for control of her body, but she managed to stay awake. She felt around to see if there was anything in the cupboard that could help her. She found a polystyrene cooler box and used the lid to manipulate the lock. She thrust the door open and sprinted as fast as she could. She neither saw nor heard any other victims in the house.

She ran outside and flagged down a passing car. She told the driver she had been kidnapped, and then finally the pills kicked in and she passed out.

When Joey and Gert returned, they discovered in horror that their latest prisoner had escaped. Knowing that the police would soon be hot on their trail, they packed up in a state of panic and fled.

Their first stop was the house of Gert's ex-wife, Aletta, who lived in Mountain View in Pretoria West. Gert and Aletta had been divorced since 1983 when Gert had come out of prison, but the two, who had had six children together, had stayed in close contact.

They told her they'd abducted a young girl but that she'd escaped.

That same day, they fled to Natal and were stopped at a speed trap near Hilton. It later emerged that 'two sleepy-looking blonde girls' were in the back of the white bakkie, and police concluded they were likely Anne-Marie and Odette. Why had Aletta not contacted the police? Had she, in fact, helped Van Rooyen with the crime that landed him in jail ten years earlier? Or was she just loyal to him? Or had she perhaps been paid to keep quiet?

By the next day, Friday, they were back in Pretoria. They made their way to the house of Joey's daughter, by then married and called Amor van der Westhuyzen, but found no one there.

Amor said she and her husband and son arrived home to find broken glass. On entering the house, they came upon the exhausted couple asleep in the living room. What had happened during that 24-hour period during which they had driven to and from Natal? Had they murdered the girls and buried them somewhere? Knowing that the police were closing in on them, they were surely doing what they could – possibly in a highly manic state – to cover their tracks. Did this include murder and burials in shallow graves?

Joey and Gert told Amor that they had tried to kidnap a policeman's daughter to extort money. When a horrified Amor said that they should rather hand themselves in, her mother replied, 'My child, you don't understand. They are going to kill us.'

Amor began to panic and the pair abruptly left. It was only later that day when she spoke to her aunt – not Yolanda's mom but another of Joey's sisters – that the pieces fell into place. The manhunt, the white bakkie, the VW Kombi …

Meanwhile, that night Joey and Gert returned to Aletta's house, slept there, and, bizarrely, attended Gert's youngest son's school athletics event on the Saturday. Perhaps this was the best they could come up with under the circumstances: blend into the crowd of other middle-aged parents at a school event.

Shortly afterwards, they left for Natal once again and made their way to a holiday spot in Umdloti that Joey had often frequented before meeting Gert.

By then, Aletta had been told by the police to leave her house as they were staking it out.

The next day, Joey and Gert headed back to Pretoria, making for 227 Malherbe Street.

In the early hours of Monday morning, 15 January, the white bakkie was spotted by police. Gert sped away and eventually slammed on the brakes before frantically pulling out two revolvers, a .22 and a .357.

Gert lifted the one revolver and shot Joey clean through the head with a single bullet. With her blood and brains sprayed over the interior of the car, it was now his turn. He lifted the other pistol to his temple and pulled the trigger.

In that single moment, with the police closing in, Gert silenced the only two people who could tell the families where their children were. Suicide was the most supreme act of selfishness. Now only the blood-soaked interior of the car stood as forensic material, robbing the police of answers to questions they were hoping to ask. Next was the house in Capital Park, not far from the small bridge where the couple had died.

When police swept the house of horrors, they found small items that were at once poignant memorials of lives once lived and also crucial evidence in a case that nonetheless went cold. Odette's home address and phone number were found written on a piece of paper hidden under a carpet in the garage. Her class-captain badge and yellow bag were also found at the house. Anne-Marie's address and the house keys that she wore on a string around her neck were also found, and, most disturbingly, so were the envelopes and paper with which the girls had been forced to write the letters home. What wasn't found, however, was any physical trace of the six missing girls themselves, alive or dead.

Their fate, once they were in Joey and Gert's clutches, could only be imagined in the darkest part of the mind. Any layers of newly exposed evidence would introduce more horrifying questions for the families and detectives alike. For example, when it came to light that the couple often travelled on the road between the Transvaal and Natal (today Gauteng and KwaZulu-Natal), an obvious question was: what happened to the girls when the couple set off to trap another victim? Were the girls left boarded up in the house of horrors in Pretoria when the couple left for Natal, or were they drugged and put in the back of the white Bantam bakkie? Or had they already been killed, their young bodies disposed of to conceal any inculpatory evidence?

As the story developed, and ever since, Joey was cast as the supporting actor in this depraved true-life drama. Always mentioned second in both broadcast and print news reports, she seemed to exist only in relation to Gert. Consistently referred to as his 'lover' or 'accomplice' or 'mistress', she was often described as the woman in a blonde wig whom Gert had 'used' to lure the young girls into his clutches. He was always the subject and she the passive party. Through this rhetoric, her agency in the horrific crimes was played down. She was, ultimately, cast as an ambiguous character, dancing in the shadows between perpetration and victimhood, and yet her role had been crucial, with no indication whatsoever that it was played under duress.

In the days between Joan Booysen's brave escape, and Joey and Gert's bloody end in a car near Malherbe Street, more news broke every day. From the details sketched out by Joan to the dramatic car chase in the early hours of the morning, the gruesome story of the predatory pair flared up in the public realm – and firmly lodged itself in the national memory.

The couple had taken their secret to the grave, but surely, everyone thought, some crucial evidence would eventually come to light.

It was simply going to be a sensational waiting game …

The revelation that the girls had been abducted by a white 'oom and tannie' went counter to every message the government propaganda machine was trying to spread in the white suburbs. The indoctrination was relentless and ranged from the subtle to the crass.

By the late 1980s, when the girls went missing, apartheid's anxiety had culminated in another state of emergency as the Nationalist government clung to power in the face of the injustice and anger it had bred. White suburbia, with its patchwork of green lawns and domestic servants, was whispering around its swimming pools. *It is coming. The end of all this is coming.*

I was in my final year of high school, barely two years older than Joey Haarhoff and Gert van Rooyen's oldest victim. My school was a sea of white adolescent females that the Transvaal education department had tried so hard to shape into the apartheid automatons of tomorrow. But the centre wasn't holding. Things were falling apart.

By then, fear and loathing were in the curriculum, and at least once a week the stern voice of the principal would come over the intercom to warn of a bomb drill. Not much later – during double maths, I always hoped – the siren would go off. And then you would see it, the shape of manufactured fear in the suburbs. Five-hundred-plus white teenage girls walking in single file down the grey corridors of the school, stripped of any critical thinking by the apartheid system.

In summer, it was almost a treat to have bomb drill – a legitimate escape from the classroom into the sunlight of a Joburg afternoon. In spring, you could see the jacaranda trees at the other end of the field. In winter, the single files would snake their way down to the lower hockey field where, as if parts of a single beast, we would sit down on the corn-coloured grass, our skin itching beneath the synthetic material of our black stockings.

These were the cogs of the propaganda machine. We were told whom to trust and whom to fear, and the former were tannies who looked like Joey Haarhoff and ooms who looked like Gert van Rooyen.

And then, with news of the manhunt, the gaze turned from the enemy who, we were taught, would try to puncture the membrane of white suburbia to plant bombs under our school desks. Suddenly, the danger 'out there' gave way to the predator within, the one who could wear a face of familiarity but drive you to your death.

Eventually, as the weeks passed and nothing turned up, the haunting photographs of the six girls began to peel from lampposts and road signs. The endless warnings from our parents not to speak to any stranger whatsoever, 'no matter what they look like', began to lose their urgency.

And slowly the case of the missing school girls went cold.

Except for the families. As time went by, their sense of loss was always at odds with the hope they held in the absence of any remains being found.

Ansie Horn, mother of the missing Joan, likely echoed what the trauma had done to every loved one for whom the disappearance had left such a devastating void. A decade and a half after Joan had vanished, she said she would spot a stranger on the street who could make her heart pound because maybe, just maybe, she was looking into the deep blue eyes of her daughter, who would have been a woman in her twenties.

She said she sometimes found herself running after someone whose hair and face resembled Joan's because 'something catches your eye and you have to have a closer look'. She added, 'Afterwards you think: that was crazy.'[5] But, in all the years after her disappearance, the face of Joan only looked at her from a large portrait that was hung in the entrance of the house shortly after she went missing.

Over the thirty years since the tragedy of the six schoolgirls, the families have had both hope and pain reignited. False sightings and eager psychics who claim to be in touch with the girls' spirits have all played their part, but the most significant have always come in the form of skeletal remains. These have the power to erase all hope that the girls are alive, but also carry the promise of closure at the very least.

In March 2007, freak waves along the coast of KwaZulu-Natal pounded the shore with such force that part of a road in the town of Umdloti was washed away. When the storm abated, someone noticed bones jutting out from the sand – newly exposed by the wave damage. It also happened to be less than half a kilometre from a cottage where Joey and Gert used to stay. These technical details, coupled with desperation, led the families to believe that the fate of their children would finally be known. For the public, too, the sensational story from almost two decades ago seemed to be reaching its long-awaited conclusion.

The police arrived. Mechanical diggers were brought in. Forensic experts began the painstaking task of removing the bones from their sandy bed. The sniffer dogs were led in as crowds of people gathered behind the incident tape strung around the site by police.

The humid air brought sweat to all who played their part, until eventually, the bones (which made up two skeletons) were safely freed. They were taken to a mortuary in Durban and then carefully transported to a laboratory in Pretoria, not far from the house of horrors itself, for testing. Again, this seemed like a logical conclusion to the story. But it wasn't. DNA testing proved that the bones came from two different skeletons, one of which was a black female adult and the other a child. Although the race and gender of the child's skeleton could not be determined, there was no match with the DNA of the missing girls. Also, just as importantly, the forensic pathologist determined that the bones had lain in the sand for ten years at most – a fact that would not fit the timeline of the abductions and deaths of the attackers.

Later that year, an ex-policeman from the Free State, Danie Krugel, got his bite at fame when he claimed to have developed a machine that used 'quantum physics' and would lead authorities to the missing girls. The way it worked, he said, was that a DNA sample could lead someone to the 'master body' if used in conjunction with his tailor-made 'Matter Orientation System'.

It's hard to imagine how Ansie Horn must have felt when she handed over a single strand of Joan's hair that she found between the pages of one of her schoolbooks. Had desperation blinded her to the absurdity of Krugel's invention?

The acclaimed documentary television programme *Carte Blanche* ran a special segment on Krugel and the missing girls. He had pinpointed a vacant plot – the size of two soccer fields – located six blocks away from Gert's house, and claimed the girls' bones were buried there. *Carte Blanche* hired experts to comb the land, but no skeletons turned up. Then the producers took it a step further and called in a clairvoyant.

Ultimately, some human bones were found, but these were not a match for the missing girls. If the families' hopes had been shredded, so too was the loyalty of many fans of *Carte Blanche*. They turned on it, saying they were outraged that such credence had been given to the fake gimmickry of Danie Krugel who they said was a quack scientist. While the fans soon moved on, the families' emotions had been stirred up once again.

Then, as if 2007 hadn't brought enough emotional turmoil to the families of the missing, there was one more event that year that held the potential to solve the mystery of the girls' fate. The owner of a property adjoining the house of horrors in Capital Park had decided to build a swimming pool. The contractor arrived and the digging began. But, before the pit was big enough for construction to begin, the workmen felt something hard beneath their spades.

As they cleared more earth away, it became obvious: they had found some bones. Once again, people began adding up the information. The house was right next to Gert and Joey's home, he owned a construction company, and now bones had been found. The fantasy, however grim, that rose up in the public mind was that Gert and Joey had disposed of the girls' bodies right near their own house, and that the skeletal remains had not been detected as they were not on the property. It was, after all, more than a decade after the Malherbe Street house had been razed and every square metre of earth dug up.

But, once again, when the results came back from forensics, the then 18-year-old mystery remained unsolved: the bones were not even human.

Each time that year, as the prospect of something definitive hit the headlines, the public intrigue would come to life. But for the families, it was just a cruel reimmersion in the tragedies that had wrecked their lives.

And that wasn't the end of it. For six years, all went quiet, but then, in 2013, a homeowner in Germiston, some seventy kilometres from the house of horrors, undertook renovations to his property. This included the builders digging underneath a pool in the garden. While working, they came across an eerie find: skeletal remains alongside a green dress, a pair of black knitted tights and a brass ring.

The fact that the swimming pool had been built in 1989 during the spate of disappearances, coupled with the fact that Gert had been in the construction business, led to widespread speculation that the bones belonged to one of the girls. Had he concealed the bones – some of which were found to have saw marks on them – under a pool built by his company?

Superficially, it would seem like a distinct possibility, but that was only because of the high profile of the case of the six missing girls. Fuelled by excessive media attention, the situation was such that many other girls who had gone missing, mainly black, had not rated so much as a mention in the newspaper briefs.

In the end, all that could be said was that the remains were definitely female, but the race of the deceased could not be determined. When it came to age, the police wrote down definitively in their case file: adult.

Once again, each family returned to the searing heartache of not knowing.

Then, in 2017, just one year shy of the 30th anniversary of the girls' disappearance, the story came to life once more. Again, it was skeletal evidence that took centre stage, but this time even the evidence itself did not exist.

A crew from *Fokus,* an Afrikaans-language current-affairs programme, had spent more than a year investigating the case of the missing schoolgirls. During their research, they came across a psychic who was convinced that the girls had been murdered and buried on the North Coast of KwaZulu-Natal.

This time, it was at Blythedale Beach, north of Durban, and once again, the proximity to where Joey and Gert used to holiday raised much interest. The excavation began after a woman in the area contacted the executive producer of *Fokus* to report that both her son and husband had seen apparitions of the young girls. A spiritualist augmented the theories of this family when she said the bodies had been buried under a construction site 'on or near Blythedale'.[6]

Further research revealed that in 1989, the second year of the disappearances, public toilets and a car park had been built near the beach. This had included the laying of a storm-water pipe from the toilets to the beach. The spiritualist had said: 'The bodies are buried under the pipe.'

This would hardly seem like the type of empirical evidence that draws the attention and manpower of the police force, but perhaps balancing it against the desperation of the families, the police resumed the search. This was fuelled in no small way by Linette Boucher and her daughter Natasha, who were desperate to know if Odette's remains could be found there.

And so, once again, the diggers, sniffer dogs and incident tape were brought in. Once again, the families wrung their hands in anxiety, while the public hung on every word of the journalists covering the story. For two days, workers excavated the site after an engineer was called in to locate the exact position of the concrete pipe.

If the previous searches had brought to light other people's bones, and non-human bones, this search brought absolutely nothing. The families' wishes for an excavation had been fulfilled but that was the end of it.

Again, the story fell silent.

And then, early in 2019, an earth-shattering claim was made by a 41-year-old woman named Lea Sloane.

She claimed she was Fiona Harvey.

This was the first time ever that the explosive new evidence did not hinge on the quackery of bad science or the supposed secrets of a buried skeleton. Here was a living, breathing human being who categorically claimed to be one of the missing girls. A number of similarities 'convinced'[7] a forensic expert and a private investigator that the woman was indeed Fiona Harvey.

Wherever the features didn't match, the two experts had an explanation: their noses were different, but this, they said, was due to Lea's description of how her nose had been broken several years earlier. Fingerprints couldn't be used for matching purposes as Joey had burnt the girl's fingers on the stove until the tips were smooth. Lea claimed she had been physically and sexually abused by the depraved couple, had eventually been released at a remote location, and had then tried to make her way back to the house in Pietermaritzburg. She had been sold into the sex trade by another man on the streets.

When Fiona's elderly parents were approached, they vehemently denied that Lea was Fiona.

'She does not have the same eyes,'[8] Fiona's father told the investigator, and asked never to be contacted again.

A parent knows. A few days later, so-called Lea Sloane was reported to be an impostor attempting to cash in on the mystery of the missing girls. Her brother had seen the story about her on Facebook, and came forward to say that her real name was Jacqueline, that she was 35 not 41, and that she had a history of 'using people' to 'gain their sympathy'. He said she had 'been off the rails' since they had lost their parents when they were very young.[9]

It is impossible to imagine the pain felt by the Harveys, now in their eighties, as they stared at a photograph of a middle-aged woman they were told could be their daughter. Since the day Fiona set off from their Pietermaritzburg home to buy milk for her mother, they – like the other families – have lived inside a well of emotional pain.

Once again, the horrific story of the missing girls from the late 1980s had made its way into the headlines. And, once again, it echoed off the walls of an empty space, faded out, and left nothing but renewed heartache in its wake.

And still, it is the elusive figure of Joey Haarhoff that looms large over this unsolved mystery. Gert has, over the decades, remained the spectre of what any community fears – the quintessential 'dirty old man' who lures children off the street and into his depraved world. Joey, by contrast, defies labelling, especially in the absence of any definitive truth of what her role was other than luring the girls into the lair.

Whether she was that rare breed, a female paedophile who sexually assaulted them, and whether she took part in their murders with her own hands are questions that will likely never be answered.

In her death, therefore, she took even more secrets to the grave than her male accomplice.

CHAPTER 5
DINA RODRIGUES

✢

Cape Town, 2007

On an autumn day in May, outside the High Court in Cape Town, a kind of macabre street party was taking place. Everyone was waiting to see if Dina Rodrigues, with her liquorice-black hair and eyebrows shaped like the wings of a bat, would finally receive the official title of murderer. Those not physically present were metaphorically craning their necks to catch a glimpse of the baby-killer accused: tuning in on radios and glued to television sets.

The only person near the courthouse who seemed oblivious, but who had been drawn to the spectacle of the crowd nonetheless, was a homeless man. In his baggy denims and torn shoes, he appeared clown-like. He inhaled deeply from the glue-soaked packet in his hand, then tugged on the nearest sleeve. 'What's going on?' he slurred.

'It's Dina. The baby killer. Today we hear.'

Inside, Judge Basheer Waglay kept those present spellbound as he neared the end of his 150-page judgment, which had taken several days to work through. It was the culmination of a 15-month-long High Court drama.

The ashes of a six-month-old baby now lay in the Garden of Remembrance, not far from the Lansdowne home where she had briefly lived and then died at the command of a young woman.

Throughout, the media had indulged in the details: the cold facts of a hired hit on a baby's life, and the jealousy-consumed woman behind it. And the more the press dished out, the more the public lapped it up.

Today was all of that, and more. Outside the courtroom, photographers strutted about with their phallic lenses, while television crews trundled technology around on their shoulders, preparing for their live crossings when the verdict came.

Inside, in the dock, Dina Rodrigues pressed her lips together, her dark eyes trained on Judge Waglay, listening to his every word. She was flanked by her four co-accused: Sipho Mfazwe, Mongezi Bobotyane, Zanethemba Gwada and Bonginkosi Sigenu. All four came from the poverty-stricken townships where most of Cape Town's black population lives. None of the men were fluent in English, and three of the four were youths. Bonginkosi, the youngest, was only 16 years of age. Zanethemba was 18, while Mongezi was 22. The eldest was Sipho, a 33-year-old taxi driver.

The judge's tone remained steady, even monotonous. He stopped from time to time to allow an interpreter to repeat it all in isiXhosa so that Dina's co-accused could understand what he was saying. To his right, he could see Natasha Norton, the mother of the murdered child, flanked by her boyfriend, parents, a brother and the nanny who had been in the house on the day in question. In solidarity, all wore tailored black outfits with pale pink shirts, and each held a set of prayer beads. They were the face of exhaustion but, today, of hope too.

Dina, impassive, never looked in their direction. She also made no eye contact with Neil Wilson, her ex-lover and the father of the dead child.

Eventually, the judge read out the verdict. Dina Rodrigues and her four co-accused were all found guilty of murder. Rapturous applause broke out in the public gallery, while members of the victim's family hugged each other tightly. Dina stared ahead blankly, as if finding it difficult to process what she had just heard.

Outside, on the courtroom steps, it was grandfather Vernon Norton's description of Dina as 'a wicked, scheming woman' that grabbed the headlines. The white middle-class woman, the puppeteer, was the focus, her co-accused quickly fading into obscurity. A tabloid front page boasted, '8 pages of Dina today'; posters shouted, 'Dina the Bitch'; a comment piece urged, 'Let the racist bitch rot in jail'.[1]

Baby Jordan-Leigh Norton's angelic and dimpled face became a cameo of tragedy, an icon of one of South Africa's most infamous murder trials.

How had it come to this? Before the notorious label 'baby killer' was attached to her name, Dina Rodrigues couldn't have been more ordinary. Raised in a Catholic family of Portuguese descent on the 'right side of the tracks' in the suburbs of Cape Town, she was the *laatlammetjie*

(late arrival) of her family and had always been indulged by her elderly parents and two older brothers as she grew up.

She attended Wynberg Girls' High School in the affluent southern suburbs, where the school principal had noted her as a young woman of integrity, someone with a 'keen sense of purpose, responsibility and loyalty, giving of her best in every undertaking'.[2] An old school friend remembered Dina being involved in charity drives, being passionate about history, and steering clear of the trouble that boys could bring to her life.[3]

At home, Dina was 'the apple of the family's eye' and had 'never given an ounce of worry',[4] according to her brother Orlando. Dina had also lived a very sheltered life. By her mid-twenties, she was still living at home with her parents and even working in the family business, a confectionary company called Dolce Lume Cape in the northern suburb of Milnerton. She had always been cosseted by her family, who held 'very old-fashioned ideas towards women in general, and unmarried daughters in particular'.[5]

Dina was also prone to the anxieties that teenage girls often experience. She worried about her weight, she doubted her looks, she lacked confidence, and was often embarrassed by her sweaty palms,[6] one newspaper said.

In 1998, she matriculated from high school. One evening the following year, she got dressed up and went out clubbing with her friends as usual. It was on the dance floor of a Sea Point nightclub called Phat Boyz that she met Kevin Richards. He was studying accounting and was not exactly lacking in self-esteem. Soon after spotting her, his mind was set on approaching her, and by the end of the evening, she was handed a till slip with his phone number scribbled across it in ballpoint pen. It had been a chance meeting with little indication of where it would go, but soon after that she called him up, and thus began a very serious relationship.

Those in the same social circle as Dina and Kevin assumed they would settle down and raise children together. Kevin told a journalist they had been 'a match made in heaven',[7] but the relationship was at times tumultuous. They were both 19 when they met, and five years later Kevin decided it was time to end the relationship. This, he said, was for no other reason than the fact that they were 'too young' when they met and had virtually done all their 'growing up' together.

Despite his deep feelings for her, Kevin felt that it was time to move on. But Dina could not accept the breakup and made several attempts to see him despite his clear resolution that it was over. In an attempt to let go, she finally decided it was time to meet other people.

That was when she met Neil Wilson, a primary-school teacher who, at 23, still lived with his family. Nicknamed 'the golden banana' on account of his success with women, Neil was known to be a philanderer who seldom remained faithful to any girlfriend or stayed in any relationship for a long time. He was, however, not the elusive or flippant type of philanderer. On the contrary, he was intense and passionate, the type of man who would declare his undying love for one woman – and possibly even feel it in the moment – while setting up a date with another whom he also found intriguing.

The chemistry between them meant that his and Dina's relationship escalated very quickly, and even in the early days of their being together, Dina became quite obsessive about him. With 'little experience of life, and even less experience of relationships with men',[8] she claimed that Neil represented her first emotional and physical relationship – this was despite her five years with Kevin – and said they were destined to spend their lives together. Although he was a few months younger than her, she perceived him as a worldly man and an 'experienced lover'.[9]

By December 2004, the two had been dating for a few months, with friends commenting on how serious their relationship seemed. Then, one day over the festive season, Neil received a call on his mobile phone. It was a voice he hadn't heard for a while but, still, it was a familiar one – and what he heard would rock his world. The call was from an ex-girlfriend – a young woman he had dated briefly much earlier that same year.

In February 2004, Neil had begun dating an attractive young woman named Natasha Norton. She was 22 at the time, and from a tightly bonded family. With her soulful eyes, prominent dimples and mane of copper-brown hair, it would have been hard for Neil not to notice this tall and athletic young woman who was studying to be a personal trainer. They dated for only three months, however, and in May of that year went their separate ways.

Natasha soon met another young man. They too became quite serious rather quickly, and when Natasha found out she was pregnant, she assumed her new boyfriend was the father.

But, by the time she gave birth to a baby girl on 30 November, she had worked out the truth of who the father most likely was.

She told Neil as clearly as possible, 'I would like you to get a paternity test.'

Neil immediately panicked. It would take some convincing for him to see that he should agree to the test. And, even then, his first demand was that under no circumstances could the paternity test be done during the week. That way, he wouldn't have to 'take time off work' or 'explain anything to anyone'.[10]

The test was set for a day in January 2005. Dina, meanwhile, was unaware of all this. Natasha moved in the same social circles, and Dina had felt some bouts of jealousy that Neil had dated her, but she saw Natasha as just another name on the list of Neil's short-lived romances.

Dina's first inkling that any news of this nature existed was when she and Neil returned from a short romantic holiday in Durban. This was not long after the phone call from Natasha, but it was before the paternity test had taken place. On their return to Cape Town, Dina had asked Neil to drop her off at a friend's house as she didn't want her parents to know that they had been away together. After all, they weren't married and she didn't want her parents to know about their physical relationship.

He obliged, and took her to the house of Arendene Fourie. Arendene happened to be another of Neil's ex-lovers, and she told Dina she had some major gossip to share: Neil was possibly the father of Natasha Norton's baby.

A number of pathology labs were contacted until one was located that agreed to carry out the test on a Saturday. When the day finally arrived, Neil not only faced the prospect of confirming he was a father, but he also got to meet baby Jordan in the flesh. In a brief moment in the waiting room, Neil slipped his index finger into her 'little fist'[11] as it rested on her grandmother's back. Natasha had no intention of trying to reunite with Neil, but thought that maybe there could be a healthy bond between her daughter and the man she suspected was the father. Perhaps he would play a role in her life?

After a short but excruciating wait, the results of the paternity test arrived. It was February by then, a year since Neil and Natasha had first started dating. As fate would have it, the fact was confirmed: Neil was the biological father of baby Jordan, then just three months old.

He made it clear he wanted nothing to do with Natasha, nor their baby, but this was of course only one aspect of it. Hot on the heels of the test results came the question of maintenance. Neil claimed that his attorney would see to this aspect, but according to Natasha's family, the amount offered for maintenance was ridiculous and 'would not even buy Jordan's milk formula'.

For Dina, the amount of money wasn't the issue. It was simply the existence of a baby that Neil had conceived with someone else. Dina's anger and emotional turmoil would rise up every time they discussed it – yet, at the same time, she wanted to know everything about it and obsessively peppered him with questions.

It was also around this time that Natasha received an anonymous text message that said she had 'ruined Neil's life' and that she was 'a slut'.[12] Natasha had as much difficulty in getting Neil to meet her to discuss the way forward as she had had in getting him to show up for the paternity test. Finally, Neil's mother, Sandra, phoned Natasha and set up a meeting – all aspects of which were to be on the Wilsons' terms. The meeting would be held at their house, and Natasha was forbidden to bring her parents or baby Jordan along. Sandra was 'aggressive' towards Natasha from the start, but Natasha tried to make it clear that her motive was not money. It was to see whether they, as Jordan's grandparents, were going to be 'a part of her life'.[13]

With the meeting set up and the Wilsons' stance already clear, Natasha still held hope, and prepared a photograph album in the belief that maybe, just maybe, Neil and his parents would involve themselves in the baby's life in one way or another and see her grow up. But on her arrival at the house, it was made clear: the meeting was going to be hostile, and Natasha returned to her house later that day with 'the photo album still unopened'.

Dina had already made it clear to Neil what his options were. He must agree to have no contact with his daughter or she would walk out of his life forever, she said. And so, faced with such a black-and-white option, he chose Dina.

Baby Jordan lived with her mother, Natasha, her grandparents, Vernon and Anastacia, and her uncle, Natasha's teenage brother, Dylan, at 15 Scout Road in Lansdowne. This had been a whites-only suburb during apartheid, but by the time Jordan was born, just a decade after apartheid ended, its character had shifted. It was inhabited predominantly by people just like the Nortons: middle-class coloured families, living the same lives as their white counterparts in the surrounding suburbs.

It was a tight-knit community, but, more importantly, Natasha had brought her baby girl into a home of boundless love and creature comforts. Vernon and Anastacia doted on their grandchild, and brother Dylan was an integral part of baby Jordan's life, as was Thobeka Buso, the nanny who cared for her as if she were her own child.

For Dina, however, baby Jordan could not be viewed as a human being – a new and vulnerable one at that. To her, she was nothing more than a hurdle in the way of her quest to be Neil's everything. Against the backdrop of an imagined idyllic future together, the news of Neil's having fathered a child had snapped her fantasy in half. She could not have imagined 'life without Wilson'[14] when suddenly presented with this information, and she was prepared to do anything to reconfigure the situation.

Over the next few months, as the maintenance issues were slowly unravelled, Neil cut Natasha off even more harshly. He changed his telephone number so that she could not get hold of him, and all the while continued fielding endless questions from Dina. As before, he made it clear he never wanted to see baby Jordan again.

Then, on 6 June 2005, Natasha's mother, Anastacia, answered the phone at the house and was told by the person calling that her name was Bobby and she was looking for Natasha. Natasha was asleep at the time, however, so Anastacia offered to pass on a message to her daughter. 'Bobby' declined the offer and said she would call again later. This she did, and when Natasha was on the other end of the phone, there was suddenly nobody there. She told her mother, 'I don't have any friend called Bobby.'[15]

There were other strange phone calls that week. Natasha was at home, off sick from work. A few times the landline rang at the house and Thobeka took some of the calls. When Natasha answered the phone or was called to the phone, there was nothing but silence.

Dina, by throwing down the gauntlet, had effectively stamped out any chance of baby Jordan being in her or Neil's life, but she could not wield the same power over where and when they might encounter Natasha. A few days after the strange phone call to the Norton household, Dina prepared to celebrate her 24th birthday. She dressed up for the occasion, applying products to her youthful face and making sure her black hair was perfect. She arrived at a restaurant in Claremont and settled in – flanked by Neil and a clutch of friends – to do nothing but eat, drink, celebrate, and open a few gifts. Among those seated at the table were two of Neil's sometime lovers, but in that moment he belonged solely to Dina and she was glowing as a result. Then in walked Natasha, and suddenly Dina's whole being was consumed with jealousy and insecurity.

She testified later in court papers that she had already begun to 'plot the child's demise'[16] in her imagination. She made 'broad hints to Wilson' of her thoughts and 'asked him how much he would "pay to get rid of the problem", or words to that effect'. She was so 'blinded by her own resentments' she would later claim, that she 'misinterpreted his reaction'.

Her choice of words was crucial. While Neil claimed to have no sense at all that a plan was being hatched to have his baby assassinated, Dina pointed a finger right at him, through omission rather than commission: she read 'his failure to condemn the sick thoughts' she harboured as 'a form of agreement with and support of my desire to rid us of this obstacle to our happiness.'[17]

This is how a Cape Town suburbanite suddenly ruptured the cocoon that had been spun around her and headed off to the taxi rank in Killarney Gardens to find some killers. This was just a few days after the creepy phone call to the Norton home and the chance encounter at the restaurant on the night of her birthday.

Given Dina's upbringing, she had probably never set foot in such a place, where the mass of South Africa's underpaid blue-collar workforce gathers early each morning and late each afternoon to travel in and out of a city where most cannot afford to live but must go to earn a living.

Dina, who had never had 'conscious contact with criminals, let alone contact with assassins',[18] arrived in the comfort of her silver Opel Corsa and began asking around for a killer the way one might ask for directions to the post office. Sipho Mfazwe, a taxi driver, crossed paths with her and asked what she was doing at the rank. She said she was trying to find someone who could 'commit a crime'. It was a crime that would involve housebreaking and killing a baby.

Clearly having already planned how the murder would unfold, it was there and then that she provided two telephone directories – the idea being that those commissioned to carry out the crime would use the annual distribution of new phone books as a ruse to gain entry into the Norton house – and put the deal on the table: R10 000 for the hit.

And so, with her 'bloodless' hands behind the sterile desk of the family business, Dina sat at work on Tuesday 14 June 2005 knowing that, not far away, her agenda was in motion. The plan was as childish as it was cruel: a man would gain access to a house by playing a trick on its owners.

And so Zanethemba Gwada, the two phone books in his hands, made his way across the brick paving and up to the portico of 15 Scout Road, Lansdowne, ready to deliver his performance.

Natasha and her parents were out that day, but inside the house Dylan pottered about while Thobeka clanked dishes in the sink. Six-month-old Jordan was safe in her cot, taking her morning nap. Hearing the bell, Thobeka walked across the open-plan living room to the front door and asked what the man wanted.

'I am here to deliver telephone directories,' the stranger replied.

Thobeka did not open the door, but instead went and passed the information on to Dylan.

As if an angel was watching over baby Jordan that day, Dylan didn't let the man in. 'We already have telephone directories,' he told him.

With the plan thwarted, information moved back along the chain of command – from Zanethemba the would-be killer, to taxi driver Sipho, and finally to Dina – so that a plan B could be devised.

The Norton family likely carried on with their daily routine, Natasha and her parents coming home before sunset, baby Jordan beaming with the joy of seeing her mother, the evening meal prepared in the kitchen, nappy changes, conversations, television, touches of exhaustion ... the entire household oblivious to the death held at bay by the random presence of telephone directories already in the house.

However, during the course of that seemingly ordinary day, the telephone had rung. When Dylan answered it, Dina put on an official-sounding voice and told him that a package would be arriving the following day for Vernon. With her plan B set for the next day, Dina then called Sipho again and instructed him to meet her in Killarney Gardens just as before. The four men – Sipho, Mongezi, Zanethemba and Bonginkosi – arrived in Sipho's taxi and waited at the allocated spot. They saw Dina's car approach from the opposite direction and park diagonally opposite. She sat waiting for Sipho to cross the road while the other accomplices inside the taxi commented on 'the beautiful white lady in the Corsa'.[19] Sipho returned holding a box and a piece of paper – the props that would replace the useless telephone directories.

Wednesday 15 June 2005. What a stroke of luck, Dina must have thought, that her role in the family business involved managing deliveries, which meant she got to handle waybills. Even in this age of digital technology, waybills provide a hard-copy record of the passage of goods crossing cities and borders and the thresholds of private houses. But, more than that, a waybill is like a key that magically opens doors for delivery personnel on motorbikes or in trucks.

Several kilometres away, Dina sat quietly at work, knowing that a bloody crime was about to take place at her request. The waybill was on its way to the house where the baby lived, all accomplices were still on board in the wake of the failed attempt, and soon she would receive the phone call to say it was done, that the baby had been murdered.

Over in Scout Road, the four men walk towards the Norton household. One holds the box and waybill. As on the previous day, Natasha and her parents aren't at home. Baby Jordan gurgles and smiles at Thobeka, who's giving her breakfast in the television room. Dylan is asleep in his room.

The bell rings. Thobeka sees the silhouette of a man at the door. He tells her he has a parcel to deliver. She goes to Dylan's bedroom and wakes him up. Without hesitating, he asks her to go ahead and sign for it. She has no reason to mistrust the caller, who looks for all the world like a delivery man.

She makes her way back to the front door, opens the security gate, and takes delivery of the box. The 'delivery man', who is actually 16-year-old Bonginkosi, asks her to sign the waybill, but she feels Dylan should do this and so she returns to his room.

Dylan emerges and walks into the lounge, where he is asked to sign the waybill. He goes off to find a pen, returns, and signs the document. Thobeka has gone back to feeding baby Jordan in the television room.

A moment later, there are three other men standing inside the house. One produces a knife with a blade as long as a ruler. Dylan, caught completely off-guard by this sudden violence in the house, is forced into his parents' bedroom.

Thobeka, unaware of what is transpiring elsewhere in the house, is spooning food into baby Jordan's mouth. Suddenly, two men burst into the television room. One snatches up the baby while the other forces the terrified woman into the main bedroom and ties her up alongside Dylan. The two are quizzed about a safe but say they have no information to share. A safe is nonetheless soon located in a cupboard of the main bedroom, and the two are pushed into the en suite bathroom and warned not to come out.

Terrified, they stay put as commanded. There are muffled sounds of voices but they have no idea of exactly what is happening.

Bonginkosi has been tasked with choking baby Jordan. The eldest of the pack, Sipho, instructs him to take the baby to a different room. He takes her as directed, but as soon as he is away from the other three men, something in him switches. The other men are sure he is about to wrap his fingers tightly around baby Jordan's neck, but as soon as he is alone with her and she starts crying, he scoops her up in his arms and begins gently rocking her. He thinks of his own little brother and can't bring himself to commit the act. Mongezi, the 22-year-old, barges in and sees that baby Jordan is still alive and staring into the eyes of her would-be killer. Mongezi asks Bonginkosi why he has not yet killed the baby, and he responds, 'Do it yourself.' Mongezi orders him to leave. On his way out of the room, Bonginkosi helps himself to the cellphone he finds lying on the bed.

Mongezi, now alone in the room with baby Jordan, raises the knife above her tiny frame and plunges it into her flesh.

Dylan and Thobeka have no idea what is happening, but when silence eventually descends on the house, they are able to free themselves from the bathroom – in a state of shock, and terrified of what they may find. The house is in a state of chaos.

Dylan's first instinct is to run into the road in search of the perpetrators. Thobeka remains inside in a traumatised state. When Dylan re-enters the house, he storms into his bedroom to look for his phone, and there, on the bed, is a sight that will haunt him for the rest of his life: under his pillow, he finds his little niece. Blood gushes from a wound in her neck and bubbles ooze from her mouth. One of her eyes is swollen from what must have been a heavy blow.

Dylan picks the baby up in his arms and runs through the house, screaming for Thobeka to take her to a neighbour who is a doctor. In a state of utter terror, he presses the panic button for the armed response.

But it is too late.

A baby lay dead as one desperate person handed her to the next. And the woman who had masterminded this, Dina Rodrigues, sat at her desk, her hands unsullied by the blood of her victim, her eyes protected from the spectre of the tiny lifeless body stabbed in the neck.

Mongezi had driven the knife with such force through Jordan's body that she sustained incisions on her spinal column. Her trachea was severed, while her oesophagus, jugular vein and vertebral artery were all badly injured. Weighing only 8 kg, and her body only holding around 640 ml[20] of blood, she must have died within just a few minutes of being attacked.

Thobeka, panicking and cradling baby Jordan in her arms, ran to Shabeeba Slamdien, the next-door neighbour. The armed-response team arrived and hurriedly bundled the two women and the baby into their vehicle before racing off to a nearby doctor's surgery.

The doctor was out, and medical receptionist Jackie Ann Davis performed CPR on the tiny body. But her attempts failed. Baby Jordan had long since succumbed to the brutal attack at the family home.

Dylan was given sugar water by another neighbour to try to calm his nerves. As soon as he was able, he called his father, Vernon, and told him the ghastly news. Vernon then had the grim task of phoning Natasha. When her phone rang and she saw it was her father calling, she was on duty at the Virgin Active gym in Constantia. When he asked her to meet him urgently at the doctor's consulting rooms, the walls of panic must have closed in on her.

When she ran through the door at the doctor's, she was met by her father and a counsellor, and shortly thereafter, a sight was engraved on her mind that nothing could ever erase. There was her baby, the dimple-faced sweetheart who that morning had been cooing and stretching her little legs out in the living room. Only now, just a few hours later, she lay motionless, lifeless and covered in blood.

There is no system to measure such trauma, nor any map that shows the journey of sorrow that lies ahead. But perhaps it can be said that the darkness of Dina's soul was equal to the devastation she caused Natasha Norton, her family, and many other people on that fateful morning.

On the very day that Baby Jordan was murdered at Dina's request, and her shattered grandfather did the official body identification at the Salt River mortuary, Dina sent a text message to Natasha, mother of the victim, that read, 'Sorry to hear about your baby. You and your family are in my prayers.'[21]

Such callous behaviour dressed up as concern did not end there. Dina also phoned Natasha that day, sometime after sending the text, and extended her condolences over the phone. What does it take to feign compassion for someone whose baby of six months you have just murdered through a hit?

In that same phone call, her possessiveness towards Neil was also evident. Natasha asked Dina for Neil's latest phone number so she could share the terrible news with him, but Dina withheld the number and responded that he already knew. Natasha said she would like to tell him herself. She was likely in too much of a state to wonder how both

Dina and Neil already knew what had happened, and simply appreciated the 'concern' that Dina had shown.

Consider this: on the same day that Dina sent Natasha a text of condolence and phoned to express her sympathies, she drove in her silver Corsa with a white envelope full of cash to pay the men she had hired to murder the baby. This was the woman whom her brother Orlando described as someone who would 'rather carry a caterpillar into the garden than step on it',[22] and as someone who protested when their mother wanted to swat flies in the kitchen because it was cruel.

The men had fled the scene of the murder and gone to Sipho Mfazwe's house. Like the others, he lived in the shack settlement known as Lusaka, in Crossroads, near Cape Town International Airport. There, they left the items they had stolen from the house before setting off once more to Killarney Gardens to meet Dina. She was already waiting for them.

She handed the envelope containing half the money to Sipho, explaining that the rest would come later. The four men then drove to a service station where they opened the envelope and helped themselves to the R5 000 inside. Each man was allocated R1 100 – one spent his share all on clothes, while the rest was allegedly spent on petrol and 'booze'.[23] Sipho assured the others that the balance would come later that day.

Baby Jordan had by then gone from being a living, breathing human being with her whole life ahead of her to a name that would be written down on an evidence sheet, a serial number allocated to a deceased body in a death register.

Dina's four co-accused had not only helped themselves to the contents of the safe and other items such as a gold pen and pencil set, a firearm and a man's watch, but had also taken baby Jordan's birth certificate. Could anything be more symbolic? They had, at the request of a callous youngster, removed baby Jordan from the book of life – erasing her future. They had also, it turned out, taken the baby bag – that all-important companion to any parent of a newborn. Baby Jordan's nappies, milk supply, changing mat and bum cream were now in the possession of the men who had killed her.

Shortly afterwards, Dina sent a text to Neil asking him to call her back. He immediately dialled the number and Dina answered. Sounding upset, she told him that his baby was dead, and that she had paid R10 000 to 'make the problem go away'.[24]

On hearing these words, his body went cold. This did not feel like reality. The news was so extreme that at first he thought it might be a hoax. He immediately remembered a message that Dina had sent some months before asking what she could do to make it 'all go away'.[25] The grim reality of it began to sink in, as did Neil's own psychological confusion as he tried to make sense of what had happened.

Dina later called from her office and told Neil that the police had arrived and were questioning her, but that they wanted to question him too. They set off to speak to Captain Esmerald Bailey, the investigating officer, at her office in central Cape Town, but they were held up in traffic and the appointment was rescheduled for the next day.

Their return to the suburbs in the late afternoon stands as proof of Neil's confusion: he allowed Dina to stay the night at his parents' house. He was also convinced by her to delete 22 possibly incriminating text messages she'd sent him.

Neil was clearly still trying to calibrate the information in his head and the feelings in his heart. That night, he 'did not question her'[26] about the R10 000 she mentioned, 'because he was still very emotional, trying to deal with the death of his baby and at the same time feeling scared and not wanting anything to happen to Dina'.[27] Right up until that very morning, she had simply been his girlfriend, someone he had even spoken about marrying.

When she and Neil turned up at Captain Bailey's offices the next day, Dina was the first to be interviewed. When it was Neil's turn, he failed to mention the most crucial evidence of all – Dina's telling him that she had paid R10 000 to make the problem 'go away'.

Finally, Neil's parents went in. As the Wilsons sat opposite Bailey, answering her questions, Dina and Neil sat outside her office in a slice of time that must have felt surreal to both of them. It was then that Dina came face to face with reality. She suddenly said, 'Oh my God, what have I done? What have I done? I'm going to jail.[28]'

Dina, who had had no material struggles in life, and no shortage of love or resources or education, finally realised the full extent of what she had done. But her eureka moment sprang not from the reality of having had a small baby assassinated, but rather from the cold realisation that she would be severely punished for the crime.

Dina Rodrigues was arrested two days after the murder of Jordan-Leigh Norton, on Friday 17 June 2005. The waybill, the magic key that opened the door of 15 Scout Road for her hitmen, was traced to Dina's place of work. It became the most damning piece of the puzzle that Captain Bailey put together in a very short time. The other crucial piece of evidence was the phone call made to the Norton residence the day before the murder, during which Dylan Norton was told that a parcel would be arriving for his father the following day. That too was traced to Dina's place of work.

Neil Wilson's confusion soon evaporated, and he cooperated fully with authorities. It was an about-face viewed with much empathy by Judge Waglay, who understood that Neil was 'undergoing severe emotional distress' after finding out that his girlfriend had organised a hit on his baby.

'Can one really blame him for postponing his decision for a few days?' the judge asked, 'I do not think so.'

The verdict in the Dina Rodrigues trial, which had gone on for 15 months, was scheduled to take place shortly after I moved to Cape Town after three decades in Johannesburg, where I was born and raised, and where I forged my career as a journalist. My husband and I moved down in 2007 with our firstborn – a two-year-old daughter whose presence in our lives was the reason we moved cities in search of a calmer place to raise her.

When baby Jordan was murdered, on 15 June 2005, my daughter was only two months old and I could scarcely bear thinking about it. I remember closing my eyes and not being able to push away the image of the murder, or the idea that her mother was now required to carry on living in this world, knowing what had happened.

Shortly after arriving in Cape Town, I was asked to cover the verdict in Dina's trial for a local newspaper. I made a conscious decision to put aside my deep-seated feelings as a mother and managed to do that. But another aspect of the trial that really hit home was the dynamic between the murder mastermind Dina Rodrigues and her four co-accused, only one of whom she had ever met.

As a reporter dedicated to exploring themes of social justice, and indeed having grown up in apartheid South Africa, I was intensely aware of the complex race relations in South Africa as a whole, and in Johannesburg in particular. But, as I was soon to discover, the inner workings of Cape Town's brand of social hierarchies are quite particular to the Mother City itself. And, as it turned out, the judgment day of the Dina Rodrigues trial provided me with my first experience of this.

A throng of journalists was packed around the entrance to the courtroom, waiting for the doors to open. A young journalist was standing behind me, clutching her notepad and looking bewildered. New to court reporting, she turned to an older journalist and said, 'I don't have any accreditation to get in here.' The older journalist replied, 'Darling, this is Cape Town. Your white skin is all the accreditation you'll ever need.'

That comment stuck with me as I got to know the city over the next few years. It also shaped my perception of the trial I was writing about. Now, up close and personal inside the courtroom, I kept an eye on the five accused from the media bench.

Seeing Dina in the dock with her four co-accused summed up the fault line in South Africa's future as designed by its past. Just like the washing of laundry and dishes, the laying of bricks, the sweeping of floors, and the patrolling of dark streets at night, the dirty work of murder had in this case been outsourced to those with far less agency over how they earned a living. That's not to imply at all that Sipho, Mongezi, Zanethemba and Bonginkosi had no choice in the matter. They did, and they chose to go ahead and commit murder in cold blood.

But, beyond those obvious facts, there was a sticky set of questions that consistently hung over the trial in a country where racialised poverty is as ubiquitous as ever. Did Dina, a relatively wealthy white woman, prey on those she knew would be desperate for the money? Were they, to quote one tabloid, 'Dina's disposable weapons to have a pesky coloured baby killed'?[29]

They all grew up in 'dire poverty' and were from dysfunctional homes.[30] Their circumstances did not cause them to commit the heinous crime but certainly placed them at higher risk of being tempted to do so. And, of course, money talked.

Sipho was a first-time offender. He had a life partner, was the father of two minor children, and had been diagnosed with HIV. Judge Essa Moosa, during the appeal process, described him as someone who 'pleaded not guilty, did not testify, and showed no remorse'.[31] In the moment of his conviction, his mother 'wept and left the court immediately'.[32]

Bonginkosi, the youngest, was still completing high school but had already earned himself a robbery conviction. Zanethemba, unemployed, had 'shocked'[33] the community with his involvement; he had a reputation for staying quietly at home and keeping well away from trouble.

Mongezi Bobotyane, 'the foot soldier who plunged the knife into the defenceless baby Jordan',[34] had an unremarkable South African background characterised by abject poverty. An orphan, he had dropped out of school due to poverty and had been working in a barber shop as an assistant. He had taken part in the murder for the money – of which he had never 'earned such a lot at one time in his entire life'.[35]

In the final analysis, Dina's co-accused acted of their own free will in a murder that was as barbaric as it was cold-blooded and carefully calculated, and one that brought 'unimaginable anguish'[36] to the family of baby Jordan.

But, it was Dina who was the 'commander-in-chief and the principal actor who sought the elimination of Baby Jordan'; it was she who took advantage of the others' 'poor socioeconomic circumstances'.[37]

Her motivation? Jealousy. Glowing red-hot jealousy.

CHAPTER 6

NAJWA PETERSEN

╬

Cape Town, 2008

It was the beginning of a hot December. Najwa Petersen wore a spotless white headscarf around her face. Her frameless glasses, as stylish as the hijab itself, seemed to float in front of her somewhat cold and narrow eyes. Her *abaya* (a long, robe-like dress), chosen carefully for the occasion, was elegantly tailored to just touch the floor. She stood in the holding cell below the courtroom, her hands shackled behind her, waiting for the command.

In courtroom one at the Cape Town High Court, the public gallery in the balcony was packed with family members of the accused, the broken and bereft looking for closure, and the regular court watchers for whom this was just another season of a real-life drama. To the right and left of where the judge and assessors would soon sit, journalists jostled for space in the wooden rows reserved for the media. Just in front of the dock, still empty and waiting for its four occupants, sat a string of soberly dressed lawyers, and to their left, the state prosecution team that had been working for months on end to see justice done.

In short, the courtroom was packed to capacity and awaited the arrival of Najwa Petersen, who would soon shuffle up the narrow wooden staircase from the holding cells below. She would face a barrage of cameramen, and take her place in the dock to hear if she had gotten away with it. But she wouldn't be alone. To her left, three other men would be present too. These were her hired hitmen. In the theatrical context of the courtroom, Najwa was always perfectly dressed, showing a definite preference for polka dots, pastel shades and sometimes the elegant simplicity of black and white. But the men might have been mistaken for stage hands, hired to move furniture around in the dark between scenes.

The entrance of Judge Siraj Desai heralded the usual 'All rise', and silence quickly fell over the courtroom. The judge nodded, sat down, and looked squarely through his glasses at the pages in front of him. 'This case relates to the untimely and brutal death of music icon Abdul Mutaliep Petersen, better known as Taliep Petersen,' he read. 'The first accused is his wife. The other three accused are men she allegedly solicited to assist in causing her husband's death.'[1]

For many in court that day, a potted history of the trial would have sufficed, followed by a short, sharp verdict that either way would send a shockwave through the room. But the criminal justice system often demands considerable patience, and everyone present settled in for the long haul as the judge placed his hands on the thick wad of paper. With 440 paragraphs to go, there would be no quick fix. Justice would unfold in the shadows of the courtroom, while outside the city of Cape Town warmed up.

The morbid appeal of the trial matched the public heartbreak two years earlier when Taliep Petersen had been murdered. Something of a national treasure, he'd made a name for himself from the mid-1970s onwards in music and theatre with a very specific flavour, alongside his close friend, the singer and composer David Kramer. Together, they'd woven together many layers of South Africa's past, with a particular focus on coloured identity and culture, in hit productions such as *District Six – The Musical*, *Fairyland*, *Ghoema* and *Kat and the Kings*. Local venues had been sold out for months on end, and invitations had poured in from top international stages in London and New York.

Taliep, with his pitch-perfect ear, was, said Kramer, the man who 'put the folk music of Cape Town back on the map'. Ebrahim Rasool, former premier of the Western Cape, noted that Taliep had been able to 'capture our entire history, express our deepest pain, articulate our joy, and demonstrate our humanity through music and drama'.[2]

Taliep's endeavours in the music world, however, were just one aspect of his life. He was also drawn to the traditional lifestyle of a family man. For the Muslim community in Cape Town, this implies a close-knit intergenerational unit, and this was something Taliep himself had grown up with. It was simply a case of finding the woman with whom he would fall in love.

That woman was Madeegha Anders. Before Taliep met her, she was a small-time performer, singing in nightclubs and appearing in amateur stage shows on the Cape Flats in the late 1970s and early 1980s. Then, in 1987, she landed a last-minute lead role in Taliep's *District Six – The Musical*, which he had cowritten with Kramer. It played at the Baxter

Theatre at the University of Cape Town, to critical acclaim, while behind the scenes a romance began to develop.

It did not take long for Taliep and Madeegha's relationship to become a committed one. They were together for almost a decade before they officially tied the knot and made the pilgrimage to Mecca (Madeegha had since converted to Islam). They had four children, and named the girls Jawaahier, Aeesha and Fatima, and the boy Mogamat Ashur.

For a period, the marriage looked as if it would go the distance, but then the cracks started showing. Taliep's father noticed that things were strained, and his son confided in him that he had been trying for several years to make it 'right' but that it was 'not going to work out'.[3]

Madeegha had a very close friend who would spend a lot of time with the Petersens. The two women had been inseparable in their childhood, and in adulthood they were like aunties to one another's children who were growing up together in the community. That woman was Najwa Petersen (née Dirk). She had been married twice and given birth to two sons, Suleiman Effendi and Achmat Gamieldien.

Soon, Najwa started visiting her old friend Madeegha's house in the morning when Madeegha wasn't there. In other words, she was spending a suspicious amount of time alone with Taliep. The illicit romance eventually became a secret that could no longer be concealed. Taliep left Madeegha and formed a union with Najwa. Thereafter the four young Petersen children lived in the same household as Achmat and Suleiman every second week, and the newly configured family became one.

The heartbroken Madeegha would have the children in the weeks in between, but as they grew older the arrangement became more flexible. For many years, she had little genuine contact with Taliep other than the administration of being co-parents.

Taliep and Najwa, meanwhile, had a daughter of their own, little Zaynab, who joined a large blended family of four half-siblings on her father's side (Jawaahier, Fatima, Aeesha and Mogamat Ashur) and her two half-brothers (Suleiman and Achmat) on her mother's side. Taliep had also fathered another daughter, Natasha, before either Madeegha or Najwa came into his life, but she had never lived with him.

By 2006, the domestic situation was stable, at least in the logistical sense. By then, Taliep and Najwa lived at 101 Grasmere Street in Athlone with seven-year-old Zaynab. Taliep's children from his marriage to Madeegha would also stay at the house for a week at a time, or longer. Najwa's sons also lived there, and in the garden was a flatlet, the tenant of which was Najwa's cousin Mogamat Riefaat Soeker.

On the surface, the family spanned two generations living under one roof. In reality, however, Najwa and Taliep's marriage was under tremendous strain. Najwa had been diagnosed with bipolar mood disorder, and over the previous four years had been admitted several times to psychiatric clinics. She became more and more difficult to live with. At the same time, Taliep and Madeegha had become close again, finding their way back to the musical connection that had started their romance all those years ago. It was Najwa's turn to experience the insecurity and jealousy that Madeegha had once felt.

On the night of 13 April 2006, Jawaahier (then 20) arrived home at 101 Grasmere Street around 11 pm. She stood in the doorway of the bedroom, chatting to Najwa about her father's upcoming birthday two days hence. He was in the bathroom doing his ablutions at the time.

Najwa had been discharged that day from a short stay in a psychiatric facility, but was 'right as rain'[4] during the conversation, and Jawaahier headed off to her bedroom. At that stage, she was living in the house permanently and no longer spending alternate weeks with her mother. She flopped down on the bed in the double-storey house, unwinding and connecting with friends through Mxit.

But, a few minutes later, the reality of home life intruded with a bump: her younger sister Fatima came into the room and said that their father, Taliep, was calling out for help.

'It doesn't sound right,'[5] Fatima said to Jawaahier, possibly too afraid to burst into her father and stepmother's room without first seeking the counsel of her elder sister.

The cries she'd heard hadn't been loud or frantic. Rather, they were muted – perhaps the sound of someone calling for help while trying to negotiate a dangerous situation.

Jawaahier moved closer to the door, her nervous ear straining to work out what her father needed. And then she heard it, the gentle voice of the musician that raised itself only in song, never in anger: 'Najwa, no, Najwa, no.'[6]

Jawaahier opened the door and stepped into darkness. She could see neither her father nor her stepmother; the television set cast its ghostly blue hue onto the bed, which had been stripped of its linen.'

'Where are you, Daddy?' she said.

'Put the light on,' he told her gently, 'but please don't freak out.'[7]

Sliding her hand up the wall, Jawaahir felt for the switch, breathing heavily with fear in the dark. And when the light came on, it was difficult to obey her father's plea not to freak out. There was blood all over the blinds, the blankets and the sheets on the floor. Najwa, kneeling on the floor, was also covered in blood. She held a knife pointed backwards over her shoulder. The knife faced directly towards Taliep, who was standing behind her. His fingers gripped her knife-wielding hand and both husband and wife were covered in blood.

As if the scene needed any more chilling aspects, Najwa had a 'demonic' look on her face and appeared 'possessed by the devil'. Her eyes were 'droopy' and, simply put, she 'wasn't herself'.[8]

But what Taliep did next would foreshadow his silence on this incident: he coaxed Najwa to let go of the knife, passed it to their domestic worker, who had also quietly entered the room by then, and said, 'Please wash it.' Holding layers of blood-soaked dishcloth to his neck, he was trying to wash away her culpability, cleanse away the red liquid that signed her name on a crime.

Jawaahier called for emergency medical help, but Taliep wasn't the only person to be whisked away by ambulance that night and driven four kilometres away to a private medical facility in Gatesville: his wife needed medical attention too, though hers was of the psychiatric kind. She was immediately transferred to the Crescent Clinic, a psychiatric facility in Claremont, where she remained for the next three weeks.

Taliep spent one night in hospital where he was treated for his injuries. The next morning, he returned home quietly and without fanfare. He immediately made it clear that he wanted to keep the incident under wraps. No public figure wants the details of his marriage put on public display. On that day in April 2006, he told his family, 'I don't want to make a big deal out of this.'[9]

The return of Najwa from the Crescent Clinic marked the start of a new era in the Petersen household. Jawaahier would henceforth stay only at her mother's house. She could not wipe the scene in the bedroom from her memory. 'I would never have been able to live and feel comfortable after that with Najwa in the house,'[10] she said. When Najwa was around, Jawaahier wouldn't let her out of her sight. The image of Najwa kneeling on the floor holding the bloody knife remained with her. From then on, constant vigilance was required.

For the other residents of the house, both permanent and transient, it was also clearly a new era. Taliep and Najwa no longer slept in the same room. Jawaahier's two younger sisters, Fatima and Aeesha, began locking their bedroom doors when they stayed at their father's house. Zaynab slept in the safe embrace of her father's arms.

Before this absurd and bloody incident unfolded, Taliep had been at his wits' end with Najwa, He had, according to family members, wanted to divorce her, as she found the marriage 'ten times worse'[11] than his previous marriage, which had itself been beset with problems.

As if the events of that night were a dress rehearsal for what could follow, Najwa now sought just the right hitman to help her do the job thoroughly. One imagines her thoughts as the cold claws of a bird of prey as it swoops down to grab something. The perfect man had to be out there. Someone over whom she had power. Someone whose moral compass could be set aside, especially if a wad of cash was involved.

That man was Fahiem Hendricks. At 42 years of age, he was four years Najwa's junior, and had known her for several years in various capacities: 25 years earlier, Fahiem's brother had worked for the Dirk family business as a driver before a car accident had left him a paraplegic. Dirk Fruit Oshakati stood at the top of the South African food chain, exporting vast amounts of fruit and vegetables to Namibia. Fahiem, occupying a position far down that chain, lived a hand-to-mouth existence selling cheap, over-processed fast food.

Najwa's previous husband was friends with Fahiem, who had visited their home on several occasions. Najwa and Fahiem were later fellow parents at the local school where Zaynab and Fahiem's son were classmates. Fahiem did not know Taliep, nor had he visited the house in Grasmere Street.

A certain level of familiarity with Najwa must have persisted, however, for when the school bell rang on 1 December 2006 – the last day before the summer holidays – Fahiem walked up to Najwa and asked her for a loan. His fast-food business was not going well.

The loan hardly put a dent in her bank account, which was receiving R100 000 at the end of every month. Not all of Najwa's income came from Dirk Fruit, however. She was also dealing in diamonds and, by her own admission, selling US dollars 'on the black market'.[12] On top of that, she was receiving payouts from a property group in which she had shares.

Fahiem, having been promised the loan by Najwa, arrived at the house in Grasmere Street to collect it. The minute that money, a sum of R10 000, was secured, a power dynamic developed between Najwa the creditor and Fahiem the debtor. Their respective businesses highlighted the different socio-economic groups from which they came, and the asymmetrical balance of power this could create.

For the Dirks, the import-export business was but one slice of the pie; the inventory of their holdings included land worth R10 million in the town of Ondangwa, in northern Namibia, two shopping centres that were leased out at a considerable profit, and several houses and erven themselves worth millions. It was also alleged that they ran a diamond-smuggling operation between Angola, Namibia and South Africa. One of the rumours that floated quietly on the wind of Cape Town for many years was that the diamonds were often hidden inside the pieces of fruit packed into the company's fleet of Volvo trucks. There was talk that the Dirk family was under investigation for tax evasion on the Namibian side of the border.

Another person who unwittingly became involved in Najwa's plan was her best friend, Mymoena Bedford. Their friendship spanned more than two decades, and Mymoena readily obeyed Najwa's strange request, shortly after the schools closed, that she pay a visit to Fahiem's house, which was two roads down from her own, to get his telephone number. It was indeed a strange request since Najwa had already given him a loan and had not asked for any security. She must already have had his contact details, though perhaps she felt having his address would suffice. At any rate, Bedford dutifully returned with the number she had procured from Fahiem's brother, since Fahiem himself was not home, and handed it over to Najwa, who now moved one step closer to securing the middleman to help her carry out the plot.

Najwa called Fahiem and invited him to the Petersen household. Seated at the dining room table, she told him what she was looking for: men who could 'do a hit'[13] for her. He understood she wanted someone killed, but at this stage did not know Taliep was the intended target. At first, he refused to have any part of the plan, but as the next few days passed that early December, Najwa chipped away at his reluctance over several phone calls until, one day, he broached the topic with a close friend of his, 34-year-old Abdoer Emjedi, from Athlone. Abdoer had recently done in a stint in jail and was staying at Fahiem's house as he was at a loose end. Unsurprisingly, he had contacts in the criminal underworld and said he would see what he could do.

This would also take time, however, but the impatient Najwa kept on calling Fahiem for updates, as if she was desperate for the hit to take place as soon as possible. Eventually, Abdoer told Fahiem he had earmarked the right men for the job – three youngsters from Hanover Park. Fahiem relayed this fact to Najwa, who summoned Fahiem to a meeting at her house. It was then that she revealed the detail that Taliep, her husband, was the man to be murdered. She said he was planning to leave her, and that in the event of a divorce, he would end up with half her money. She also claimed that he had lost a lot of their money in a bad deal.

What she didn't mention, though it was likely on her mind, was a R5.3-million life-insurance policy that had been taken out in Taliep's name just a few months earlier. The sole beneficiary of that policy, in the event of the musician's death, would be Zaynab. None of Taliep's other children were listed as beneficiaries, and since Zaynab was only seven, it was Najwa who would manage the money on her behalf until she came of age.

Najwa promised a sum of R100 000 for the job, and, absurdly, it was decided that a 'deposit' of R30 000 would change hands during a staged robbery, while the rest would be paid later, once all policies had been cashed.

By 13 December that year, Cape Town International Airport was the hive of activity it always becomes over the festive season. South Africans

from other provinces and travellers from all over the world were flocking to the Mother City by the thousands to enjoy the white-sand beaches and long summer days. The scorching December sun was practically melting the streets, but Taliep Petersen was far from his home city. Bundled up in a warm jacket, he was in London, where he had been since the beginning of the month, preparing for the opening of his and David Kramer's latest musical production, *Ghoema*.

When it was time to return to Cape Town, Taliep made his way through the various checkpoints at Heathrow Airport, boarded the aircraft, and settled into his seat. During the long flight, he read, slept and gazed out the window. Soon he would touch down in the city of his birth. Perhaps he shuffled past other passengers down the narrow aisle of the plane, his feet in flight socks, padding towards the small toilet. Perhaps he freshened up with a splash of cool water, or slipped his hand into his daypack to check that Zaynab's gift was still there. Or perhaps he merely tilted his head back and closed his eyes, waiting for the final descent.

But, waiting at the other end for him was a wife who wanted nothing more than to end his life. A fake hijacking, she had thought, was the perfect solution, and so she arranged to meet him at the airport, which was not far from the house in Grasmere Street. Over the course of the previous day, while Taliep had been preparing for his flight home, Najwa placed no fewer than 26 calls to Fahiem, 22 of them from the comfort of the family home. What is the texture of a conversation that unfolds between two people when the one is plotting the imminent murder of her husband, and the other is the supervisor, the one who will wrangle the killers while not getting any blood on his own hands?

While Taliep's plane flew over South Africa, Najwa appeared to all the world as just another person waiting for a loved one to touch down – a wife waiting for her husband at an airport. But, in truth, her brain was working overtime on how best to murder him in as authentic-seeming a hijacking as possible. It was during these moments at Cape Town International Airport that she placed the last four calls to Fahiem.

Despite her best efforts, however, the murder did not come to pass. Fahiem repeatedly told Najwa the same thing – Abdoer had done his level best to round up the three youngsters from Hanover Park, but they were difficult to get hold of, and did not have their own transport. So, that day, through sheer disorganisation, Taliep's life was spared.

Having come so close to a murder, Najwa might have had pause for thought as to what she was planning. A reality check of sorts.

But, no. The very next day, she came up with a new plan.

That night, 15 December, a day after his return to Cape Town, Taliep was preparing to make one of his most treasured dreams a reality. He would be performing with his son, Mogamat Ashur, on stage at the Luxurama Theatre in Wynberg. Mogamat Ashur was only 14, and this was to be his first public performance.

This, Najwa calculated, was an opportune moment to carry out the murder. Claiming illness, she said she would arrive at the theatre for the second half only, during which father and son would be playing together.

She waved goodbye to her husband as he left for the theatre, confident this would be the last time he would ever be leaving the house.

But, again, that evening the plan failed. Just as before, Fahiem told Najwa that Abdoer could not get hold of the three young men from Hanover Park. All along, Najwa's first plan had been a staged robbery. With both the hastily planned hijackings having failed, she put her mind to the original plot.

Abdoer, in the meantime, had procured two other men to replace the would-be assassins. Later that evening, after the Luxurama plan had failed, Abdoer (along with his girlfriend) arrived at Fahiem's home with the new hitman. He was Waheed Hassen, aged 30, from Belhar, some 15 km away. Abdoer pulled up in his sister's car, with Waheed behind him in a bakkie. Seated next to Waheed was Jefferson Snyders, 30 years old and from Mitchells Plain, who worked for him. While Jefferson remained in the bakkie, the three other men stood locked in serious conversation: Fahiem explained to Waheed in front of Abdoer that a staged robbery had to take place, and that the father of the household had to be murdered. Abdoer, his girlfriend, Fahiem and Waheed then left and headed off to 101 Grasmere Street to map out what would happen. Jefferson stayed behind in the bakkie, and on their return, they went their separate ways again.

On Saturday, 16 December 2006, Najwa, Taliep and the rest of the family were scheduled to attend the 21st-birthday party of Najwa's sister's twins. But, once again, Najwa said she felt ill and would not be able to join them. Taliep set off from the house, inadvertently giving Najwa an opportunity to stay in contact with Fahiem.

He spent a few hours at the party, chatting to family members, eating the delicious food that was served, and celebrating the milestone birthday of the twins. Then, still tired from the busy schedule he had had in London, or perhaps worried about his 'sick' wife, Taliep said his goodbyes and left the party.

On arrival at home, he found her under the blankets in one of the children's rooms. Not long after that, Najwa's daughter-in-law Insaaf returned home. She and Achmat, Najwa's son, were staying at the house with their newborn baby. When Insaaf walked in, she found Taliep praying with Najwa. The rhythmic chant, known as *thikr*, resounded softly through the house.

A little later, around 9 pm, Taliep sat down in the kitchen with Najwa's cousin Mogamat, who lived in the flatlet on their property. Najwa joined them briefly, and the three of them sat casually chatting for a few minutes, drinking tea and eating the cake that Taliep had brought home from the party. Then Najwa said she was turning in for the evening, said her goodnights, and headed upstairs, leaving the men in the kitchen.

Taliep and Mogamat, cousins by marriage, were close friends and had much to talk about. Najwa, meanwhile, soaked in a candlelit bath upstairs, perhaps cogitating on the plan and going through the checklist of how the 'robbery' would unfold.

Again, just as on the two previous days, she stayed in intermittent contact with Fahiem. She placed a call at 9.20 pm, not long after she had padded upstairs to run her bath. Around the same time, downstairs in the kitchen, Taliep was confiding in Mogamat about how the stabbing incident had shifted the dynamics in the blended family. It upset him that the children no longer wanted to stay over, and he indicated that he was considering getting another property. The two men discussed the marital problems further and at around 11 pm went their separate ways, Mogamat to the flatlet and Taliep to an upstairs room with a television.

When he switched the television on and settled into his chair, he was doing exactly as Najwa had told Fahiem he would do. It was either that or he would head to his studio, she had predicted. Fahiem passed the information on to Abdoer that Taliep was upstairs watching television.

Over the course of that evening, before and after Taliep came home, Najwa made several calls to Fahiem, asking after the hitmen.

Finally, he told her that they (Waheed and Jefferson) were on their way.

Earlier that evening, Abdoer kept calling Waheed to find out if he had obtained a gun for the job. Waheed eventually did, but hoped that Abdoer would do the actual killing. Abdoer had no such plans, however. Having secured the men to carry out the hit, and having repeatedly called them, he did not accompany them to the scene of the crime. Waheed hatched a plan to stage the robbery and make off with the spoils, but not to actually kill Taliep. Jefferson, sitting beside him, still had no idea that a murder was even on the cards.

With Fahiem once again as the 'remote control' to the murder, he listened by phone as Najwa emphasised, 'Nobody else must be injured. Only Taliep. He must be shot.'[14]

The standing arrangement at the Petersen household was that the last person home would activate the security system in the house. On this night the task fell to Suleiman, Najwa's older teenage son, who was still at the party. This meant that the two men making their way to the house would have easy access. Najwa had also made sure any other security measures would be disabled that evening.

As the car drew nearer to 101 Grasmere Street, Waheed and Jefferson covered their faces with balaclavas as per Najwa's instructions.

On any other night, Taliep would have checked all the doors and windows before everyone went to bed, but not everyone was home from the party by that stage. The gate was ajar and the door was unlatched.

Najwa made her last call to Fahiem just before 11.30 pm, shortly before the nightmare began.

Taliep was sitting watching cricket on television when the men burst into the room. 'Stand up! Hands up! We're here to rob your place!'[15] one said.

In one short, sharp moment, Taliep went from being a man with a belly full of cake, happily watching cricket on his own, to a helpless victim as his arms were bent behind his back and his hands joined together with cable ties.

Najwa emerged from her bedroom, pretending to be a fellow victim, wearing an expression of desperate concern. She walked towards the terrified Taliep and tried to hug him. But Taliep had realised what was happening, and he head-butted her away.

Jefferson kicked Taliep squarely in the face, sending him falling backwards onto the floor, blood streaming from his face and mouth. As the attackers turned him over onto his stomach, Najwa moved forward and tried to kiss him. She also spoke softly to him, but her words, layered over by the sound of his crying, meant nothing. Knowing what she was about, he rejected her feigned affection.

After this, the events of the night unfolded at a breathless pace. Only Taliep's hands had been tied before, but then, deciding he was moving too much, the attackers decided to restrain him further. He was tied up with a tablecloth just swept off a nearby coffee table. While Waheed pressed his knee into Taliep's back, it was left to Jefferson and Najwa – her pretence abandoned – to tie his feet.

Waheed lifted Najwa from the floor and asked to be taken to the safe. As they entered the main bedroom, she said, 'My baby is sleeping. You mustn't make a noise.'[16] Zaynab lay curled up under a duvet just metres away.

Najwa led Waheed through the darkened room to the bathroom,

dimly lit by the candles still flickering faintly around the bath. She opened a cupboard and produced, from the safe inside, a large white bank bag. Waheed tried to see what else was in the safe, but Najwa obscured his view. He peeked into the bag to make sure it was real money and saw wads of crisp new R100 and R200 notes. She told him there was R27 000. When he questioned the amount (it was R3 000 short of what he had been told would be there), she said, 'You have got the money you came for, and now you must finish the man.'[17]

Waheed said it would look more authentic if they took other items too, and Najwa quickly gave him her watch.

'Is there anyone else in the house?'[18] he asked. She responded that her son, his wife and their baby were staying in the house. She led him to Achmat and Insaaf's room, where their newborn baby lay fast asleep. Achmat and Insaaf were still awake, their eyes wide with terror. In another bizarre display of fake empathy, Najwa began comforting her crying daughter-in-law.

'We are six people robbing this house. If you cooperate nobody will be hurt,'[19] said Waheed, pointing the gun at them. He hastily picked up some jeans off the floor and yanked money out of the pockets. Next he helped himself to a camera off Insaaf's bedside table. He was just about to leave the room when he saw the baby lying in the cot. In a strange echo of Najwa's show of affection for Taliep a few minutes earlier, Waheed bent down and kissed the baby on the forehead. He then tried to manoeuvre them all to the main bedroom, where he intended to lock them up. But, as the baby began crying, Insaaf pleaded to be locked up in their own room instead. Najwa left the room, followed by Waheed, who locked the door.

Najwa could now drop the pretence of victimhood and resume

pushing for her agenda: she threaded her arm around Waheed's and egged him on: '*Kom julle moet nou klaarmaak met die man, julle moet hom skiet, julle moet hom vanaand skiet*' (Come, you must now finish with the man, you must shoot him, you must shoot him tonight).[20]

Jefferson, meanwhile, had remained with Taliep, at some point stuffing one of his gloves into the terrified musician's mouth, but also wiping the blood and tears from his face and reassuring him that he was going to survive the ordeal. And that was what Jefferson believed. It was just a robbery, he had been told by the others. When Najwa and Waheed reappeared, he took the glove out of Taliep's mouth. In his final moments, Taliep began reciting the *kalima* (an Islamic declaration of faith) while Jefferson sat on his knees beside him, still wiping his face and reassuring him he was not going to die.

But, when Najwa told the men to murder her husband downstairs instead of upstairs, Jefferson rose to his feet in panic as the real plan was suddenly revealed. Waheed told Jefferson to leave the room and sent him to be a lookout instead.

Waheed disappeared into another room, leaving the married couple alone in one another's company for one last time. He came back holding a pillow, folded it in half, placed it over his arm and inserted the gun. The weapon was pointing down towards the man bleeding and bound on the floor two steps away.

Taliep Petersen, celebrated musical director, loving father, betrayed husband, repeated, in the moments before his gruesome death, '*Allāhu akbar.*' Najwa stood in close proximity, looking on with compassionless eyes. Waheed hesitated, but Najwa's hand quickly moved into the folded pillow where it found his hand. She placed her hand over his, and a single shot went off.

In the hours, days and months after Taliep Petersen's senseless murder, Najwa Petersen had to give the performance of her life in roles that included traumatised robbery victim, witness to murder, adoring mother comforting her little girl after her father's murder, and bipolar sufferer whose shaky mental health had been exacerbated by a horrific ordeal.

Straight after the execution-style murder of her husband, Najwa was locked in her bedroom to give credence to the theory of a robbery gone wrong. When Taliep's younger brother Igsaan arrived with his son at the house shortly after the murder, he found his brother lying dead in a pool of blood, his hands and feet bound. He and his son kicked down the door of the bedroom where Achmat was locked with his wife and child, and also of the main bedroom where Najwa was locked up with Zaynab.

When he entered the room, he found Najwa sobbing on the bed, her arms wrapped tightly around the traumatised little girl.

This was the very picture of grief, the symbol of a murder that rocked the entire nation and would be on everyone's lips for weeks on end. The senseless killing, the unknown thugs who had broken into the house, the opportunistic nature of crime ...

Then, six months after the gruesome murder, Fahiem Hendricks did an about-turn: he decided to confess and tell the world who had really plotted to have Taliep murdered. This he did of his own volition.

He was whisked away into witness protection, and given immunity from prosecution for his role in the sequence of events. All he had to do was dish up the details.

The next time he saw Najwa Petersen was in a courtroom, and when that moment came, the two could not have presented a starker contrast. The woman from whom Fahiem had borrowed money, taken instructions, and then received a handsome payment, stood in the Cape Town High Court, impeccably dressed. She seem to revel quietly in the limelight. But, as elegantly as Najwa was dressed, so did the man who had revealed her role in the murder seem uncomfortable in his own skin. Fahiem sat in the courtroom looking 'dishevelled' and in an 'awkward position'[21] – not helped by the clunky bulletproof vest that he wore under his clothing. His voice barely audible, he stared ahead, as if danger could come from any part of the room if he made eye contact while telling his story.

Throughout the protracted trial, with Fahiem implicating her at every turn, Najwa clung to her story of a surprise attack by the balaclava-clad robbers. Interestingly, she also changed counsel four times, with those in the legal profession quickly realising that representing the changeable Najwa was a poisoned chalice.

Najwa tried to paint the marriage as a happy one, in order to claim that she had no motive. During the eight months between the stabbing incident in April and the murder in December, she said the couple 'did everything together' and it was 'just when it came to sleeping time' that they 'slept in separate bedrooms',[22] and this at her husband's request. She conceded that Taliep took issue with her smoking and felt slighted that she still called herself Najwa Dirk rather than Najwa Petersen.

She conceded, too, that differences had arisen around the various children they had each brought into the marriage, and even the little girl they had created together. But, according to her, those were just sideshows to what was a normal and loving marriage.

The harmonious relationship she described in court did not match what Taliep had told his family members. It also didn't match up to the image of her standing with a demonic look on her face and a bloody knife that she had driven into Taliep's neck eight months before the murder.

While she presented herself as a bereft widow cruelly separated from her husband by a violent death, evidence to the contrary became overwhelming. Apart from Fahiem's turning state witness, both Waheed and Jefferson made detailed and damning confessions that corroborated the testimony of Fahiem and many others. Added to this were the crystal-clear telephone records, the paper trail of money changing hands and the massive holes in the stories built by Najwa and her different lawyers.

For some, the truth was a revelation. For others, it was merely confirmation. Taliep's brother Igsaan had found the scene of mother and daughter sobbing on the bed on the night of the murder utterly heartbreaking – as did the medical emergency service personnel who sedated Najwa – but, at the same time, right from that night onwards, he 'found the circumstances suspicious'[23] and suspected that the Dirks had killed his brother.

Likewise, the first detective on the scene of the murder, Brian Hermanus, said that while Najwa was 'clearly distraught' and 'her sorrow appeared to be genuine',[24] he had suspicions within hours of the murder and believed his 'gut instinct' about her involvement.

In early December 2008, exactly two years after she'd sat at her dining-room table and asked Fahiem to find some hitmen, Najwa was found guilty of murdering her husband. When she was sentenced in February the following year, Judge Desai said, 'This was a contract killing, in itself a most reprehensible offence. The contractor, in this instance, remained on the scene to ensure that the hired killer carried out her instructions.'

Najwa Petersen, who'd so desperately wanted her husband dead and then had tried to hug him when the moment came, was sentenced to 28 years behind bars.

CHAPTER 7

CELIWE MBOKAZI

━┼┼━

Muldersdrift, 2007

Celiwe picked up her husband's coffee cup from the small table on the stoep. The dregs lay at the bottom like fresh mud. Letting out a sigh, she walked inside the house, ran some cold water into the cup, and splashed some on her face. She could already feel the morning heat rising, and wondered if a thunderstorm would follow in the afternoon. Everything about this place on the Highveld was different from the rural village in KwaZulu-Natal from where she had come twenty years earlier as a girl of 15, except for the thunderclaps and forks of lightning streaking in the sky. Those made her feel right at home.

If it rains later today, she thought to herself, it will wash things away.

As soon as the water from the tap had cooled the skin on her cheeks, she looked at the clock. There was still time to cook some oats before

Franz, her husband, whom she often called 'the old man', came back to fetch her and the kids. But just before going to the kitchen, she went back to her room and flopped down on the bed, pulling the cool white sheets around her as if they might mop up some of her irritation. For the briefest time, she drifted back to sleep. It was a strange sleep, light and feverish.

The sound of 13-year-old Nosipho padding down the passage towards the bathroom brought her out of it. Instead of calling to Nosipho, as she might have done on any other morning, Celiwe lay there quietly, hoping she wouldn't pop her head in. Nosipho was technically her niece, but since she was raising her, she allowed herself the irritation that parents sometimes feel for their teenagers. She also remembered herself at that age – passionate, dreaming of something bigger – and wondered if Nosipho felt the same.

How could she? she thought to herself. I was in a rural village. Nosipho is in the lap of luxury.

She looked at her watch.

'Too late to make oats now,' she sighed.

It was time to make the phone call. She moved her hand down towards her belly and began rubbing it. At first, she rubbed slowly and almost lovingly, as if she was stroking the downy skin of the baby's head within. But too many thoughts pushed their fingers into the crevices of her brain, and she found herself rubbing angrily the skin that stretched around her belly button. Then she reached for her cellphone.

On that day, 28 November 2007, Franz Richter, aged 80, had woken up early next to Celiwe to prepare for the day. Nearly four decades in the tourism industry had taught him the value of always dressing neatly. A short-sleeved white button-down shirt and a pair of brown shorts had been neatly laid out for him by Celiwe the night before. He got dressed and combed what was left of his hair. He felt fit, despite the pacemaker inside his body. People often told him he looked 70.

He stepped out onto the stoep. It was going to be a hot day. Celiwe Mbokazi, 45 years his junior and his customary wife, brought him a strong cup of coffee. He searched her face for some affection but she gave nothing away.

'I'll see you later,' she said. 'Please call as usual before you head back from the lodge so I can make sure we're ready.'

After swirling the last sip around in his mouth, he headed from the house to the lodge. A punctual man, he walked through the doors into the dark interior of the dining section at exactly 8 am and seated himself at a table. Soon, a hearty breakfast was placed in front of him: fried eggs, sliced potatoes, a pile of bacon, two sausages and sliced tomato fried in garlic butter and black pepper. As he ate, he looked out the window to watch the zebra drinking water from the swimming pool, their long eyelashes dipping down, catching the morning light of the Highveld. He never tired of this image, and nor did the countless guests who passed through the gates of the safari lodge.

Back at the farmhouse, Celiwe thought about the first time she'd seen Franz, 20 years before. He had arrived in a bakkie in the tiny village, tucked behind the mountains near Eshowe in what is now KwaZulu-Natal, where she grew up. She and the other villagers had seen the lumbering vehicle kicking up mud on the mountain road from several kilometres away, and the word spread quickly: the businessman from Johannesburg was coming to choose traditional dancers to live and work in the cultural village at his tourist lodge.

Twenty minutes later, she was standing opposite him in a long line of youngsters, wishing that his eyes would fall on her and that he would whisk her away for this golden opportunity.

They could not have come from more different worlds. Orphaned at the age of five, Franz had grown up in Romania. He left his native country two years before the communist takeover got under way, and spent several years in Germany from the age of 15, including service in the German forces during the Second World War. In 1952, he saw an advertisement for job opportunities for gold miners in South Africa, and hoped against hope he would be chosen: there were 1 000 applicants and space for only 80 men.

When the news came through that he had been selected, he immediately boarded a ship, leaving Europe behind. With his ruddy cheeks and neat smile, he arrived in the strange land of South Africa as a young man in his twenties.

At first, he worked underground at Crown Mines in Johannesburg, venturing 2.7 km below the surface on a regular basis. He had signed a contract with the South African government 'binding him to work in the mines for a minimum of four and a half years',[1] and eventually he was promoted to the position of shift boss.

By then, apartheid's iron fist was pushing its way through the social fabric of a city that by its very nature was diverse – not just in terms of race, but ethnicity, nationality, language and religion too. Despite being a foreigner, Franz would have found himself among other like-minded men hoping to carve out a future for themselves.

That didn't mean his ties to Europe had been severed. He soon found himself a penfriend in Germany, and one day a young Munich seamstress, Hedwig Sedlmayr, received a ticket to join him in Johannesburg. This she did, carrying nothing with her but a sewing machine, a suitcase and the hope of an adventure. They were married 16 hours after they met.

After working on the mines, Franz turned to his other trade. Before he had left Germany, he had qualified as a motor mechanic, and now he 'took his tool box to a number of workshops before opening his own Richters Motors garage'.[2] He eventually grew the business to four garages in Johannesburg, and also managed a team of mechanics at the Kyalami racetrack.

Throughout the 1960s, while Franz had been working tirelessly as a mechanic, he had also been saving up whatever he could to invest in a piece of land. He was passionate about conservation and wildlife, and became interested in establishing a safari lodge. Finally, in 1970, he signed the letter of purchase: 1 100 hectares of pristine land in Muldersdrift, northwest of Johannesburg. He built a lodge and purchased game, and as the years rolled on, Heia Safari Ranch acquired a reputation as an accessible destination near Johannesburg for game drives and nights in a rondavel.

He and Hedwig had two daughters and a son who grew up in the warmth of the family homestead, and for some years life was good – delicious food, game drives, lolling by the pool next to the restaurant.

Then, in 1983, when Franz was in his mid-fifties, Hedwig suddenly died. This was an emotional turning point for him, and he poured all his energy into the business.

With Hedwig's death, however, the safari lodge itself seemed to get stuck in time. As design trends changed, the lodge remained the same. Even the tiles in the bathroom had not been modernised since Hedwig's days, and there was no longer any pretence of serving up gourmet food. But perhaps Franz felt such change wasn't necessary when the drawcard was simply the wildlife.

To cash in on tourists' interest in getting a glimpse of traditional life, Franz established a 'cultural village', Phumangena uMuzi, four years after Hedwig's death. It was opened by King Goodwill Zwelithini, the Zulu monarch. Visitors could watch Zulu dancers perform, and while for many locals the lodge and cultural village were a curio-shopped version of Africa, for tourists it was a one-stop shop for an African sunset, a game drive and a cultural treat.

At the turn of the century, Franz took another bold step and created one of the biggest hand-built stone dams on the continent. After that, as the Muldersdrift area attracted more attention, offers began to pour in from developers. From golfing estates to gated communities, it seemed like every entrepreneur had an eye on his land and was waving wads of cash around. But each time he said the same thing: he was going to hold on to his land and carry on doing what he loved. He developed a reputation as a big-hearted philanthropist whose entrepreneurial flair was matched by his ability to connect positively with his staff and the surrounding community.

Over the next decade, Muldersdrift become known as the 'wedding belt'. Brides and grooms in search of a tranquil setting not too far from Johannesburg would choose it as the backdrop for their big day. Tucked behind every farm gate was a wedding venue complete with a large thatched hall, a stone chapel and a garden in which to sip champagne and throw petals ...

At Heia Safari, however, Franz remained resolute that nature, game drives and accommodation would be all that was on offer. The food was bland, and the rondavels drably decorated, but most people would leave talking about the wildlife they had seen. Franz had no interest in the booming wedding industry, nor in the luxury spa experience, in which visitors pay a handsome sum for a hot-rock massage and a pedicure. For Franz, the most important thing was the sheer beauty of the surroundings, which gave his guests a sense of being in the bush and encountering exquisite animals without having to trek to the Kruger National Park, several hours' drive east of Johannesburg.

Though perhaps not obvious to many of those working at Heia Safari, an unlikely romance had developed between Franz and one of the much younger Zulu dancers he had brought in from Natal. It had begun in 1987, four years after his wife's death. Celiwe Mbokazi, along with 19 other dancers, had been recruited to live in the cultural village, where she and the others would dance for tourists. She was only 15 when she arrived at the lodge, while Franz was already a man of 60.

By 1995, at age 23, she had moved into the farmhouse. In apartheid South Africa, the romance would have been deemed illegal by the authorities had they known about it. Interracial sexual relations were not unheard of but were certainly rare because of the regime's social engineering and the racist legislation that went with it. The strangeness of an older Romanian-German man becoming involved with a much younger Zulu woman, a teenager from a rural area, would certainly have raised questions. Staff members, including Celiwe's twin brother, Mcelwa, said the relationship was obvious, but Franz's own children, most notably his daughter Gaby, who helped run the tourism enterprise, said otherwise – that Celiwe was simply a housekeeper.

Perhaps the lines were blurred. By the time she was living at the farmhouse, in 1995, one year after apartheid ended and eight years after they had met, Celiwe was still on the payroll but was also identifying as Franz's significant other. He had paid lobola to her extended family back in KwaZulu-Natal, and it was, for all intents and purposes, a customary marriage. She and Franz 'resided together as husband and wife',³ and he also committed to building her a homestead in her home village.

Over the years, Celiwe and Franz would also become the unofficial adoptive parents of five children, all originally from KwaZulu-Natal. Nosipho, Celiwe's niece, had been involved in a terrible car accident in 2004, at the age of ten, and had been brought to Muldersdrift to be nearer to better medical care. Franz paid for all her medical expenses, and she lived in the farmhouse with the couple: the young girl came to regard them as her father and mother.

Siyabonga, a year older, seemed close to Nosipho, who was like a sister to him. He similarly regarded Celiwe and Franz as his parents.

There were another two younger children, Lindokuhle and Thabang, who were in primary school, and then there was little Bheki, who hadn't started school yet. Not officially adopted, they nonetheless were raised and cared for by Celiwe and Franz.

In a small office near the dining room in the lodge, Sandra Wenman sat behind a wooden desk carefully counting out money. In front of her were several small brown envelopes. She sorted the cash into equal portions before running her thumb along the lip of each envelope to seal the money inside. Having worked at the lodge for 15 years since 1992, she, like the others, was a loyal employee who appreciated the care Franz put into maintaining warm friendships with everyone who worked for him.

She knew Franz's routine well, and especially the monthly ritual of wage day. He would arrive early and chat to staff members before tucking into a hearty breakfast. At a few minutes before 10 am, he would come into her office. They would chat for a few minutes, and he would collect the self-sealing brown envelopes containing the wages. By then, the money would all be neatly stacked inside the metal stationery box, after she'd checked the full amount (R23 213.00) and included a list with the name of each dancer, who would later sign to acknowledge receipt. The box would then be clipped firmly closed.

That day, Franz was running a few minutes late. Perhaps the hot November weather had slowed him down. Finally, he pushed his chair back from the table and walked over to his office, where he made a few calls. A few minutes later, he entered Sandra's office, gave his usual warm greeting, and picked up the small metal box.

At the front of the lodge, the receptionist also had an oft-repeated role: on seeing Franz setting off with the money, she would phone the main farmhouse to let Celiwe know that her husband was on his way.

Franz set off in the vehicle along with a young man called Terence. Like Sandra, Terence had worked for Franz for several years, knew his routine, and counted him as a kind and caring boss.

At the farmhouse, Celiwe had spent a few minutes alone, during which she had spoken quietly on the phone to Dumisani Xulu, a man with a long face and a smooth bald head with whom she had intermittently been in contact since the beginning of the month.

As Celiwe lifted herself from the cool touch of the sheets and exited her room, she found Nosipho, already scrubbed and ready, sitting in the living room with her legs curled under her and a glass of milk in her hand. Celiwe ran her fingers over the top of Nosipho's head and asked her if she'd slept well. Nosipho nodded while taking a large gulp of milk, and stretched her legs out.

Siyabonga was outside sweeping the verandah. When the phone rang and the receptionist told Celiwe that Franz was on his way, Celiwe knocked on the window next to the front door, motioned for Siyabonga to come inside to get dressed, and walked down the passage. She'd forgotten to make breakfast. 'I'll feed them later,' she said to herself.

Celiwe quickly went to her room, pulled off her nightie, and found a loose white shirt and a soft pair of pants that would make her feel as comfortable as possible. I'll be able to run more easily in these, she thought to herself, and then pushed the thought from her mind.

She made another brief phone call, told the other children in the house to make some food for little Bheki, and joined Nosipho and Siyabonga waiting in the living room. Celiwe opened the front door and noticed how the sun was already pouring over the stoep. She felt her nerves tighten as she looked out and saw the Nissan game-drive vehicle, the one they all called the 'zebra', approaching, kicking up stones on the gravel road. She drew in a deep breath for a few seconds until calm returned to her body.

The image of this vehicle, used for family transport, game drives and ferrying eager tourists around, was so engraved on her brain that she wondered if it would ever go away. How many times had she sat beside

Franz on their way to the Zulu dancers? How often had she seen the metal box with the envelopes inside bouncing along as they travelled the gravel roads? How might her life have been had she not moved into the farmhouse and instead remained up at the village waiting for her own brown envelope to arrive?

Her silent questions were interrupted by the vehicle's quick hoot as it pulled up at the gate. Nosipho and Siyabonga immediately went outside. Staying inside, she made another hurried phone call before slipping into the car beside her husband.

Not far from the farmhouse, from where the 'zebra' set off that day towards the Zulu village, a small group of men were stationed behind the mottled green curtain of foliage. One of these men was Dumisani Xulu, the man to whom she'd spoken earlier on the phone. Standing next to him, breathing slowly as he waited for the vehicle to come in sight, was Johnson Chirwa. At 23, he was the youngest of the group and was known as a bit of a gambler. Also with Dumisani and Johnson was a man older than Johnson but younger than kingpin Dumisani. He came from North West province and his name was Gilbert Mosadi. Like Johnson, he was a father, but his commitment in that regard was purely financial. Like Johnson, he had taken to gambling.

Franz has his hands on the wheel. Celiwe is next to him in the front passenger seat, with the metal box placed between them. Behind them, in the middle row of the game-drive vehicle, Nosipho and Siyabonga sit next to one another, looking out at the scenery. The manicured lawns around the farmhouse soon give way to open veld. Terence sits in the back row, one hand on each knee, as he too looks out across the veld. He knows this is likely to be the most relaxing part of his day, the three-kilometre drive from door to door when there's nothing to do but just enjoy the ride. The weather could not be more pleasant, nor the clouds more willing to stay away for at least a few more hours.

There's a fence that runs along the edge of a section of the game farm. Not all the animals are herbivores; some are carnivores, and the fence is needed to keep them where they're supposed to be. Each time the family does the drive along the gravel road, there's a gate that must be opened. On this day, with the sun already climbing high in the sky before 11 am, it's Siyabonga who alights from the vehicle to open the gate. The vehicle drives through.

Terence gets out of the vehicle to assist Siyabonga in closing the gate, and suddenly, a scatter of three men bursts out from behind the bushes. Their faces are covered by balaclavas, and as they appear from the tangle of foliage, it is clear that they are armed. Two stomp along with bent knees waving guns about; the other runs on tiptoes like a dog on hot concrete. For a few quick seconds, they're all silent, as if every move has been agreed on beforehand.

The hearts of those in the vehicle are pounding furiously as the men move towards the car. Someone lets out a gasp. Nosipho is terrified and grabs the seat with both hands as if they're about to crash. Terence's legs shake under him as he stands by the gate. Should he run away, run back to the vehicle, hide, or confront the men to protect his boss and his family? Siyabonga feels like this is a bad dream, like the world is melting in front of him. He feels as if the power is draining from his body and only grabbing onto the gate will keep him upright.

'Voetsek! Voetsek!' the men shout, gesturing menacingly.

Franz is in a panic but draws a deep breath and holds it in. He feels responsible for the lives of every person in the vehicle and makes a quick assessment in his head. The money will get rid of the attackers, he thinks.

Celiwe lets out a scream, but it sounds different to how she thought it would. She raises her palms to her ears as she suddenly sees the silhouette of the gun. One of the attackers fires into the air, the loud bang echoing off the surrounding landscape.

Suddenly, all three men are standing next to Celiwe's side of the vehicle, looking five times their actual size. One puts his fingers on the handle of her door, yanking it so abruptly that she too feels off-guard now. Franz quickly grabs the metal box and shouts to her, 'Give them the money!'[4]

But one of the men shouts back, 'We don't want the money! We want the man!'[5]

Another assailant thrusts a gun into Celiwe's face while her door is properly yanked open. Someone pulls her out of the vehicle, digging strong fingers into her flesh and pushing her to the ground. She feels her handbag being pulled away from her and sees her cellphone being sought within.

Then the men are at Franz's window, a gun in his face.

Nosipho hears a second gunshot. Then a third. Unlike the first, these are not 'warning shots' fired into the air. She panics even more, throws herself from the vehicle, and begins running, the sound of her feet on the gravel sounding like more gunfire. Almost no breath left inside her, she ducks down behind a clump of bushes, too terrified to cry. Then she hears her mother's scream and runs back along the short stretch of gravel. Grabbing her mother's arm, she pulls her up and they begin running towards the lodge. By then, the men have run off, pulling open the metal box at the same time. Siyabonga and Terence have run off in another direction to get help.

On their way, Celiwe and Nosipho see Gaby striding in the opposite direction. Next to her is a panic-stricken Terence, who has just called to her for help ...

They all arrive on foot at the scene of horror not far from the lodge. The metal box that held the brown envelopes lies empty on the grass nearby. The chemical smell of gunfire is still in the air. The vehicle is a few metres from the gate, stationary, under a tree off the road – it has been pushed there. Franz is in the driver's seat, only his back and shoulders visible from outside. Slumped down, he appears lifeless, his shirt soaked with blood.

It's eerily silent.

The events leading up to that day began around a year earlier when, in September 2006, Celiwe met Ronnie Khumalo, a man with a long face, narrow eyes and a neat beard and moustache. Just like herself two decades before, he'd been recruited as a Zulu dancer to perform in the cultural village. At 28, Ronnie was closer in age to Celiwe and was someone to whom she could relate. It wasn't long before they fell in love. When nobody else was around, Ronnie would make his way to the farmhouse and the two of them would meet inside the tool shed.

Keeping a sexual and romantic relationship secret was one thing. Concealing a pregnancy was quite another. And this was the cold-shiver revelation that came to Celiwe when her period didn't arrive. She was acutely aware of what was at stake: a long-term marriage, a lifestyle to which she had become accustomed, resources for five children and being part of a successful business. With so much at stake, she decided to seek an abortion and travelled to the small town of Nigel on the East Rand. But, instead of visiting a legitimate health facility where she could have had a legal surgical abortion under sanitary conditions, she found an unregistered practitioner who promised to assist with a chemical abortion. There's no shortage of such 'service providers', and nor is there a shortage of women who, for reasons that range from fear to gullibility to mistrust of government health officials, prefer to visit these unreliable and dangerous backstreet abortionists.

Celiwe took the risk and dutifully drank the concoction given to her by the practitioner, but as the weeks went by, it dawned on her that the baby was still growing. Her secret was not concealed from everyone, though. Nosipho for one had noticed her swollen belly, and certainly Celiwe's sister was aware of the attempted abortion. Ronnie also knew of the pregnancy, but for the first months there were others who were oblivious to it.

By August 2007, however, the pregnancy had become obvious to even the most unobservant. No choice remained to Celiwe but to break the news to her husband. Franz was shattered. With anger and sadness, he told Celiwe that she should return to KwaZulu-Natal to give birth to the child she was carrying, and that after that she should go to Johannesburg and look for 'work with other people'.[6]

The fate of the five children also hung in the balance. Would Franz, a man of 80, raise them on his own in Celiwe's absence when they all hailed from the same family and village? Come mid-December, Celiwe would be making the journey back to the rural land she came from. There she would give birth to the baby that represented betrayal to her husband. She would also be taking the five children with her, to a place where all the luxuries of Heia Safari would be nothing but a memory.

In hindsight, one thing is certain: the news of the pregnancy resurrected the former power relation that had existed between Franz and Celiwe. No longer the wife with whom he shared a home and co-parented five children, Celiwe was once again thrust into the role of an employee, a younger subordinate on the payroll. She was, as Franz's daughter called her, 'the housekeeper'.[7]

╬

A man named Lindikhaya, who had been working on the farm since 7 am that day and was a mere hundred metres away when the attack took place, had looked up when the gunshots sounded and seen a small group of men darting off into the bushes. A few moments later, a security guard pulled up and Lindikhaya jumped into his vehicle. The two of them set off in search of the fugitives, with Lindikhaya describing in detail what he'd witnessed as they drove.

And, suddenly, there they were, attempting to pick their way down the side of a small mountain. The pursuers quickly alerted the police.

Muldersdrift is a large and sparsely populated area, and the police station is several kilometres away. The police got there as quickly as they could, however, and found the men still on the side of the small mountain. When the men saw the police, they quickly dispersed – two of them into the bushes, and the third man in the opposite direction.

From that point the police presence swelled, as Franz lay dead in the car and investigators began to collect and photograph evidence around him. One bullet was found near the vehicle, and two others were later found lodged in Franz's body, having passed through his chest and upper arm. The shots had been fired from around two metres away, on the right-hand side of the car, exactly as described by Terence, Nosipho, Siyabonga and Celiwe herself.

Police teams hunted for the killers, picking their way through the area near the Crocodile River on foot for hours. Helicopters were brought in, and the policemen on board circled overhead with eagle-eyed concentration. But still there was nothing.

Several hours passed, and hope of finding the killers began to wane. But then, towards 4 pm, community members insisted that the men must be hiding among the dry but dense reeds below the hills on a nearby farm. It didn't take long before police, dogs, community members and security guards were heading down to the reeds.

The thick reeds provided cover for the fugitives, a maze through which they could creep to avoid arrest. But then it was decided that the reeds would be set alight. The men who had killed Franz Richter would be smoked out. Starting a fire was a risky move, but it paid off: within ten minutes of the vegetation being set ablaze, Johnson Chirwa emerged from the area in his black jeans and T-shirt, with his hands over his head. He fitted the description the police had been given.

Johnson was searched and wads of cash were found – more than R1 000 inside his trousers, over R4 000 inside one takkie and R2 000 in the other, as well as smaller amounts in his back pockets. When R50 was taken from his right back pocket, Johnson protested that it was his own money and should not be confiscated. As for the other amounts, he kept quiet. He was led away to a police vehicle and bundled inside.

A policeman and a member of the private armed-response company entered the reeds themselves on foot. There they found a terrified Gilbert

Mosadi crouched on the ground. As the police closed in on him, he tried to crawl away, but it was too late. The manhunt, for him, was over. As he stood up and moved out from the reeds, money tumbled from his clothing onto the ground. He was frisked and more money was found in his back pockets. He claimed that it was his own cash, but was arrested on the spot.

After being questioned, Johnson travelled with police officers to the impoverished Video informal settlement in Nooitgedacht, not far from Heia Safari. Johnson led the police to a shack where they found Dumisani Xulu, the man who had recruited the others and planned how the attack would unfold.

Next to be arrested was Ronnie Khumalo, Celiwe's secret lover. A tipoff said that he was likely at the gate of the Garden Lodge, about a kilometre away from Heia Safari. When the police arrived, he was told to lie on the ground and was searched from head to toe.

At the funeral held at Heia Safari on Monday 3 December 2007, less than a week after his brutal murder, Franz was laid to rest. Celiwe stood in the summer heat playing the role of the bereft widow, with tears running down her cheeks.

Franz's remains were buried with those of Hedwig on the vast property that now had a shroud of sadness hanging over it. His motto, according to Gaby, had always been 'Live in Africa, with Africa.'

Barely a week later, Celiwe confided to a friend that she feared arrest. This was said to a young woman named Amanda, who was only 22 years old and who considered Celiwe a mentor.

Events soon moved quickly, proving that Celiwe's fear was not unfounded.

Battling with the shock and grief of losing her father in such a violent way, Gaby still had to keep the administrative wheels rolling. A few days later, she noticed something suspicious in the business's phone records. The landline at the farmhouse where Franz lived with Celiwe and the children was connected to the switchboard of the lodge. It was all part of the same telephone system, and detailed records were kept so that guests staying overnight could be charged for any calls made. Included in the dataset were the date, time and telephone number of every call made. This was printed out daily so that the correct amount could be charged to each guest.

While trawling through the telephone records, Gaby noticed some unfamiliar numbers that had been called repeatedly from the farmhouse in the days leading up to her father's murder. She alerted the investigating officer and handed over the data, which revealed many calls made from the landline to Dumisani Xulu. Celiwe had phoned Dumisani in early November, which was possibly when the bloody plan was first conceived. She called him again on 22 November, just six days before the murder. After that, the frequency of the calls picked up; she called him on 25 and 26 November, and then on the day of the murder, just before 8 am. Between 9.20 am and 10 am, she placed no less than four calls to him.

As one investigator went through Celiwe's landline and cellphone records line by line, behind another closed door Dumisani sat opposite a policeman and spared no detail. He told the policeman straight – he had acted in cahoots with Franz's own wife.

On 7 December, just a few days after the funeral, Celiwe Mbokazi was handcuffed and arrested for the murder of her 80-year-old husband. For the Muldersdrift community, the news came as a relief (showing that the murder hadn't been a random act of violence) but also as a shock.

But how shocked was the murderess herself? Did she believe she had gotten away with murder, or did she know it was just a matter of time before the police arrived at the farmhouse? At her trial, the judge observed, 'The fear she expressed [to her young friend, Amanda] is contrary to what one would expect of a complainant and state witness which is what accused number five was at the time.'[8] Without blinking an eye, Celiwe flatly denied even knowing the young woman on the witness stand.

But, fortunately, in the criminal justice system, different forms of evidence can revolve around the same suspect like moons circling a planet. Celiwe could deny knowing about a will in which she was promised R1 million. She could deny knowing Amanda. She could even deny knowing Dumisani, with whom she had conspired to have her husband murdered.

The phone records handed over by Gaby, however, spoke for themselves. But Celiwe had a story to explain those too. Those calls, she told the judge, were actually made by her secret lover, Ronnie, who had come to the house on the morning of the murder. She claimed she did not know and had never in her life uttered a single word to Dumisani. Ronnie, she said, had called him from her cellphone and then the landline when her airtime ran out.

Ronnie tried to protect Celiwe by corroborating this story, claiming that he had slept in the tool shed and had asked to use his lover's cellphone and then the landline to call Dumisani. But Nosipho, who

169

had been at home the entire time, had not seen Ronnie come into the house nor standing outside using a cellphone, and nor had Siyabonga.

When it came to motive, the issue of Franz's will, coupled with the context of the pregnancy, the affair and Celiwe's being told to return to KwaZulu-Natal, became something of a perfect storm. Franz had updated his last will and testament just a month before Celiwe broke the news of the pregnancy to him.

On 10 July 2007, nearly six months before the murder, he had signed the will, which was witnessed by Sandra. The trust fund detailed in the will amounted to R1 million. It was stipulated that, in the event of his death, Franz wished the interest from that money, or the capital itself, to be spent on Celiwe for accommodation, medical expenses, travel, 'reasonable pleasures', the payment of taxes, and general welfare and benefits. She was also to be provided, at no cost, free daily meals and beverages at the lodge. A further trust of R500 000 was created for the five children. Franz, knowing that Celiwe was often concerned about his health as he got older, had discussed the will with her in order 'to give her peace of mind'.[9]

Later in court, however, knowing that the will and details of the trust appeared as the perfect motive for murder, Celiwe denied any knowledge of it. She claimed that she had only been made aware of a will when behind bars at Johannesburg Prison following her arrest.

Gaby said in court that she found this claim absurd, as did the judge, who said that it was 'highly improbable' that Franz would not have told Celiwe about his will when 'they lived together as a family', she was his wife, and Franz 'very much cared for the children'. He said also it was clear that they loved him as their father.

When the trial finally began in 2009, Celiwe was the mother of an

18-month-old daughter, her love-child with Ronnie Khumalo, with whom she was still romantically involved.

Gaby, who for so many years had helped her father run the lodge, denied that Celiwe had been her father's customary wife. 'I confronted my father on numerous occasions. He denied anything was going on. She was his housekeeper. There is no marriage documentation,'[10] she said. She described Celiwe as someone who 'did cleaning and ironing – what a normal housekeeper does – and making sure the orphans get bathed and that they were looked after'.[11]

Her claim was, of course, contradicted by several facts: the lobola paid by Franz all those years ago; the fact that the couple were living and caring for the children together; and various testimonies that were given in court – not to mention the house being built for her in her village, and the R1 million that had been left to her in the will. Did Gaby not know they were involved, or, in the wake of his tragic death, was she trying to make sense of it by distancing her father from his much younger and, as it turned out, murderous partner?

When it came to her father's will, 'Because she has blood on her hands, whatever was bequeathed to her will fall away',[12] Gaby said of Celiwe. However, the money placed in trust for the five children was sent to them every month in KwaZulu-Natal, where they had all returned, until they were 18.

In January of the following year, yet another man was arrested. He was a warder at Johannesburg Prison by the name of Vincent Dlamini, and he was implicated in the attack by three of the others on trial. Some of the eyewitnesses reported that there had been four attackers and not three, raising the suspicion that Vincent was the fourth man. However, there was not sufficient evidence against him, and his constitutional rights were also violated during his arrest and questioning. As the trial unfolded, the judge was clearly not impressed with him, and described him as an 'unreliable' and 'untruthful'[13] witness, but he did not feel it was proven beyond reasonable doubt that Dlamini had been involved, and he was duly acquitted of being involved in the robbery and murder.

And so, of the six people tried for the murder of Franz Richter, two were set free. One of these was Vincent Dlamini and the other was Ronnie Khumalo. The judge described the latter as 'a most unimpressive witness' whose evidence, like that of Dlamini, was also untruthful and unreliable throughout. He had 'adjusted his evidence when the shoe pinched'.[14]

Celiwe, Dumisani, Johnson and Gilbert were all found guilty of murder and robbery. Celiwe, said the judge, had 'acted like someone who planted a bomb and watched as it exploded'.[15]

She was sentenced to life behind bars.

CHAPTER 8

CHANÉ VAN HEERDEN

✝✝

Welkom, 1997

The rifle felt cold and heavy in her hand. He'd warned her that the first time would feel strange, but that's the thing about strangeness, her mother had said as they packed the bakkie that morning: you can know it's coming but it still pounces on you. Only the smell of the gunmetal was somehow familiar, reminding her of the handrail of the staircase at the mall. Grown-ups' fingers always looked like vultures' claws there, curled around it. She recognised the smell, but wasn't sure she liked it. Iron and blood smell the same, she thought, and just hoped she could stay on her feet as a dizziness came over her.

But as soon as she saw her finger on the trigger, and spotted the neat row of small buck springing past some hundred metres ahead of her, she felt a rush of excitement that rooted her to the spot, her legs suddenly feeling like sturdy poles that could withstand even the worst hurricane.

'Just wait,' said a voice in her ear. 'Just be patient. And calm.'

'But they're right there. I can shoot them now,' she whispered back to her stepfather.

'No,' he said. 'It's your first time, Chané. You must get a feel for it, not shoot the first group that comes past you.'

His hands were on her shoulders and every now and then she caught a whiff of his breath: yesterday's beer and Peter Stuyvesant cigarettes.

'Chané. Just. Wait,' he said again, pressing her shoulders harder.

But, as one buck turned its head and looked at her, the finger on the trigger felt like something over which she had no control. It squeezed, and the shot ruptured the silence of the blue sky arching over them. She closed her eyes, expecting her stepfather's wrath, but instead she heard him give a single hard clap of his hands.

'You're a natural,' he said, flicking her on the back of the head.

The smell of the gunshot made her mouth water. She carefully placed the rifle down next to her, facing away, just as she'd been taught. An aircraft overhead drew a line across the sky like a flat white signature of approval. Its faint hum drew her eyes up and her head back until she was looking straight up at the sky.

'Come,' said her stepfather, drawing her back down to earth. 'Now comes the best part of all.'

She fell in behind him, echoing his every footstep as they walked to where the dead animal lay. The smell of fresh meat entered her nostrils as they got closer. Pleasure pumped through her body in time with her own heartbeat, until she was standing right over the motionless buck.

Her stepfather went off to find a suitable branch from which they could suspend the animal. Chané squatted down right next to it. The buck looked young. She drew her hand over one thigh, brushing the fawn-coloured fur this way and that, now velvet, then rough, as the hairs prickled against the palm of her small hand. She moved her hand to the other thigh, which lay flush against the ground, like a neat sack of flour. She ran her fingers along the contours, half expecting the animal to respond like a dog, grateful for the affection. But it was the stillness of death that pleased her far more. She saw the sticky film of blood that had formed over the softness of its belly, crimson over silver-white, and she stretched out until she was lying flat on her stomach, her face right up to that of the creature. Its nose against hers felt like a soft leather purse that had lain on the grass at twilight, quickly turning from warmth to cold wetness against her skin. She closed her eyes for a second, and recited her favourite verse from the Bible. 'All flesh is not the same flesh: but there is one kind of flesh of men, another flesh of beasts, another of fishes, and another of birds.'[1]

She opened her eyes as wide as they could go, and set them directly opposite the eyes of the dead buck. She stared into the glassy orbs, as if the life in her own eyes might jump-start the dead animal. The pupils were black as ink, still wide with fear from the seconds before death as it sensed the man and child among the thorny bushes.

There she lay for some ten minutes, so mesmerised by the up-close spectacle of death that she almost licked the creature's eyelashes, which seemed like some sort of ancient paint brush.

When she finally heard the approaching crunch of her stepfather's boots, she drew herself back up into a squat, and quickly pushed her finger into the single bullet wound just above the animal's belly to see how far it would go.

Back at the house, in the kitchen, her mother gave her a cold hug before disappearing into her bedroom, as she always did when her stepfather came back from hunting.

She heard him laugh behind her. 'Ag shame, your mother doesn't like the dead animals in the house,' he said.

Chané hoped her mother would ask how it had gone, but she also knew she could only tell her half the story. There wasn't, after all, another soul in the world with whom she would want to share her experience of lying there on the ground with the just-dead creature in front of her, the smell of its fear still hanging above its body. She followed her stepfather to the scullery, where he carefully laid the animal down on a stainless-steel table.

'Ja,' he said, looking pleased, 'your mother has scrubbed this table clean for us.'

He held a pair of gloves against Chané's hands. 'They might be a bit big for you,' he said, holding them up against her fingers like a dressmaker holding a sample against the figure of a bride-to-be.

'It's okay,' she said, 'I don't need them.'

'What? You're going to help me skin it with bare hands?' he asked, passing her a plastic apron.

'Ja,' she said. 'Is it all right?'

He shook his head.

'Germs,' he said, and she knew to obey immediately.

✠

She stands rooted to the ground once more. He turns the dead animal onto its back, its four stiff legs pointing to the ceiling. He holds the ones closest to him in one hand, and tells Chané to take the others. The limbs feel much colder now, as if the veins have frozen into rivets of ice. He checks the blade of his knife (the third time now, Chané has noticed) and begins slicing carefully through the animal's genitals, loosening the penis from the tufts of soft white fur around it. He places it in a stainless-steel bowl.

Next, the glands. 'These,' he says, with hands cupped over them as if he both designed and manufactured them, 'are the glands that make all the right smells to get himself a female.'

As her stepfather starts cutting through the glands, the room is filled with the smell of fresh, wet mud just scooped up from beneath brown-green water.

'Musk,' says her stepfather. 'That's the scent of musk.'

Several minutes pass. She's mesmerised by the work of the blade as it pushes between the fawn-coloured fur like tufts of grass being pulled apart by the world's most careful gardener. Her stepfather barely blinks, and with her small hands she helps him loosen each part of the animal's extremities, the blood oozing between her fingers. The muscles are cold and smooth, and she feels nothing but pleasure pulsating through her body.

But the best is yet to come. For this, her stepfather asks her to move her hands away from the main action so she doesn't get injured. Transfixed, she watches as the blade slices the skin away from the bed of flesh, carefully loosening it from the biological fibres that hold it together. It's the most beautiful material she's ever seen – coarse with fur on the top, translucent underneath, white, with the slightest hint of purple.

She looks into the animal's eyes once more, and no longer does she see its face as a whole. Instead, she imagines that the two marble eyes are protruding from behind a mask that has been carefully placed in the perfect position, just waiting to be skinned away.

†††

As a child, Chané inhabited a lonely world in which she felt unloved by her mother. It seemed that her two older siblings – a brother and a sister – were planned, and cherished accordingly, whereas she was nothing but a mistake that her mother refused to accept. Her mother would allegedly 'tear up pictures of her unplanned baby and cry herself to sleep'.[2]

She had an imaginary friend who was a demon, and at night, because of her fear of the dark, Chané would blindfold her dolls and bind them with shoelaces because her mother told her that they came alive at night.

When her parents finally split up after years of a dysfunctional marriage, her mother became involved in a series of abusive relationships. Chané began self-mutilating, cutting lines into the flesh of her arms. She moved back and forth between her mother's and father's houses, and became sexually active 'at a very young age'.[3] She also began experimenting with drugs, and by age 12 was sniffing benzene and taking ecstasy. She socialised with teens who were much older than her.[4] When she was 15, her mother emigrated to New Zealand with her partner. Chané went to live with her father but never found her way back to a stable life and soon dropped out of school.

Not far from where Chané grew up, in a featureless suburb of Welkom, in the Free State, another soul who would soon cross her path was battling his own demons. It was clear from early on that there was something different about Maartens van der Merwe. He had a photographic memory, was a top achiever in his class, and was always ahead of his peers in mathematics and chess. But always his academic achievements and his social aptitude were poles apart. At age ten he was still wetting his bed, and found it hard to hang out in groups with other children.

As early as the foundation phase at school, he began to hallucinate and had difficulty discerning what was real from what wasn't. His family dogs used to maul stray cats in the yard and he would have to clean up the mess. He once came across a live cat that had slunk into the yard while he was cleaning up, and he picked it up and broke its neck. He became a miserable and reclusive child who would seek solace in endless computer games.

At age 14, Maartens was diagnosed with schizophrenia. Delusional, and often thrown off course by the hallucinations, he also showed clear signs of disorganised thinking and speech, as if all logic had been drained from his body. He was put on a maximum dose of medication, which eased the symptoms at times, except for one: sudden bouts of aggression. These were attributed by doctors to a form of epilepsy that complicated his psychiatric disorder.

In and out of hospital, Maartens's life was characterised by psychotic episodes, emotional withdrawal and mental instability. He was a perfect magnet for someone like Chané, who had kept the darkness of her soul mainly hidden from society.

When the two met in 2010, Maartens, then aged 24, had been staying with a friend who was nursing a broken heart after a bad breakup. It was a characteristic of his personality to attach himself to another person, especially someone who needed his support, so that he was taken out of his own loneliness.

Chané, then aged 20 and working as a graphic designer, had also been a lonely child who'd never fitted in. By age 16, she had dropped out of school, and as she got older her twisted fantasy world became more apparent in both her art and her writing. Her artwork portrayed faces with their mouths stitched closed, while one of her poems read, 'I will tear off their faces to see the truth.'[5]

She had also been obsessed with the act of skinning for as long as she could remember. As a young teenager, she wrote in an essay, 'When I woke up this morning, I realised I had nothing to wear. So I thought for a while, and came up with an idea that would change the world forever. I remembered I had some old material in the back of my cupboard. I think it's called skin. Since I had some time to spare, I stitched some skin together forming a suit. It was quite a tight fit so I had to stitch it to my flesh, otherwise it would slip off and that could get quite messy.'[6]

Welkom, where both Chané and Maartens grew up, is the second-largest city in the Free State. An entirely planned community established to serve the once-flourishing gold and uranium mining industries, Welkom retains the air of a sleepy mining town, a quilt of flat suburbia long past its heyday. It has always had an eerie, non-organic feel about it, and its traffic circles, parks and grid of suburban streets look the same all over the city, which, ultimately, is without much character at all.

It was against this backdrop that the pair threw themselves into a passionate relationship or, as some might call it, a 'disastrous partnership'[7] that would 'create the platform' for the despicable behaviour that was to follow. Soon after they met, they moved into an apartment in the working-class suburb of St Helena.

While another couple might come together through a common

interest such as history or hiking, Chané and her lover were said to have studied occult literature together. Not the types to watch *Sex and the City*, they were instead drawn to *Dexter*, a television series that makes a hero of a serial killer, and took delight in how the main character kept up the appearance of normality, working as a forensic technician while living a double life as a killer. Chané and Maartens mirrored this: they put in regular appearances at Bible study groups, while behind closed doors they ritualistically killed and sometimes crucified innocent animals, especially cats. At some point, the couple declared their love for one another by dipping a set of rings into a small bucket of their own blood.

None of this behaviour was apparent to the outside world. Chané had remained close to her father after her parents split up, and when the time came she introduced him to her new beau. Her father promptly invited them on a boating trip on the Vaal Dam, and witnessed Maartens's joy when he 'caught his first fish ever'[8] – an experience that made him as excited as 'a little boy'. Once they were on the shore, Chané and Maartens posed with the freshly caught fish. She held it between her hands like a child with a trophy, and he stood by soaking up the new experience.

Chané's family liked Maartens, whom they described as a 'nice chap': well-mannered, intelligent and a 'total gentleman'.[9] He certainly looked nothing other than ordinary, and had arrived for the fishing trip in a pair of faded blue denims and a navy T-shirt. Chané for her part wore a striped spaghetti-strap top, a pair of black pleated shorts, and her hair in a ponytail.

But despite this outward show of normality, Chané decided they should 'move on'[10] from killing cats, and put in a call to an animal welfare organisation. But, as the woman took down her details over the phone, Chané could not bring herself to offer a desperate dog a 'loving' home when she had every intention of killing, skinning and dismembering it.

'We then decided to look for a human victim,'[11] she said.

She and Maartens conducted meticulous research on what they would do to that victim and spent countless hours exploring 'everything to do with the dark side of humanity'.[12] The ritualistic killings of animals, it would soon become apparent, had simply been 'trial runs' for what they planned to do with their human victim.

With cold deliberation, Chané created a profile for herself on an online dating site – a honeytrap through which she could lure an unsuspecting victim into her lair.

Michael van Eck was from a very close family. He lived with his parents, Henriette and Naas, and was the golden boy in a family of four sisters whom he adored. He had three older sisters, Natasha, Bianka and Michelle, and then there was Hendriena, the youngest sister, with whom he shared a close bond. The family would go out fishing together, or invite friends over to braai in the garden at their family home. At 24, he had a stable job as a mining engineer. A handsome, dark-haired young man with a winning smile, he had a naturally warm personality. As his older sisters left home one by one, he became his mother's 'right-hand man and greatest confidant'.[13]

In early April 2010, Michael told both his mother and his boss at work that he'd met someone on the internet. His mother felt relieved as he had been rather blue since a recent romantic breakup. He said he would be taking his date to a movie that evening. During the day, he travelled with his mother from Welkom to Virginia, 25 km away, to the house of one of his sisters, where they borrowed a trailer and hitched it to the car.

Later that evening, he ate dinner at home with his parents. Then, excited at the prospect of what the night might hold in store, he showered and put on his jeans and a grey-blue T-shirt. This was in preparation for meeting the petite, dark-haired 20-year-old that he had met online.

There was, however, one aspect of the date that Michael felt was somewhat strange: they were to meet at the cemetery, of all places. His boss had warned him to consider cancelling the date because of this strange request, but he did not take heed. Apart from simply being an odd setting for a date, the cemetery was also very isolated – situated near the mine dumps and surrounding farmlands, several kilometres away from any venue that a fun evening out might include. His mother noticed, as he drove off, that he headed left and not right towards St Helena, where he said the young woman lived.

Michael gives himself one last look in the rearview mirror of his parked car, gets out, and walks towards the entrance to the graveyard. He cannot tell where his excitement ends and his first-date nerves begin. Texting and photographs are in the mix of internet dating, but there's still nothing like that first moment of chemistry – or lack thereof – to bring out the human instinct of anticipation. What would she be like in person? Would they connect easily? Would the conversation flow?

Chané waits for him in the shadows. He walks towards her, a hopeful bounce in his step – but soon a freezing cold fear grips his entire body. She has someone with her, and by the light of the moon he sees a weapon in the other person's hand. It is a hunting knife, and before he can escape he feels it plunging into his flesh.

He tries to run away, but the two pull him down. The young woman takes a butcher's knife and joins the stabbing frenzy. As he struggles, the two knives cut into him 33 times in a matter of seconds until he can fight back no more.

Under the dark night sky, among the gravestones and with the hard gravel beneath him, he takes his last breath.

As Michael's body slowly turns cold, Chané and Maartens drag him almost two hundred metres away towards the trees that line a section of the graveyard. Eventually they stop. With Maartens at her side, Chané kneels over Michael's dead body. She begins slicing through his neck, making her way through a landscape of flesh, oozing blood, muscle and, eventually, bone. She severs his right arm and cuts through both his muscular legs at the knees.

Absurdly, using just kitchen cutlery, they dig a shallow grave and bury Michael's torso and denims in it. They leave his bloody T-shirt – now ragged from all the knife work – at the entrance to the cemetery, making no genuine attempt to hide the evidence of their deeds.

They carry Michael's head away as they leave the ink-black cemetery behind them, indifferent to the fact that, just a few minutes before, it had been attached to the body of a hopeful young man who had gelled his hair and brushed his teeth and chosen the 'right' outfit for a date. Back at the rented apartment where they lived, 'they descended on the body of their victim, Michael van Eck, like hyenas tearing a buck apart'.[14]

Michael's body parts became a hierarchy of sorts – some prized as trophies, others the detritus of a murderous frenzy. In the dark of night, they dug into the earth of the small yard next to their semi-detached apartment and lowered Michael's right foot and left arm into it. Also placed inside the haphazard grave were two dead cats.

The morning brought new horrors. Chané began stitching up the mouth of Michael's severed head, an act that she had practised in her dreams and her artwork for many years. She had considered doing it to her boyfriend, but she 'loved him too much'.[15] She had, however, practised her other arts on him. Their sex life had involved much cutting, sometimes going so deep on Maartens's body that it was way beyond the point of 'fun'.

She carefully cut off both of Michael's ears and placed them in a bottle of water. Then she went about removing his eyes from their sockets, perhaps symbolically snuffing the light from his being, and similarly put them in a bottle of water. She placed both bottles in the freezer.

Next, she engaged in the job of 'tearing off his face' so she could 'see the truth'.[16] She did this 'so precisely that one could easily have confused the skin with a real mask'.[17]

With Michael's body now broken down into the sum of its parts – divided between the cemetery, the fridge, the cupboard and the backyard – Chané concluded her work. She had thrown herself into the deepest pit of her desires, with the loyal Maartens a most worthy assistant.

But, after the brutal stabbing, the dismembering, the skinning, the dropping of the eyes into water, an emptiness came over her. This was all she had dreamed about, and yet she found she got no kick out of it.

It was a disappointment after all the 'positive accounts'[18] from serial killers she'd read about. They all described a rush of excitement.

She felt nothing.

Michael's parents were unaware that he had not come home that night. They had gone to bed, assuming that everything would be as usual: Michael would come home, park his silver Peugeot in the usual spot, quietly open the door to his flatlet, set his alarm for his Sunday shift at the mine, and fall asleep. He would likely rise before them and set off to work before they were even awake.

But, over at the taxi rank several kilometres from their house, the first clue to a crime had already turned up. In the early hours of the morning, a security guard had spotted an abandoned car on the side of the road. He had immediately called the police. With the sun just coming up, the police soon arrived at the rank.

On closer inspection of the vehicle, they found that the keys were still in the ignition – and thus began their search for its owner. It wasn't anything complicated. They merely had to run the number plate through the computer system, find the person in whose name the car was registered, and make a turn at the corresponding address.

This could easily be just a simple case of car theft, they thought, as they drove across Welkom to the more upmarket suburb where the Van Ecks lived. But, as soon as Naas and Henriette appeared in the driveway – at first half asleep and then suddenly shocked at the news that their son's car had been found abandoned – the police began to suspect this was something more sinister. Henriette immediately ran to the flatlet to check if her son was there. He would have been at work anyway by this time, but she thought perhaps she would find him asleep in his room. Instead, she was met with the sight of an untouched bed, the duvet still pulled neatly over the sheet and mattress, the pillows still carefully plumped up at the top. It was obvious he had not been home at all.

The last hope was that he was safely at work and that his car had been stolen without his knowledge. But they were told that Michael hadn't shown up for work. It was just assumed that he had had car trouble and was running late. Michael's parents were in a state of panic as they headed off to the taxi rank with the police. On their arrival at Michael's car, a man with a wooden leg was busy trying to steal it, and everyone assumed he was behind whatever grim events had led to this moment. But he was just an opportunist.

More clues turned up, joining one gruesome dot to the next. Michael's boss reported on his conversation with Michael about meeting his date at the cemetery, so Michael's mother and his older sister Natasha went rushing over to see if they could find him there. Perhaps he was badly injured but alive, they tried to comfort themselves.

By the time they arrived at the low cement pillars of the cemetery entrance,[19] the first gruesome evidence had already been spotted. A maintenance worker named Daniel Ranthimo, who was pushing a lawnmower, came across a 'large, fresh pool of blood'[20] in the sand. There were also blood smears along the paving, 'splashes of blood on the grass'[21] and what looked like a piece of material soaked in blood. Daniel had immediately reported this to his boss, Ephraim Morolong.

As Henriette and Natasha arrived on the scene, Henriette's eyes immediately fell on the blood-soaked material that had once been part of Michael's T-shirt. She lifted it up and began pleading and sobbing for her son.

Anxiety then turned to furious action as Henriette, accompanied by Ephraim, began to search the grounds, her heart skipping a beat every time she looked into the graves that had been dug in anticipation of that week's burials. Surrounded by some 10 000 graves, her anxiety reached fever pitch.

But still there was no sign of Michael. Not then – and not when the police arrived and began combing the area. Hours would pass before a warrant officer named Ernst de Reu arrived from another town with his sniffer dog, Xander. By then, the Van Ecks were desperate to know Michael's whereabouts.

It did not take Xander long. He found the spot near the trees and began digging. But nothing could prepare the police for the news they would have to break to the family: a torso had been found, but the head and other limbs were missing.

Across town, in the unassuming suburb of St Helena, a young couple who shared a deadly secret decided to get engaged. They invited Chané's father to a restaurant, and there Maartens, stuttering as he went, asked for Chané's hand in marriage.

Her father did not hesitate to give them his blessing. The two seemed perfectly in love, as if Chané's spirits had been lifted for the first time in years.

But, try as they might to conjure up a sense of normality, a world in which people go out for supper and plan for a wedding, it didn't take many clues to lead the police to the killers. Chané had switched her cellphone off for two days, but on the Tuesday she answered it. In a very simple sting operation, the police lured her and Maartens to the local hospital. From there, they were driven in separate vehicles to the apartment.

In the small courtyard garden and in the kitchen, Chané calmly walked the police through her exhibits of Michael's cruel death. Without a flicker of emotion, she showed them Michael's missing limbs in their shallow grave with the two dead cats, his eyeballs in a jar of water in the freezer, his sliced-off ears and, most disturbingly, the mask of his face with the mouth sewn shut, which she had carefully placed inside a plastic bag between two bags of frozen vegetables.

The following year, when the trial began at the Circuit Court in Virginia, Chané's appearance was disappointing to those who had bought into the occult narrative surrounding the murder. As ordinary-looking as could be, she appeared in court in a plain purple T-shirt and jeans. More telling, however, was the blank canvas of her face, held without effort in a neutral position as one gory detail of her acts followed another. Behind closed doors, too, when she shared the story with a social worker, she detailed the murder as if she had 'read it in a book'.[22]

Maartens looked directly at Michael's family, who had positioned themselves in the first row of the public gallery, and pleaded for forgiveness. Maartens's mother simply shook her head.

Chané, by contrast, showed no remorse at all during the trial. According to Brigadier Gerard Labuschagne, who wrote a report on behalf of the police service's Investigative Psychology Section, Chané would best be managed as a serial murderer. He said that psychologically motivated crimes, likely to be repeated, were characterised by trial runs such as the ones Chané and Maartens had carried out on animals, and by the 'bodily trophies'[23] that the pair had taken from Michael's corpse.

It was very possible, concurred Dap Louw, a forensic psychologist who testified for the state, that Chané would go out and kill again in the brutal manner that she had that night. 'I wouldn't want her as my neighbour and I am sure nobody else would want that either,'[24] he said.

Her father said, 'The daughter we know and love is not capable of these things.' He described her as 'beautiful, and full of love and laughter'.[25] He described how much his 'normal' daughter loved art and how well her job as a graphic designer was going. He proudly spoke of her commitment to Bible classes, about her passion for wildlife documentaries, about how she enjoyed discussing quantum physics and the solar system. 'She isn't a person who spoke about baking cookies and stuff like that,' he said. 'She does wear black, but not all the time, and it's not a religious statement, it's a fashion statement,'[26] he insisted.

Dap Louw said he'd never before encountered a person like Chané, where the gap between her public persona and her interior world of emotion and thought was so large.

Chané, called a 'monster' by the state advocate, was sentenced to 'indefinite imprisonment'[27] for a minimum of 20 years, after which her case would be reevaluated and in all likelihood 'reaffirmed',[28] since her chances of rehabilitation were so slim.

She did not move a single muscle in her face when she heard the judge's words.

Maartens, who was tried separately, got a life sentence. 'I thought

I would experience something that made me understand death,'²⁹ he told the judge, 'and I was hoping Chané would be happy with me if she had Van Eck to cut up.'

CHAPTER 9
PHOENIX RACING CLOUD THERON

†††

Knysna, 1998

The little girl sits down on the ground at the bottom of the two steps leading into the caravan. Tufts of grass have grown around the wheels, and the middle part of each step has worn away, the metal now smooth as a pebble. For the grown-ups, the stairs are a doddle. For little Phoenix Racing Cloud, they're a challenge: she must lean forward, place two small hands on the step above, then pull one leg up at a time.

She climbs up on all fours like this at least ten times a day, but sometimes, after carefully making her way up, she pushes the door open and finds nobody there. Today is one of those days. She steps inside. The wind is blowing through the caravan, sending her mother's colourful scarves billowing across the narrow passageway between the two beds, throwing lines of red, pink, orange, lime-green and yellow up in front of her eyes. Her mother's clown outfit is dangling from a hanger off the ceiling, the arms flowing out like a diva performing an aria. Phoenix takes fright at first, thinking that this apparition is a real person.

She toddles to the toilet cubicle where she finds the set of little wooden steps with the hearts painted all over it. She drags it across the floor and places it next to the bed. One step. One foot. Another step. Another foot. She grabs onto the fluffy blanket on the bed to pull herself up. It slips and her feet tap down on the step again. She grabs hold of it again, but this time her fingers are also pinching the material of the mattress. She holds on, her feet climbing up the side of the bed like a frantic mountaineer on a rescue mission.

Finally, on the bed below the window, she sits and waits, just as her mother told her to do if she was alone. She moves the rainbow curtain to the side. There are strings of pink beads hanging down the centre. She curls the fingers of both hands around them and makes a parting in the middle. She looks out the small window but can't see her mother. She sits staring for a few minutes, then flops over on her side, one small foot dangling off the bed. Her tummy grumbles with hunger but she doesn't want to climb down again. She sits for another minute, and then decides, yes, she will climb down to look in the fridge for some food. She eases herself off the bed onto the steps, and then onto the floor. She stands on tiptoes and tugs hard at the fridge handle. Inside, she finds a half-filled bowl of oats and sticks three fingers inside. It's much colder than she thought it would be.

She decides not to eat it, and slowly makes her way back onto the bed. She curls up on her side and falls asleep.

When she wakes, she rubs her eyes, then rubs her blanket between her fingers. 'Mommy?' she says, not sure if a reply will come.

'I'm here, darling, in the bathroom.'

She slides her bum to the edge of the bed and plops her feet down on the steps. Climbing down, she goes to the small bathroom of the caravan and looks up into the mirror. There, she sees her mother's reflection. Her mother's eyes meet hers in the mirror and she smiles back. The girl stands staring, mesmerised by the movements of her mother's hands as she applies the clown make-up. The white layer – the canvas. The black sweetheart lips. The dark eyebrows. The thick black liner just under the lashes.

Phoenix was born in 1994 in Noordhoek, a laid-back coastal suburb of Cape Town just below Chapman's Peak. Her mother, Rosemary, then only 20, was a hippie drifter living precariously from one festival to the next; her father, also a hippie, shunned the idea of a suburban life at a fixed address. The family of three lived in a small caravan, although they would sometimes leave even that behind and travel all over the country on a rickety wooden cart drawn by a horse, peddling hand-sewn puppets and camping temporarily in abandoned buildings and vehicles.

It seems that her parents enjoyed their freewheeling lifestyle together, going from one trance party to the next, while also attending 'rainbow gatherings'[1] where they and other hippies would camp out in remote forests 'running wild in the woods naked while searching for an entirely new view of the world'.[2]

At these events, Rosemary – or 'Rosie',[3] as she was affectionately called – made many social connections, and her warm personality instantly drew other people to her. It was, however, a subculture in which dagga and psychedelic drugs were commonly used, and this atmosphere did not make for attentive parenting. When Phoenix was three, her parents' relationship ended abruptly. She found herself living in a caravan once more, in a community on a farm near Knysna. The community followed a lifestyle free of structure or responsibility, and Phoenix often went hungry while her mother 'meditated'.[4]

Around 2000, Rosemary delivered her daughter into the arms of the child's father and set off to seek adventure in South America. During this period, her father may have offered her a more stable existence compared to what Rosemary had, but Phoenix became an object of sexual abuse to more than one of the adults around her. At first, it was one of her father's friends who started sexually assaulting her. Then, her grandmother's boyfriend violated her too.[5]

A year later, a pregnant Rosemary returned from South America and reclaimed Phoenix, then six years old, from her father. Having given birth to a baby boy named Taki, whose father was in South America, Rosemary moved with her two small children into a clapped-out bus in the Oude Molen Eco Village in Cape Town. This is a rustic piece of land near the city centre where abandoned buildings and horse paddocks share space with a few low-key businesses and not-for-profit organisations.

Rosemary fell pregnant for a third time, and by a third man, in 2005, when Phoenix was eleven and Taki four. When Rosemary returned from hospital with Phoenix's brand-new baby sister, Charial, she immediately handed the tiny bundle to the 11-year-old and went off for a long sleep. Thus began a pattern of the young Phoenix's having responsibilities far beyond her age as she fed, washed and saw to the general well-being of her two younger siblings, while Rosemary continued her bohemian lifestyle.

Phoenix's primary-school years were a mix of home-schooling, self-schooling and no schooling at all. Moving between her parents, neither of whom was particularly dedicated to her formal education, also meant that any system she embraced would soon be interrupted by another move.

A few years later, Rosemary married a man with whom a toxic relationship soon developed. As a young teen, and with two younger siblings, Phoenix would witness both physical and emotional abuse. Though her schooling was still patchy, to say the least, she was enrolled at Fish Hoek High School, but then went to live with her father again in Knysna, and at age 16 was placed in Grade 10 at Knysna High School.

Here, however, away from the responsibilities of caring for her younger siblings, Phoenix went into full-scale teenage rebellion – drinking, taking drugs and having unprotected sex. She was, perhaps not surprisingly given her dysfunctional background, drawn to a broken young man who could relate to her past. Kyle Maspero was from a broken home, had lost his mother when he was five, and had lived temporarily with members of his extended family, as well as in two different foster homes. He became addicted to tik (crystal meth) and was expelled from school after being caught using drugs, but managed to find a place at another school. There, however, he committed theft on more than one occasion – probably to fund his drug habit – and again was kicked out. He did a stint in a rehabilitation facility and was accepted into yet another school on condition that he stayed clean. He didn't. Finally, he was expelled by a principal who called him 'troubled' and 'challenging'.[6]

He finally ended up in the care of a third foster parent, a writer in Knysna named Martin Hatchuel, who tried his best to provide a stable home. Kyle also enrolled in a photography course and was well-liked by those who taught him.

But in January 2013 Phoenix discovered she was pregnant. By that time, she and Kyle had been involved in an intense romance for several months in Knysna, and they decided, much to the sadness of Kyle's foster father, to relocate to Cape Town. They moved in with Rosemary and Charial, by then eight years of age, in a rented house in Clovelly, a suburb in the greater Fish Hoek area. Rosemary was making a precarious living as a clown and face-painter, and occasionally working on film sets. The previous year, 2012, Taki had been sent to South America to live with his father, whom he scarcely knew. Phoenix sought a termination of pregnancy in Cape Town, and after that she and Kyle stayed on in the Clovelly house.

It was an early-autumn morning in March 2013, two months since the teens had joined the household, when the southeaster finally stopped blowing for the season. Already a line of cars could be seen on the coastal road below Clovelly, where Rosemary Theron rented a white and windswept house. Beachgoers, hikers, cyclists and brunchers were all heading along the curved seaboard of False Bay, embracing the warm weather that would soon give way to a cold and rainy winter. But inside the Theron household, the day held no such wholesome promise, only the likelihood of more conflict. Fights had been flaring up constantly between Kyle and Rosemary, to the point that Rosemary, a few weeks earlier, had asked the couple to leave. For a short spell, they lived on the mountainside, but they felt unsafe there and were robbed of their belongings. They had returned to the house, asking Rosemary to put them up again – and here they were, with tensions rising once again on a daily basis.

Kyle reached his arm out from under the duvet, feeling around on the cluttered pedestal next to the bed for his version of a security blanket: some rolling papers and a small bag of dagga. Propping himself up against the headboard, he pulled a paper from the small orange box and began to line it with dagga. Catching a whiff of fresh weed, Phoenix also sat up, her eyes bleary and her throat aching for a cup of coffee. It didn't take Kyle long to roll the joint – he'd had plenty of practice – and they lay in bed, taking turns smoking it. The smell instantly took Phoenix back to her childhood: musty sheets and marijuana.

Sometime later, Kyle climbed out of bed and walked to the bathroom, closing the door behind him. Within seconds, another familiar smell crept into the bedroom: tik. Phoenix knew that Rosemary, also lying in her bed not far away but likely still fast asleep, would comment on how she hated crystal meth being smoked in the house. Not that Phoenix cared too much about her mother's reaction; she was in no position to comment on the perils of drugs, even though Rosemary kept insisting that crystal meth was in a league of its own when it came to destruction.

Phoenix lay with her eyes closed but heard Kyle go to the kitchen, and she padded down the passage after him. Plopping down in a chair and resting her elbows on the wooden table, she called her little sister, Charial. Preparing food for an eight-year-old wasn't easy, but her sister was only too pleased when a square meal was presented to her, and unlike many other kids, wasn't too fussy about what went onto her plate. Nor was she too fussed about the chaos around her. She had never been taught by her mother to stay clean or wear laundered clothes, and she knew nothing else but to take each moment as it came. This was her life. This was her world. With the dagga wearing off for both of them, but the tik kicking in strongly for Kyle, they sat eating their food as if the day ahead was blank. And, in fact, it was. With nothing planned and their hunger satisfied, Phoenix and Kyle returned to the bedroom where they immediately enfolded themselves in the sheets and blankets. Again, they smoked a joint, and Kyle smoked more tik. This made him over-focused, and he went back to the kitchen, where he manically scrubbed and sorted and swept. Phoenix also went about cleaning. In her bedroom with Charial, Phoenix made some order out of the chaos.

A couple of hours later, Rosemary finally emerged from her bedroom and came into the kitchen.

'There is just way too much noise in here,' she complained.

Kyle turned, thumped his hands on the table, and fixed his eyes on her.

'Oh really?' he snapped. 'So says who? The person who is sleeping the day away while I try clean this fucked-up kitchen?'

'It is my kitchen, and anyway, it will only get dirty again when we eat our next meal, so don't bother!' she said loudly.

He let out a low growl.

The heated exchange served to remind Rosemary how little she wanted this tik-addicted young man in her house or in her daughter's bed. The argument continued, and as their voices rose, Charial was drawn out of the make-believe game she was playing in her bedroom and into the kitchen. Seeing the adults fighting, she covered her ears, and tears began to stream down her face.

Kyle picked up the little girl and took her to Phoenix. The elder girl hugged her sister, thinking about how to broach the subject of Charial's education with their mother. Had her life been more conventional, Charial would have been in Grade 3. Instead, she was being home-schooled by Rosemary.

Phoenix went to Rosemary's room and tried to discuss it with her. But Rosemary barely looked up from her computer as she checked to see if any new gigs had been booked. She burst out laughing and said, 'She'll just run away from school like she did last year.'[7]

This infuriated Phoenix, who remembered how her mother had turned her against her own teachers, telling her that they were evil and that the other children at school were strange.

Rolling another joint, Kyle and Phoenix sat in their bedroom and discussed what a terrible mother Rosemary was. Kyle, whose own difficult childhood had fuelled his disapproval and dislike of Rosemary, said, 'It would actually be better if your mother wasn't around at all.'[8]

After thinking about it for a few moments in a fog of dagga smoke, Phoenix said, 'Yes, I agree.'

Back in the kitchen, Rosemary felt upset by the words that had been thrown at her. It really got to her how Phoenix and Kyle would shout her down as if she were a child in her own home. She found their presence in the house a constant intrusion. She also knew how tik addicts could behave – Charial's father was cut from the same cloth – so she knew there was no reasoning with Kyle when he'd been smoking. And, as for Phoenix, what had happened to the free-spirited little girl she'd raised, the one who'd travelled all over the country with her as a baby, happily fitting into life on the road? The young woman who'd moved back into her house was sulky, obstinate and, quite frankly, unwelcome.

All things considered, though, Phoenix was her flesh and blood and she loved her no matter what. But, with Kyle around, she felt like she was being pushed up against the walls of her own home. She knew her rhythms were not exactly conventional, but why should they be? What person earning their living as a clown and stilt-walker would want to keep the regular hours of a conventional life and be told what time to wake up in the morning? Why should she feel bad if she slept in after working until late the night before?

She had felt particularly annoyed at how Kyle had been clanging the pots and dishes around in the kitchen while she was trying to sleep. But, more than that, it was the way he reacted to her request that he tone it down. It was her house, after all. Sure, it wasn't a mansion, but the two should really have been grateful to have a roof over their heads. She also knew that cleaning a kitchen wasn't exactly deviant behaviour, but she sensed an anger in his movements, and it unnerved her.

Just a few days shy of her 40th birthday, Rosemary didn't feel she needed to explain to anyone why she had no interest in the kitchen being spotless. Or why she slept so late in the mornings. Or why she didn't want her eight-year-old daughter to have to handle the rigidity of a formal school curriculum.

She looked out the window, and let out a sigh of exhaustion. Thank goodness for her work. It took her out of herself and paid the bills. Wearing the face of a clown provided the perfect façade behind which to hide. Her stilts, too, lifted her above the crowd and into the realm of fancy. Out there, at parties and gatherings and festivals, she felt comfortable being in painted skin. It was at these events that she found her kindred spirits: fire-breathers, jugglers, hippies and hangers-on.

Knowing that her lift would be arriving soon, she applied herself to the task of putting on her make-up. First, the white layer – the canvas. Then the black sweetheart lips. The dark eyebrows. The thick black liner just under the lashes.

That day's gig was several kilometres away in Claremont, in Cape Town's southern suburbs, where a street carnival was being held. Her performance involved the use of an angle-grinder, which pushed her adrenaline up when the machine sent sparks flying into the air close to her skin as she danced about in front of the crowd. After a long and busy day of street bands and the smell of boerewors, she was keen to get home. She got a lift from a colleague's boyfriend who dropped her right outside the house.

<hr />

Rosemary, exhausted from work and ready to flop down on the couch, opens the front gate and steps into the small garden. She can see the door of the house standing open. It's just after 7 pm, and the sun has fanned out its last rays across the sky, which has turned the rich blue of early night. The stars are coming out, and it's time to put the kettle on.

She sees Phoenix emerging from the house. Is she coming back for another screaming match? Rosemary hopes not; she doesn't have the energy to take on these angry youngsters who want to tell her how to run her life. She braces herself for more harsh words, but is pleasantly surprised. Phoenix walks towards her with the sweetest smile on her face. She points out a star in the evening sky and gently puts her arms around her mother in an affectionate hug.

'I'm so sorry about this morning,' Phoenix says quietly.

Relief floods through Rosemary's whole being. Her daughter has finally understood that she and her boyfriend are being too aggressive.

Kyle approaches from behind, holding a rope he has taken out of a pot plant, but quickly loses his nerve. Phoenix, picking up on his hesitancy, shoots him a cold glance. Rosemary is about to respond to the kind gesture of an apology when something suddenly chokes off her words. She can't breathe.

Kyle has stepped forward and followed the script of murder they'd written between them during the day between bouts of smoking dagga and, in his case, tik. Phoenix's suggestion was to kill her mother by hitting her over the head with a spade. Kyle said it would be more humane to strangle her – and now it's all happening.

The rope is firmly around Rosemary's neck. Shocked and terrified, she begins to struggle, but her daughter's hug turns from affectionate embrace to the vice-like grip of a killer.

The two teenagers 'walk'[9] Rosemary through the open door into the house and into her bedroom. With the rope held tightly around her neck, she keeps struggling, kicking her legs, and trying to wrench her slender frame free of the hands of her killers.

Phoenix keeps her arms tightly around her mother as the two of them fall onto the bed. She instructs her boyfriend, 'Don't look at her face. Just count off four minutes before you let go of the rope.'[10]

He obeys.

Minutes later, Rosemary emits a 'huge sigh'.[11] Kyle recoils from her but Phoenix reassures him it is simply the last of the 'trapped air' in her lungs leaving her body. She lies completely still.

The teenagers lock eyes, as if even they are taken aback by what they have just done.

The sky outside shifts from deep blue to black.

Phoenix and Kyle crept into Charial's room straight after the murder to check on the sleeping child, and then returned to the issue at hand – the dead body. Each taking a side, they carried Rosemary's body through the house, navigating the narrow passages with hardly a word passing between them. Phoenix wanted to bury Rosemary before her body was even cold, but Kyle refused.

Once the body was outside in the back garden, they placed it in some black rubbish bags and covered it with a large tarpaulin dragged from a storage cupboard.

Phoenix went back inside to clean the blood off Rosemary's bed. She had bled from the ear onto the duvet during the strangulation, and her daughter wanted to remove the traces. Kyle, meantime, went to have another hit of crystal meth.

After this, they got into the bed where, just that morning, they had hatched the plan for the murder. They had Charial in the bed with them too that night. Phoenix fell asleep next to her, but Kyle was too wired and went off to smoke some more dagga and crystal meth, which he continued to do throughout the 'entire night'.[12]

When Phoenix woke up the next morning, they had two tasks: to convince the eight-year-old that all was well, and to dispose of the body of the eight-year-old's mother. But Kyle could not go through with it, and blamed his reluctance on the wild and windy weather. The day after that, however, was warm and mild, and proved more fruitful. Rosemary's body could be wrapped in a pink blanket and moved to what both Phoenix and Kyle thought would be her final resting place. Kyle left the Clovelly house carrying a spade and, not far away, began digging a grave. Before he managed to get very deep, he and Phoenix took the body to the designated spot. Once Rosemary's body had been lowered in, Kyle began covering it up with soil.

┿┿

With her mother's body decomposing in the ground, Phoenix was free to play the role of the anxious daughter, suddenly thrown into a world of fear after her mother had failed to return home. A few days after the murder, she walked into the Fish Hoek police station and told the officer behind the desk, 'My mother has gone missing.' She told him that her mother had left home at around 9 pm, getting into the white Mercedes-Benz of a strange man. She'd been wearing jeans, a waistcoat, a black top and brown boots. The news spread quickly, both by word of mouth and the 'missing person' poster that began circulating on social media. It bore three images of Rosemary, with her mane of brown hair, deep brown eyes and beautiful chiselled features – the perfect canvas for her face-painting.

As the days turned into weeks, Rosemary failed to turn up at a few gigs she had been booked for, which was highly unusual for her. Despite this, many people still held out hope: Rosemary's life had often been nomadic. She had also often dumped her three children with other people for days on end, and so, some argued, this could simply be her latest trick of reneging on her responsibilities in pursuit of fun. They also said that come 11 March – Charial's ninth birthday and Rosemary's 40th– she would reappear or at least phone home. But the day came and went, and still there was no sign of Rosemary.

Phoenix, in the meantime, was cashing in on the situation. The public felt sorry for the children abandoned by their feckless mother and wanted to help, particularly after a call went out on social media for money to help them pay rent at the end of the month. Kyle was teaching surfing in Muizenberg, apparently, but the money he earned barely covered the basics. The people of Fish Hoek responded generously, collecting money and groceries for the bereft family.

Rosemary's disappearance mystified the community and the police more and more with each passing day. Meetings were held regularly at the Fish Hoek police station to share information on whether any clues had turned up that could shed light on the case. Rosemary's mother, Denise, and her sister, Angelique, gutted by what had happened, refused to give up. They stayed in constant contact with the authorities, and their exhausted faces were a feature of the meetings at the station.

But, as investigators looked for the cold facts of the case, rumours and theories developed a life of their own. Some said Rosemary had been take into the 'sex trade';[13] others said a vengeful ex-boyfriend had nabbed her outside her house; while some thought maybe she had just done a runner, defeated by the responsibilities of adulthood, parenthood and earning a living. Her sister was 'adamant'[14] that this was not the case, and the search continued.

The police continued trying to unlock the truth. More money poured in from the community, but slowly, as no clues came to the fore, the broader public began to lose interest. Through it all, one thing was for sure: nobody suspected Phoenix Racing Cloud of being her mother's murderer.

✝✝

By July 2013, when the days had grown short and the Cape Town winter rain had set in, hope had faded. So too had the cash donations, and Phoenix and Kyle, short of money and anxious, decided it was time to move on.

Relocating to Gordon's Bay, about sixty kilometres away on the far side of False Bay, Phoenix and Kyle began building a new life. They rented a flat for themselves and nine-year-old Charial on the property of an acquaintance, Godfrey Scheepers. Phoenix crowed on social media about their 'beautiful new home',[15] and noted that Charial was going to an 'epic' school where her teachers thought her 'the loveliest girl in the world'.

But Kyle's mind wasn't at ease, and, possibly in a tik-induced obsession, he began to worry that Rosemary's body might be discovered. Somehow, he persuaded Godfrey to help him move the corpse. The two young men travelled from Gordon's Bay to Clovelly, where they went about removing the decomposing body from its shallow grave, located barely a kilometre from the police station where she had been reported missing. They loaded the body into Godfrey's car, and, under cover of darkness, drove for about 15 km along Baden Powell Drive. This long road runs through the desolate landscape along the False Bay coastline before turning northeastwards. Along the route is the unremarkable Strandfontein Pavilion, a beachfront 'leisure' building built in the 1980s for people of colour who were forbidden from using the whites-only beaches on the Fish Hoek side of the bay. The gritty wind constantly blows through tufts of grass and mounds of sand that stretch as far as the eye can see. It is a place where a dead body could remain untouched for many years.

It was not far from the pavilion and its desolate surroundings that

Kyle and Godfrey reburied Rosemary's remains. The teens who had killed then felt confident: they had literally gotten away with murder.

But, after a while, Godfrey found he could not shake off his guilt. He began jotting down the various facts of the murder as told to him by Kyle, as well as detailing his own part in moving the remains. This didn't prove cathartic, however, and by September, two months after helping Kyle move the body, he was spending sleepless nights thinking about it. One morning, he simply got into his car and drove to the Fish Hoek police station, stood at the exact spot where Phoenix had once reported her mother missing, and said he had a confession to make. He spared no details, handed over his notebook in corroboration of his story, and told the police he would cooperate with any aspect of the investigation going forward.

The police vehicles made their way along Baden Powell Drive. They arrived at the place where a body was presumed buried. The southeaster sent eddies of sand up and around the open veld. The police demarcated the area pointed out by Godfrey with yellow incident tape – and the digging began.

It took some five weeks for DNA tests to reveal that the body unearthed at Strandfontein was indeed that of Rosemary Theron. With Godfrey's story now watertight, Phoenix Racing Cloud Theron and Kyle Maspero were arrested on a warm day in late September and charged with murder.

For many, the news that Rosemary's body had been found was a blessing. 'May we also find peace now that we know Rosie is happy and ultimately free,'[16] said one of her friends. But the shock of discovering that her daughter had been behind her murder tempered any feelings of relief.

※

When Phoenix and Kyle first appeared in the Simon's Town Magistrate's Court in early October, they were the picture of teen imperviousness. Phoenix 'rested her head'[17] on Kyle's shoulder as the two 'giggled softly' together, while next to them in the dock sat the sullen-faced Godfrey Scheepers, the young man who had helped move the body and who had then gone to the police.

The case was rescheduled, and at the next court appearance, just over a week later, reality had clearly begun to bite. Kyle, in his holed T-shirt, simply stared ahead throughout the proceedings. Phoenix, in a tracksuit top with her honey-brown hair hanging to her shoulders, was clearly overcome with emotion. The two had abandoned their bail applications, and as Phoenix was led from the dock back down to the holding cells, she wept uncontrollably. In the public gallery, Rosemary's friends and community members, who had come to see justice in action, kept their eyes glued to the trio in the dock and stood around outside the court afterwards to discuss what had unfolded.

In the meantime, a number of memorials were held for 'Rosie', who had many close friends in the various bohemian communities where she had lived at different times during her life. One such memorial service began on the grounds of the Oude Molen Eco Village, a day after Phoenix and Kyle stood in the dock charged with her murder. The site of the event was marked by a shrine draped in a red cloth to represent 'blood shed' and 'mother earth'.[18] In keeping with the life she had lived, incense was burned, and music was played by those from her colourful community who pitched their tents around the village and settled in for a weekend-long commemoration.

Another memorial was held on Solar Beach in Plettenberg Bay, where her friends created an altar in the sand by drawing and decorating a big mandala, and planting memorial flags all around it. They also sang songs of 'love and life',[19] and meditated together in commemoration of their lost friend.

The case was set to resume on 2 May 2014 after further investigation had taken place. But, for those who settled into their seats for what was meant to be a climactic trial, the stage was bare. As soon as court was in session, Phoenix's advocate announced that his client, then 19 years old, would be taking a plea bargain. It was a move that surprised Kyle's defence counsel. Phoenix pleaded guilty to murder and attempting to defeat the course of justice, and it was here, in her bid for mercy, that her advocate read out the details of her unconventional childhood of neglect. She also turned on Kyle, stating that he had masterminded the murder and that she would be happy to testify against him.

She was sentenced to 20 years in prison, with five years suspended on condition that she did not carry out any violent crimes. 'This is a very serious offence – the planned and premeditated murder of her mother,' the judge noted. 'The sentence agreed upon is, in my view, just. This case is where she killed someone near and dear to her, her mother, and it will haunt her for the rest of her life.'[20]

Godfrey had all charges against him withdrawn, while Kyle – who had controversially been released and placed under house arrest in the care of a member of his foster family in March – appeared in court in early June. With a cigarette hanging from his mouth and a beanie pulled over his mop of hair, he stood outside the High Court in Cape Town that day looking like an old man, with sagging skin around his eyes.

Once in the dock, he was expected to plead, but instead, in a surprise move, his advocate claimed that he was 'failing to recollect material aspects of the offence'[21] because of his heavy use of crystal meth over a long period of time before Rosemary's murder. The judge ruled that he would be sent to Valkenberg psychiatric hospital, in Cape Town, for an evaluation as soon as a bed became available. The case was duly postponed.

It was only in the following year, 2015, that a bed became available at Valkenberg. Kyle arrived with his small suitcase of clothing, and thus began his 30-day evaluation, which would play a crucial role in how the criminal justice system would deal with him. When the report was finally compiled, it stated clearly that Kyle was fit to stand trial and to be questioned on the details of the murder.

When he appeared in the dock in October that year, it was exactly two years since his first court appearance with his then girlfriend Phoenix. He followed in her footsteps and opted for a plea bargain, not only admitting to his part in the murder but also detailing exactly how it had unfolded, as well as the copious amount of crystal meth he had smoked that day. In his statement, he concluded with these words: 'I have no excuse for my conduct and acknowledge same to be culpable.'[22]

Kyle's plea bargain earned him an effective 13 years behind bars. 'Were it not for your age, you would be the perfect candidate for life imprisonment,'[23] the judge told the 20-year-old. Kyle, with dark circles under his eyes, sobbed in the dock, wiped his nose on his sleeve, and asked for a glass of water. 'I would also be crying if I were going to prison,'[24] the judge said.

For some, justice had been served. For others, the sentences, particularly Kyle's, were not harsh enough. But for Rosemary's family none of this mattered. Her brutal murder was a traumatic event too difficult to overcome and one that could not be erased by any amount of punishment meted out to her killers. Rosemary's mother sank into a deep depression after the murder, and needed treatment at a psychiatric hospital, as she had not been able to cope with the loss of her daughter. Then, she lost her other daughter too: Rosemary's sister Angelique, who had been devastated since the day Rosemary went missing, hanged herself one Sunday morning. She was 35 years of age and the mother of three sons.

When Michelle Searle, a visitor to the prison, broke the news to Phoenix that her aunt Angelique had taken her own life, Phoenix wept. Searle had become the guardian of Phoenix's three young cousins, and perhaps nobody said it out loud in that moment, but the suicide was yet another chapter in this ghastly sequence of events that began with the decision to end Rosemary's life.

But, by then, enclosed in the prison walls and with every waking hour available to think about what she had done, weeping had become a way of life for Phoenix.

'Phoenix just cries. She cries every single day. She's very upset. She realises her actions, and realises it was the biggest mistake,' said Michelle.[25]

CHAPTER 10

INSIGHTS

✢

Why are so few killers female?
The statistics speak for themselves: 95 per cent of people who commit murder are male. That's at the global level and is 'consistent across countries and regions'[1] regardless of the type of murder or weapon used. This is what makes the stories of the murderers in this book all the more unusual: they come from the small five per cent of killers who are female.

But why is this? What is it about males that places them at a higher risk of killing someone?

Some have argued, rather simplistically, that male aggression is linked to the male hormone testosterone. There is no doubt that high levels of testosterone can increase levels of aggression, and it has been found, for example, that in prisons those who are the most violent also have higher levels of testosterone.

But it is much more complicated than that, and several other factors play an arguably bigger role than this biological reality. As journalist Christopher Mims puts it, 'testosterone is less a perpetrator and more an accomplice'.[2]

Giada del Fabbro, a well-known South African forensic psychologist, places great emphasis on the role of socialisation. First, females have more ways in which to 'deal with their emotions'.[3] Because it is more acceptable for girls to talk about their feelings, they are 'able to resolve their emotional difficulties more effectively'. They are, generally speaking, raised to 'have a greater familiarity and engagement with their emotions and can resolve and process these better on the whole as a result'. Males, on the other hand, might resort to physical violence in response to unresolved feelings.

But what happens when negative feelings persist? How might a female act? When they do struggle with difficult feelings, says Del Fabbro, 'females are more likely to direct their self-loathing towards themselves than towards others', and when that isn't the case, they usually express their aggression and anger differently from males.

Del Fabbro says that it is more 'socially acceptable for a boy to deal with conflict and anger through physical violence than for a girl to do so'. With girls, violence is more likely to become 'social and emotional through manipulating the social arrangements they are a part of'. They are more likely to ostracise others and humiliate them as a means to express their anger or aggression.

Another aspect, says Del Fabbro, is also that 'men are physically able to commit violence more easily than women in terms of their general greater physical strength'. In this way, 'masculine physiology also plays a role in the predominance of violent male killers in comparison to women'.

It is important to remember, however, that while the statistics illuminate the masculine in homicide, females are just as capable of committing murder. Our society's notion of women only as nurturers makes no allowances for the horrific acts that women can also carry out if the right confluence of factors comes into play.

Micki Pistorius, who was South Africa's first serial killer profiler, writes, 'Throughout history the opinion seems to have prevailed that women are not inclined to commit violent crimes.'[4] She says little research was conducted on the subject of female criminality before the nineteenth century, and that the current thinking that it is 'against a woman's nature to commit an act of violence'[5] is simply a 'remnant from the Victorian era'[6] when women were considered 'paragons of virtue'.[7] When women did deviate, says psychologist Adelene Africa, they were invariably considered 'mad'. In other words, violence by women was always 'pathologised', placing them 'at the mercy of their biology' rather than seeing them as active participants who had chosen to carry out their deeds.[8]

So, as we analyse the murderous acts of certain females in South Africa, Pistorius reminds us that 'it is time we recognise that some women are quite capable of committing violent crimes simply because they want to'.[9]

Do female murderers and male murderers kill for different reasons?'
Today, there is as much fascination with female killers as there was in the era of Daisy de Melker, but our understanding of the psychology behind such behaviour has grown. An interest in female killers over the past few years has produced some uncomfortable theories on how we've evolved across gender lines.

Marissa Harrison, an evolutionary psychologist at Pennsylvania State University, led one of the biggest studies on female killers to date; her research[10] focused on 64 American female serial killers between 1821 and 2008. The study concluded that 'men kill for sex, women kill for money'. Harrison argued that women, with their finite supply of eggs, have 'limited reproductive potential' and have thus 'evolved to place a premium on securing resources'; men, with their 'relatively unlimited sperm', are likely 'predisposed to seek a vast number of sexual opportunities'.

These findings relate directly to evolutionary psychology – how the human brain and psyche have developed over millennia as a way of adapting to the environment for survival of the species. This would include innate gender-specific roles in keeping the species alive.

Other studies have come to the same conclusion. An Australian study[11] that looked into 149 homicides in that country found that the vast majority were committed by men and were motivated by a variety of reasons. But the murders committed by women were classified as 'gain' homicides. From the murder, the killer would derive a resource or benefit, such as money, personal advantage or even a professional advantage.

Daisy de Melker: Ticking the 'female serial killer' boxes

In Harrison's study (described above), common traits begin to emerge among the profiles of the female serial killers. From this, we can see how Daisy de Melker fits the profile so perfectly. While there were variations, the killers explored by Harrison and her team typically had a caregiving role (nurse, stay-at-home mother, Sunday-school teacher, babysitter), and were well-educated, middle-class and white.

The female serial killers 'knew all or most of their victims, and most were related to them'. In all cases, 'they targeted at least one victim who was a child, elderly or infirm – those who had little chance of fighting back', and in most cases they killed primarily for money, despite always being from upper- or middle-class families. By contrast, male serial killers 'tend to stalk and kill strangers'. Harrison says from her study it seems that male serial killers are 'hunters' whereas the females are 'gatherers'.

Daisy de Melker, as a nurse, used her intimate knowledge of medication to wipe out her nearest and dearest, with a plan to get her hands on the purse strings. Harrison found that 'almost all (92 per cent) knew their victims, almost all were white, and their most common means to kill was poison, while the primary motive for murder was money'. Daisy is thus a textbook example of a female serial killer.

Harrison's study explored some notorious cases that resonate strongly with that of De Melker. There was, for example, Jane Toppan, a nurse at Cambridge Hospital in Massachusetts, who carefully administered deadly morphine cocktails and other poisonous substances to over thirty people. In 1901 she confessed to the murders. While most of her victims were patients in her care, they also included her best friend from childhood and her foster sister.

Another example was Dorothea Puente, dubbed the 'Death House Landlady', who ran a boarding house for the elderly and infirm in Sacramento, California, during the 1980s. She would cash her tenants' social security cheques and kill them off in cold blood if they complained about it. Police eventually discovered seven bodies buried in her backyard.

Del Fabbro says Daisy de Melker was 'most likely a psychopath who did not feel empathy and who was cold, hard and callous and exploited her position of power'. Some research suggests that these traits are inherited,[12] and also that they relate to the development of different areas of our brain. Studies have shown that in psychopaths, the prefrontal cortex and amygdala do not communicate properly with one another. The prefrontal cortex is near the front of the brain and is the 'part of the brain responsible for sentiments such as empathy and guilt',[13] while the amygdala is an almond-shaped group of neurons set deep inside the brain that 'mediates fear and anxiety'.[14] The two structures work together to regulate emotion and social behaviour, but in psychopaths seem 'not to be communicating as they should'.[15]

According to Del Fabbro, 'Psychopaths do not actually feel fear in the way that others do, which means they aren't inhibited from behaving in ways' that others know to be unacceptable. It also means that they 'seek out bigger thrills to get the kicks that would come from less dangerous activities in the average person', she says.

Marlene Lehnberg: An anomalous love-triangle murder

More than four decades later, what do we make of a teenage girl from an ultra-conservative family who murdered her lover's wife with a pair of scissors? In the simplest of terms, it was a classic love-triangle murder. But, within the statistics of that genre, Marlene Lehnberg was an outlier. It is normally the spouse who has been cheated on who does the killing, and when a woman is the killer, she normally kills her partner rather than her rival.

In a study[16] on love-triangle homicides by American sociologist Richard Felson, even the opening question of the research shows that the jilted partner is assumed to be the perpetrator: 'Who are people angry at when they come home unexpectedly and find their partner with someone else?' One example of such a homicide is the 2018 murder of Meredith Chapman, a candidate for the Delaware state senate, who was gunned down in her home by her lover's wife, Jennair Gerardot, who then also turned the gun on herself.

But, in the case of Marlene, we have the unusual scenario of the female lover killing the spouse of the unfaithful partner. Stereotypically, Marlene was the 'rival', the young and fertile interloper who, on a primal level, posed a major threat to the older Susanna, who was a homemaker and a mother. Statistically, Susanna (like Jennair Gerardot) might have been the one to act out of anger towards her husband's teen lover, but she was, on the contrary, compassionate towards her. Marlene's rage was unleashed when it was clear that the marriage between her lover and his wife would not end. Suddenly perceiving herself to be the rejected one, she sought to remove what she saw as the obstacle to her own happiness.

Pistorius describes Marlene's crime as a case of 'cold-blooded murder',[17] meaning that it was carefully planned and not done in the heat of the moment. Marlene met Susanna and 'found her amicable',[18] but still developed no empathy for her. Also, despite her apparent religious convictions, she could not actually 'view Susanna as a human being',[19] according to Pistorius.

The other glaring anomaly in Marlene's story is around the choice of victim. Felson found that a male perpetrator in a heterosexual love-triangle homicide normally kills his rival (the other male). When the perpetrator is female, however, she is far more likely to kill her male lover than her female rival. But Marlene's murderous thoughts were always and only directed towards Susanna and never Christiaan.

Where Marlene is less of an anomaly is simply in the portion of female-committed homicides that are motivated by a love triangle. Certainly, men commit far more murders as a result of love triangles than do women, but that's because men commit far more homicides in general. But, of the homicides that females commit, love triangles show up far more frequently as a proportion than they do for men.[20]

Finally, there is the issue of age. At 19, Marlene was not a child offender, but she was young enough for some to believe that her lack of maturity blinded her to the consequences of her actions. There was hope that, on her release, she would look back in shame at what she had done. But, even after 12 years in prison to contemplate what she had done, she took no responsibility, instead blaming both her lover and her accomplice for what had happened.

According to Pistorius, after more than a decade behind bars, Marlene at 33 still 'manifested the same narcissistic selfish attitude'[21] she had as a teen. Pistorius says she was 'more concerned about her looks and following the latest fashion than repenting for having taken the life of a mother of three and the damage she had caused to [Marthinus] Choegoe wife's and children.'[22]

Charmaine Phillips: The undefinable spree killer

Charmaine Phillips, like Daisy de Melker, was involved in the deaths of multiple victims. Her family background was horrendous, and she was also still in her teens when she committed murder. Furthermore, the dynamics between her and her older lover, Pieter Grundlingh, were the subject of much debate. Also, her own personality was the cause of much disagreement among experts. All these factors make hers a highly complicated case, one in which the psychology behind the murders is difficult to pin down.

The first thing to note is the 'high' that came with the murders, and in this regard it is useful to note the difference between a serial killer and someone who goes on a killing spree. Criminologist Scott Bonn[23] defines the terms 'serial murder' and 'spree killing' as follows: serial murder, on the one hand, 'involves at least three murders and crime scenes', each separated by a 'cooling-off period' that may be 'weeks, months and, in rare instances, even years'. Think Daisy de Melker. Spree killers, on the other hand, commit 'multiple homicides at two or more locations with almost no time break in between the events'. Bonn notes that 'spree killers do not come down from the high', and that the 'maximum duration between murders in spree killing' is generally seven days.

In the case of Charmaine and Pieter, four murders over 16 days meant they didn't 'resume their seemingly normal lives in between killings as serial killers do'[24] and were likely still on the high they'd got from the previous homicide when they went about committing the next.

From a statistical and criminological perspective, Charmaine is a rare breed: women rarely take part in killing sprees, and when they do alongside a male accomplice, the power dynamics are always highly complicated. Pistorius describes an abusive relationship in which the older Pieter held sway over the teen Charmaine. In that scenario, she would be an unwilling accomplice, a subservient sidekick to a psychopathic man who physically and emotionally abused her.[25]

But, in court, she portrayed herself as a street-smart murderer. She confessed to all the murders, describing how in each case the men had infuriated her and how she had wiped them out. Pieter, however, took responsibility for the murders himself in a letter written shortly before he was hanged, and so the truth remains unclear.

Likewise, it was unclear whether Charmaine could be classified as a psychopath or not. According to psychologist Shirley-Ann Maritz,[26] several of the expert witnesses were 'at loggerheads' with regard to this. But what was clear was that 'she had a drive towards immediate impulse gratification', was 'emotionally superficial', had no regrets about the murders, and very easily became aggressive.

Psychopath or not, main perpetrator or subservient accomplice, Charmaine made choices that mapped out her future. She remained with Pieter after the first gruesome scene unfolded, took an active part in the murders that followed, and at no point made a serious attempt to escape. The judge said she was the best example of 'inherent evil'[27] but did take her upbringing into account when he decided she shouldn't hang. Since Pieter was hanged and she wasn't, she had free rein to create whatever narrative about the past that she wanted.

The one thing that is clear is her wretched childhood. She grew up with a family background of mental illness, violence, drug abuse and alcoholism. While still a child herself, she became homeless, used drugs, and earned her keep as a sex worker.

That Charmaine was not able to break away from the patterns in her own family and her story, says Maritz, is a 'culmination' of both nature and nurture, as these together brought her to her 'destructive and disturbing actions'.[28]

Joey Haarhoff: More than just a sidekick

As is often the case with a murderous male-female pair, Joey was portrayed as the assistant or secondary force in the acts of criminality. She was consistently described in relation to Gert van Rooyen rather than in terms of her own identity, and most media outlets at the time described her as being 'used' by Van Rooyen to lure the victims into his car. She was always described as Gert's lover, never he as hers. She was thus always portrayed as a less powerful sidekick in the matter, with some even speculating that she was coerced by Van Rooyen into playing her role in the crimes.

It was only with the 2016 publication of a tell-all book, *Battered, Abused, Shamed: Joey Haarhoff Was My Mother*, by her daughter, Amor van der Westhuyzen, that Joey's violent personality was laid bare to the world. Joey was far from a passive victim who was manipulated by a twisted man to do his bidding. She had been an extremely violent mother herself, and clearly had sadistic tendencies.

Joni Johnston, an American forensic psychologist who has worked in maximum-security prisons doing insanity evaluations, describes some of the myths that float around characters such as Joey Haarhoff who are accomplices to male deviants such as Gert van Rooyen. She writes, 'When it's a serial-killing male-female duo, the woman tends to be portrayed as the gullible innocent who, but for the devious influence of a Machiavellian male, would have lived a law-abiding life.' Such scenarios can and do exist, Johnston notes, and there are 'female members of a deadly duo' who are coerced into a pathological relationship by an abusive spouse. But the female accomplice isn't always 'a reluctant sidekick to a violent, predatory male'.[29]

In Joey's case, given her violent behaviour in the past, and her choice of husband before Gert, and then also of Gert himself, she clearly had a deep attraction to men who used sexual violence as a currency of power. She had her full faculties when she turned a blind eye to her previous husband's sexually violating their daughter, and then played an active role in whatever depraved acts of violence Gert carried out.

According to Del Fabbro, there is a 'sexist bias' in implying that female accomplices have little agency over murders when working alongside a male. 'If we look at the United Kingdom with some of the research done around Fred and Rosemary West, or Ian Brady and Myra Hindley (the Moors Murderers) there are some very strong hypotheses and reports that the female members of these serial killing duos were more influential and sadistic in terms of directing the actions of their male counterparts,' she says. (Between 1967 and 1987, Fred and Rosemary West tortured and killed at least a dozen young women and girls – some of them their own children – at their home in Gloucester, and buried some of them in the garden or in cement under the patio. Ian Brady and Myra Hindley murdered five young children and buried them on the desolate moors outside Manchester in 1963–1965.)

The thinking is that 'their male partners almost served as a conduit for the violent and sadistic fantasies' that they always harboured but had felt unable to act out because of 'social norms and socialisation or just physical strength', says Del Fabbro.

Because they died before police could arrest them, we will never know what the dynamic was between Joey and Gert, but we certainly cannot assume she was less active in the crimes than he was.

Dina Rodrigues: The cold contract killing of a baby
Was Dina insane when she hired contract killers to murder a baby? In other words, was she so severely mentally ill that her perception of reality was distorted? The answer is a resounding no. According to Johnston,[30] 'A person who hires a contract killer may be desperate, greedy, psychopathic or drug-addicted, but is not insane.' This is borne out by the fact that she 'clearly understands that the idea behind the intended action is wrong'.

So what drives a contract killing? Anger, says Johnston. The typical examples of anger she cites occur in situations when someone is resentful about giving away half their assets to an estranged spouse, or when someone is tired of an interfering ex. Although Natasha Norton was far from an interfering ex, the existence of little baby Jordan was viewed by Dina as a major threat from a past relationship.

The rest of us might harbour feelings of anger at various points in our lives, even feelings of extreme anger, but we generally don't rush out and hire hitmen to carry out a murder. This, according to Johnston, is because someone like Dina has a sense of entitlement and 'lacks empathy underneath the façade'. She writes, 'This is a person who believes she deserves to get what she wants, no matter what the cost to others.'[31]

Del Fabbro believes that in the case of Dina, 'there is definitely an antisocial or borderline personality disorder' component to consider. She says, 'Antisocial personality disorder refers to a lack of compliance with social rules and regulations – basically a sense of being above the law and doing anything to get what one wants.' Borderline personality disorder, in a nutshell, refers to 'difficulties with rejection and feelings of abandonment'. Regarding Dina, Del Fabbro says, 'I think that this combination was a big part of the explanation underlying her actions.'

Another point to consider in the case of Dina was how she preyed on the socio-economic imbalance between herself and the hitmen. A study by researchers at Birmingham City University has identified four types of contract killers: the novice, the dilettante, the journeyman and the master. The men hired by Dina fit perfectly into one of these categories. Although they were all novices in the sense that they had not carried out a hit before, they were not doing it in the hope of building a future life out of contract killing. Certainly, none was a journeyman, who is 'capable, experienced and reliable'. Nor was any a master, who usually has a military background, leaves no trace, is highly skilled, and is unlikely to be caught. Dina's contract killers were clearly dilettantes; she knew this, and preyed on the situation. 'This type of hitman does not necessarily come from an offending background and only seems to have decided to accept a contract as a way of resolving some form of personal crisis,' the study says. 'More often than not, this crisis was financial.'[32]

Dina was, according to Del Fabbro, going to 'do anything to get what she wanted'. In a country of such dire inequality as South Africa, once she had made her plan it was not difficult to find a group of dilettantes to remove that which stood in her way. The fact that it was a baby was of no significance to her.

Najwa Petersen: Flipping the script on intimate-partner homicide
Why was Najwa Petersen so hell-bent on murdering her husband? She appeared to have everything her heart could desire: a beautiful home, shares in a highly successful business, a loving husband who also took care of her when she was sick, children who seemed happy and healthy, a newborn grandchild. What was she thinking?

The two most interesting elements of the story of Najwa Petersen lie in the question of mental illness, and in the reversed gender roles in a country where intimate-partner homicides are rife.

At the time of her trial, Najwa's mental health featured strongly in court proceedings. She was diagnosed with bipolar mood disorder, for which she had been receiving treatment for four years. Psychologist Adelene Africa[33] said Najwa was 'alternately constructed as avaricious and mentally disordered as the media (and public) tried to make sense of her role in the execution-style killing of her spouse'. Members of Taliep's family were also angry that Najwa hid behind her mental illness to evade questions that would incriminate her if answered truthfully.

She was eventually sent for 30 days of psychiatric observation, and the unanimous report from three psychiatrists and a psychologist stated that she was 'fit to stand trial and could be held criminally responsible for her actions'.[34] She was not, 'by reason of mental illness or defect', incapable of understanding court proceedings or mounting a defence. The experts also found that she was not mentally ill at the time of the offence, putting paid to any notion that she was insane and thus could not be held responsible.

Also of note is that Najwa's is an unusual story when it comes to intimate-partner homicides. Gerard Labuschagne,[35] the former head of the South African Police Service's Investigative Psychology Section, says that studies have shown that 77 per cent of intimate-partner murderers are male, and only 23 per cent are female. According to the South African Medical Research Council, a woman is murdered every four hours in South Africa, and half of those victims are killed by their partners. The rate at which South African men kill their intimate female partners is five times the global average.

Community psychologist Dr Malose Langa[36] notes that it is important to analyse how we 'critically interrogate' what is 'scripted' for black men from poorer communities, compared to white men from middle-class communities, in the minds of the public. If we apply the same idea to gender, asking ourselves what is 'scripted' for men compared to women when it comes to murder, we begin to understand our morbid fascination with someone such as Najwa Petersen. Najwa's story disrupts our stereotypical narratives of intimate-partner murders, which we immediately think of as being committed by men.

Najwa might have flipped the gender script, but she did not upturn the typical characteristics of a 'pre-planned intimate-partner murder' when compared to a 'spontaneous one'. Labuschagne says the former are staged – 'often in the form of a hijacking or house robbery', involve the use of a third party or 'hired hand', and tend to occur 'late in the evening', 'often at the deceased's house'. The only box Najwa didn't tick was that of 'removal of evidence' such as fingerprints and weapons.

Where Najwa also flipped the script was in her motive. Most female perpetrators of intimate-partner homicides have been abused by their partner before killing him, and 'during sentencing such evidence is often led for mitigating purposes', says Labuschagne. However, in the case of Najwa and Taliep, there was no suggestion whatsoever that he had abused her.

Celiwe Mbokazi: The killer who subverted her unequal status
Cold-blooded murder is deliberate and carefully planned, and is a rare phenomenon when it comes to black women. Why is this? In terms of race, says Del Fabbro, the 'traditional gender roles are more entrenched where there is a patriarchal cultural background that is still in strong operation'. As it is, socialisation means that the acceptable ways in which women express 'aggression and violence' are different from those of men, and she says that this is 'even more pronounced' in traditional cultural backgrounds such as that of Celiwe. Countries such as India and China, where patriarchy is still strong, see far fewer female killers 'in comparison to the United States where we see proportionally more

of this'. Against this backdrop, we can see how unusual Celiwe Mbokazi is as a murderer.

Another interesting aspect of this murder has to do with power relations. Celiwe was a black female teenager, from a village with few resources, when she became involved with Franz Richter during the apartheid era. He was a white European male who had far more wealth than her, was 45 years older, and was her employer. These facts make it tempting to see her as a victim of circumstance.

But, says University of Cape Town public law expert Kelly Phelps,[37] 'the same law applies to all accused persons, irrespective of race, class, gender or power'. These factors might form part of the consideration of whether the accused could or could not appreciate 'the wrongfulness of their conduct', as well as sentencing, which 'revolves around the concept of individual blameworthiness'. But, in general, the courts cannot make excuses for people because of the social and economic problems that plague South Africa. 'It is important to remember that the vast majority of offenders who appear before a court come from poor socio-economic and troubled backgrounds', but this simply underlines 'the need for far more time and resources to be spent on prevention of crime and social upliftment'. The courts are not responsible for this.

In terms of Celiwe, says Del Fabbro, we cannot discount a possible diagnosis of psychopathy, 'which is made more with men than women but occurs with women nonetheless'. She says that 'in the case of psychopaths, people are seen as a means to an end'. We could strip Celiwe of all power in the background to the story and see her as a powerless teen from a rural village with no sway over what life would bring her. But there is another, and somewhat opposite, way to look at it – a perspective that sees Celiwe as capitalising on circumstance and using Franz to get what she needed. 'Initially the older husband may have served her purposes of getting access to a better life,' says Del Fabbro, 'but after a while, she probably saw that she could gain even more by getting him out of the way.'

In this perspective, 'the callous unemotional traits of a psychopath would have made arranging a hit on her husband that much easier, so, in some ways, she was able to exploit and subvert the power inequalities in their relationship'.

Del Fabbro says that psychopaths are all about 'power and control over others', and that with women, sexuality can be a means of exerting that power. Celiwe might initially have been viewed as 'a victim in terms of age, socioeconomic status, class, race and gender', but ultimately, 'she exploited her position in an expedient way to gain the upper hand over him and get rid of him'.

Chané van Heerden: A shared psychosis
There are two standout features of the bizarre and cruel act carried out by Chané van Heerden. The first is her unusual obsession with skinning a human being. The other is the chemistry between her and her boyfriend, Maartens van der Merwe, and how this catalysed her descent into murder.

That their 'disastrous partnership created the platform for their behaviour'[38] is an established fact. According to experts, theirs was a case of 'shared psychotic disorder'. This is a rare mental illness in which one person takes on the delusions of another with a psychotic disorder such as schizophrenia. The one person is out of touch with reality and cannot function in daily life. The other, once emotional ties have developed, takes on these delusions too. In the case of Chané and Maartens, it was particularly complicated: he was the one with schizophrenia and bouts of delusional behaviour, but it was she who had the dark fantasies of skinning and stitching human faces, and mutilating bodies.

According to Professor Dap Louw,[39] head of the Centre for Psychology and the Law at the University of the Free State, who was a state witness at the trial, Chané could not unequivocally be classified as a psychopath but likely had several psychopathic tendencies. These might have remained in the abstract world of fantasy, but when the schizophrenic Maartens crossed her path, an opportunity to make them a reality unfolded. Louw described this as a moment when something just 'clicks', and two people in shared psychosis begin planning the practical expression of their fantasies. There is also little doubt that it was Chané who dominated the proceedings as they went from the morbid to the macabre.

Louw said, 'These two people made each other far sicker than they would have been on their own.' Maartens seemed to agree. 'We pushed each other to commit a murder. We would never have done it individually,' he said. A post on his Facebook page before the arrest also foreshadowed their strange connection: 'Sifting through the facts, I sometimes believe I see that life is two locked boxes, each containing the other's key.'

Looking more closely at Chané's long-standing obsession with skinning, this is a highly unusual fetish. When Louw testified during the trial, he said a crime in which the victim's face had been skinned was 'unheard of locally', and also rare internationally. 'The uniqueness of this case must be mentioned,' he said. Louw had contacted three international experts about the nature of the crime, and had also sifted through thousands of court records and research reports. He had concluded that although 'mutilation of the body is not rare', the way in which the victim's face was skinned 'was unique'.

The very few precedents that exist, however, point to an insatiable appetite for such practices, and an enormous risk of repeat offending. Particularly chilling is the case of the American murderer Ed Gein,[40] also known as the 'Butcher of Plainfield'. Driven by a similar fetish for human skin, his gruesome crimes far outnumbered those of Chané, and suggest that she might well have gone on to commit more such acts of horror herself.

When Gein became a suspect in the disappearance of a woman in 1957, his home was searched and his grisly collection of 'bodily trophies' revealed: a headless body hung upside down and prepared like a dead deer; many objects made from human skin, including a corset, leggings and masks; chairs upholstered in human skin; skulls on the bed posts; vulvas in a shoebox; a belt made from nipples; and a pair of lips on a window-blind drawstring. After his mother died, he began to create a 'woman suit' out of human skin that he could crawl into. This was similar to Chané's fantasy writing in which she described creating a skin outfit that she could wear like a garment.

Like Chané, Gein confessed and remained emotionally detached as he spoke of what he had done and as detectives looked on in horror at his bodily trophies. He too was found guilty of murder but, unlike Chané, he was declared insane and placed in a mental health facility (rather than prison) until his death in 1984.

Phoenix Racing Cloud Theron: When a teen commits matricide
How unusual is it for a teenage girl to kill her mother? There are no statistics for South Africa, but according to Johnston, it's a rare phenomenon. Johnston notes that in the United States, of all the murders where a child kills a parent, only 15 per cent involve a daughter killing a mother, and of those, less than a fifth involve a mother dying at the hands of her teen rather than adult daughter.[41]

Johnston adds that of the small number of teen girls who kill their mothers, almost half do so with an accomplice, and often that person is a boyfriend who 'sees himself as a rescuer'.[42] This resonates strongly with the case of Phoenix: the murder was rare in the sense that it saw a teenage girl killing her mother, but she had an accomplice in the form of Kyle Maspero, and he certainly posited himself as a 'rescuer' when he suggested they kill Rosemary, as both she (Phoenix) and her younger sister would be better off without her.

Another familiar component in situations where teenage girls murder their mothers is the type of home they've grown up in. Johnston writes that 'family dysfunction exists in virtually every household where a teen girl kills her mom'. But, she cautions, this is a risk factor and not a cause: 'There are a lot more problem-filled households than murderous teens.'[43]

That said, the more dysfunctional the home, the more the chance there is of matricide. Johnston says that girls can suddenly snap, and those who end up committing murder usually come from homes where 'family violence, substance abuse and multiple forms of abuse and neglect are present'.[44]

It is common cause that Phoenix experienced major neglect as a child, was sexually abused by two different people, and had no stability in her life whatsoever. All these might have impacted on her decision to commit murder. Del Fabbro says that 'the nature of trauma and severity of abuse that one may have experienced growing up' will vary between individuals and then intersect with their 'respective innate vulnerabilities' in terms of temperament or underlying psychiatric problems.

There are also individuals who come from an equally bad or traumatic background but do not follow the path that Phoenix chose. In such cases, 'there may have been some kind of moderating factors' to keep the person on track. These could include the influence of positive adults or caregivers such as 'family members or teachers', or the intervention of social welfare or healthcare services or 'even the criminal justice system earlier in their lives'. But, generally, 'the role of an abusive and neglecting upbringing in the development of personality pathology cannot be underestimated', says Del Fabbro, and frequently offenders have been victims of such behaviour in their early life.

Her childhood experiences and her youth were all taken into consideration when Phoenix was sentenced to an effective 15 years in prison. Says Phelps, 'Courts cannot be blunt tools of revenge' and must 'dispense with cases involving youths' in a way that increases their chance of 'successful rehabilitation to avoid repeat offending'.

Final word

The women in this book all committed murder, but they are all, as illustrated above, extremely different. During the writing of this book, I have immersed myself in their worlds. I have stayed up late and woken up early to delve into their lives, their relationships, their psychological histories and, ultimately, their acts of murder.

Many friends have asked me how I managed to process so many

harrowing stories in my mind over a relatively short space of time. That gave me pause for thought. These stories have certainly taken me into dark places where I have been shaken by what these murderers chose to do and how they went about doing it.

But the ironic twist is this: I have come out of the process with a very upbeat perception of the world, of humanity, and of women in particular. That's because stories like these are so few and far between.

Each time I emerged from my writing 'bubble', it was amazing to be out in the world surrounded by people who are just living their lives, without giving a single thought, as far as one can tell, to murdering another person.

The world is teeming with people who do not commit murder. For that we should all be grateful.

ACKNOWLEDGEMENTS

I would like to acknowledge the team at Jonathan Ball, especially Ester Levinrad and Aimee Carelse, for their consistent feedback and advice. My thanks also go to Jeremy Boraine and Ceri Prenter for their support, as well as to Alfred LeMaitre for the careful editing. I would also like to acknowledge forensic psychologist Giada del Fabbro, public law expert Kelly Phelps, and former South African Police Service forensic psychologist Gerard Labuschagne, for giving up their time for me to interview them for the Insights chapter. I am also very grateful to the Southern African Legal Information Institute for the invaluable court records they keep, as well as to Vanja Karth at the University of Cape Town for helping me source legal papers that were not readily available. I am further grateful to forensic profiler Micki Pistorius and many other experts whose academic and written work played a crucial role in my working through these stories. I am especially grateful to the various journalists, too many to mention here, whose reports on these murder cases were a rich source of information.

NOTES

CHAPTER 1 DAISY DE MELKER

1. MZ Tomlins, 'Daisy de Melker: South Africa's first serial killer', *Crime Magazine* (online), 2 December 2007. Available at www.crimemagazine.com/daisy-de-melker-south-africas-first-serial-killer-0, accessed on 26 May 2019.
2. 'Fanny Augusta Mathilda Hancorn-Smith', Geni online genealogy resource, 23 May 2018. Available at www.geni.com/people/Fanny-Hancorn-Smith/6000000009331802065, accessed on 19 April 2019.
3. B Grogan, 'Perceptions of Daisy de Melker: Representations of a sensational trial', *Journal of Southern African Studies*, vol 42, no 6 (November 2016), pp 1125–1142.
4. J Snow, 'Arsenic as a preservative of dead bodies', *The Lancet*, 10 November 1838.
5. R Marsh, 'South Africa's most famous poisoner', *Famous South African Crimes*, 2003. Available at www.africacrime-mystery.co.za/books/fsac/chp6.htm, accessed on 19 April 2019.

6   Ibid.
7   Tomlins, 'Daisy de Melker'.

CHAPTER 2   MARLENE LEHNBERG

1   'In the shadow of the noose: The Scissors Murder', *Flatnote Magazine*, 21 December 2015. Available at flatnote.co.za/scissors-murder/, accessed on 19 April 2019.
2   R Marsh. 'The "Scissors Murder"', *Famous South African Crimes*, 2009. Available at www.africacrime-mystery.co.za/books/fsac/chp18.htm, accessed on 19 April 2019.
3   Ibid.
4   'In the shadow of the noose'.
5   Ibid.
6   Ibid.
7   Ibid.
8   Ibid.
9   Ibid.
10 Marsh; 'The "Scissors Murder"'.
11 'In the shadow of the noose'.
12 Marsh, 'The "Scissors Murder"'.

CHAPTER 3   CHARMAINE PHILLIPS

1   Staff Reporter, 'Charmaine Phillips's love-child laid to rest', *IOL*, 25 March 2006. Available at www.iol.co.za/news/south-africa/charmaine-phillipss-love-child-laid-to-rest-270678, accessed on 19 April 2019.
2   E Ellis, 'Bloody trail of couple who put death on road', *Cape Argus*, 5 August 2004.
3   S-A Maritz, 'Women who kill: A psycho-legal literature review', unpublished MA thesis, Department of Psychology, Rand Afrikaans University, October 2003.
4   E Holtzhauzen, 'In court I understood why he killed for her', *Sunday Times Lifestyle*, 15 August 2004.

5   F Bridgland, 'Paintings are the path to killer's 20-year rehabilitation', *The Scotsman*, 23 August 2004.

6   Staff Reporter, 'Partner in crime's date with death', *Sunday Times Lifestyle*, 15 August 2004.

7   J Ancer; 'A bonny day for Charmaine Phillips', *IOL*, 8 August 2004. Available at www.iol.co.za/news/south-africa/a-bonny-day-for-charmaine-phillips-219135, accessed on 19 April 2019.

8   Bridgland, 'Paintings are the path to killer's 20-year rehabilitation'.

9   J Ancer, 'Trendy salon employs ex-con', *IOL*, 21 August 2004. Available at www.iol.co.za/news/south-africa/trendy-salon-employs-ex-con-charmaine-220043, accessed on 19 April 2019.

10 G Hosken, 'Brother of victim angry over killer's release', *IOL*, 21 August 2004. Available at www.iol.co.za/news/south-africa/brother-of-victim-angry-over-killers-release-220044, accessed on 19 April 2019.

11 Ibid.

CHAPTER 4   JOEY HAARHOFF

1   SABC Digital News, 'Daughter of notorious Haarhoff speaks', *Fokus*, 8 July 2016. Available at www.youtube.com/watch?v=AUKkS-Kdv6M, accessed on 25 April 2019.

2   J van der Merwe, 'Gert van Rooyen victim: Mom speaks', *You*, 6 July 2017.

3   SABC Digital News, 'The search for Gert van Rooyen's victims', *Fokus*, 18 June 2017. Available at www.youtube.com/watch?v=L5fqNr9sdbM&t=913s, accessed on 25 April 2019.

4   Uitenhage Forum, 'One who got away tells of her kidnap by Van Rooyen', blog post, 23 November 2009. Available at uitenhage.org.za/2009/11/one-who-got-away-tells-of-her-kidnap-by-van-rooyen/, accessed on 25 April 2019.

5   L Magnus, 'Happy sparks hope', *News24*, 23 May 2003.

6   B Stephenson, 'Psychic leads hunt for 6 girls missing for 30 years', *The Citizen*, 24 June 2017.

7   C Keeton, 'I'm a missing Gert van Rooyen girl', *Sunday Times*, 27 January 2019.
8   Ibid.
9   K Pillay, 'Fiona Harvey woman is an imposter', *The Witness*, 11 February 2019.

CHAPTER 5   DINA RODRIGUES

1   T Farber, 'The white lady of the necrothon', *Mail & Guardian*, 10 May 2005.
2   K Maughan, 'My little baby sister's no killer', *IOL*, 1 July 2005. Available at www.iol.co.za/news/south-africa/my-little-sisters-no-baby-killer-245263, accessed on 3 May 2019.
3   N Davids and B Makwabe, 'Moment of truth for baby killer Rodrigues', *Sunday Times*, 3 June 2007.
4   Maughan, 'My little baby sister's no killer'.
5   F Schroeder, 'Dina: Why I killed baby Jordan', *IOL*, 17 August 2013. Available at www.iol.co.za/news/dina-why-i-killed-baby-jordan-1563905, accessed on 3 May 2019.
6   Ibid.
7   K Maughan, 'I believed we were a match made in heaven', *IOL*, 8 May 2007. Available at www.iol.co.za/news/south-africa/i-believed-we-were-a-match-made-in-heaven-351917, accessed on 3 May 2019.
8   F Schroeder, 'Dina: Why I killed baby Jordan.
9   Ibid.
10 K Maughan, 'Book sheds light on baby Jordan', *IOL*, 1 December 2007. Available at www.iol.co.za/news/south-africa/book-sheds-light-on-baby-jordan-380971, accessed on 3 May 2019.
11 Ibid.
12 D Caelers and J Steele, 'I'm praying for you – Dina', *IOL*, 1 February 2006. Available at www.iol.co.za/news/south-africa/im-praying-for-you-dina-265151, accessed on 3 May 2019.
13 Maughan, 'Book sheds light on baby Jordan'.

14 Schroeder, 'Dina: Why I killed baby Jordan'.
15 Caelers and Steele, 'I'm praying for you'.
16 Schroeder, 'Dina: Why I killed baby Jordan'.
17 Ibid.
18 Ibid.
19 Farber, 'The white lady of the necrothon'.
20 W Roelf, 'Jordan-Leigh Norton: Anatomy of a murder', *Mail & Guardian*, 2 February 2006.
21 Caelers and Steele, 'I'm praying for you'.
22 Maughan, 'My little baby sister's no killer'.
23 High Court of South Africa (Western Cape High Court), *Mfazwe and Others* v *State* (A562/07) [2009] ZAWCHC 160; 2010 (1) SACR 504 (WCC) (29 October 2009). Available at www.saflii.org/za/cases/ZAWCHC/2009/160.html, accessed on 25 April 2019.
24 Ibid.
25 Staff Reporter, 'Father of murdered Baby Jordan testifies', *Mail & Guardian*, 8 February 2006
26 B Makwabe, 'Squalid lives of men hired to kill Jordan', *Sunday Times*, 13 May 2007.
27 Ibid.
28 Ibid.
29 Farber, 'The white lady of the necrothon'.
30 Makwabe, 'Squalid lives of men hired to kill Jordan'.
31 High Court of South Africa (Western Cape High Court), *Mfazwe and Others* v *State*.
32 Ibid.
33 Ibid.
34 Ibid.
35 Ibid.
36 Ibid.
37 Ibid.

CHAPTER 6 NAJWA PETERSEN

1. High Court of South Africa (Cape of Good Hope Division), *State* v *Petersen and Others* (02/08) [2008] ZAWCHC 64 (1 December 2008). Available at www.saflii.org/za/cases/ZAWCHC/2008/64.html, accessed on 25 April 2019.
2. BBC News, 'SA celebrity murdered in robbery', 17 December 2006. Available at news.bbc.co.uk/2/hi/africa/6188061.stm, accessed on 25 April 2019.
3. N Davids, 'Taliep Petersen: Tale of two wives', *Sunday Times*, 24 June 2007.
4. Staff Reporter, 'Taliep's daughter takes stand in Najwa trial', *Mail & Guardian*, 5 May 2008.
5. Ibid.
6. Ibid.
7. E Smook, 'Petersen intruders not real robbers', *Cape Argus*, 6 May 2008.
8. High Court of South Africa (Cape of Good Hope Division), *State* v *Petersen and Others*.
9. Staff Reporter, 'Taliep's daughter takes stand in Najwa trial'.
10. Staff Reporter, 'All I could see was blood', *News24*, 5 May 2008. Available at www.news24.com/SouthAfrica/News/All-I-could-see-was-blood-20080505, accessed on 3 May 2019.
11. Ibid.
12. K Breytenbach, 'Najwa's diamond scams', *IOL*, 29 July 2008. Available at www.iol.co.za/news/south-africa/najwas-diamond-scams-410124, accessed on 3 May 2019.
13. High Court of South Africa (Cape of Good Hope Division), *State* v *Petersen and Others*.
14. Ibid.
15. Ibid.
16. Ibid.
17. Ibid.
18. Ibid.

19 Ibid.
20 Ibid.
21 Ibid.
22 Ibid.
23 Ibid.
24 Ibid.

CHAPTER 7   CELIWE MBOKAZI

1   C Barron, 'Franz Richter: Pioneer of game tourism in SA', *Sunday Times*, 2 December 2007.
2   Ibid.
3   South Gauteng High Court, *State* v *Chirwa and Others* (SS118/2008) [2010] ZAGPJHC 168 (5 March 2010). Available at www.saflii.org/za/cases/ZAGPJHC/2010/168.html, accessed on 29 April 2019.
4   Ibid.
5   Ibid.
6   Ibid.
7   K Hawkey, 'Cleaning lady link to R1m fund', *Reef Metro*, 27 January 2008.
8   South Gauteng High Court, *State* v *Chirwa and Others*.
9   Ibid.
10 B Fraser, 'Family nightmare is finally over', *Sowetan*, 16 March 2010.
11 Hawkey, 'Cleaning lady link to R1m fund'.
12 Fraser, 'Family nightmare is finally over'.
13 South Gauteng High Court, *State* v *Chirwa and Others*.
14 Ibid.
15 Ibid.

CHAPTER 8   CHANÉ VAN HEERDEN

1   1 Corinthians 15:39.
2   J van der Merwe, *Grave Murder: The Story Behind the Brutal Welkom Killing*, Penguin Random House South Africa, 2015.

3   Sapa, 'Woman skinned occult victim', *IOL*, 22 November 2011. Available at www.iol.co.za/news/woman-skinned-occult-victim-1183921, accessed on 29 April 2019.
4   Van der Merwe, *Grave Murder*.
5   V Attwood, 'Under the skin of a killer', *Sunday Tribune*, 27 November 2011.
6   S Naik, 'Serial killer jailed for at least 20 years', *Saturday Star*, 26 November 2011.
7   Sapa, 'Occult killer shows no remorse', *Daily News*, 21 November 2011.
8   I Mahlangu, 'Loving pair held over grim killing', *Sunday Times*, 10 April 2011.
9   Ibid.
10 Naik, 'Serial killer jailed for at least 20 years'.
11 Ibid.
12 Van der Merwe, *Grave Murder*.
13 Ibid.
14 Attwood, 'Under the skin of a killer'.
15 Staff Reporter, 'Cemetery killer: We did it together', *News24*, 30 October 2012. Available at www.news24.com/southafrica/news/cemetery-killer-we-did-it-together-20121030, accessed on 29 April 2019.
16 Naik, 'Serial killer jailed for at least 20 years'.
17 Attwood, 'Under the skin of a killer'.
18 Sapa, 'Occult killer shows no remorse'.
19 All the details of the search effort were originally documented by Jana van der Merwe in *Grave Murder*.
20 Van der Merwe, *Grave Murder*.
21 Ibid.
22 Sapa, 'Occult killer shows no remorse'.
23 Naik, 'Serial killer jailed for at least 20 years'.
24 Ibid.

25 Mahlangu, 'Loving pair held over grim killing'.
26 For all direct quotes in this paragraph, see Mahlangu, 'Loving pair held over grim killing'.
27 Staff Reporter, 'Murderer to appear in 20 years', *The Citizen*, 28 November 2011.
28 M Simasiku, '*State* v *Chane van Heerden and Maartens van der Merwe*: The Welkom Cult Murder', *Khasho*, November/December 2011. Available at www.npa.gov.za/sites/default/files/newsletters/Khasho-November-December-2011.pdf, accessed on 29 April 2019.
29 Van der Merwe, *Grave Murder*.

CHAPTER 9   PHOENIX RACING CLOUD THERON

1 P Nombembe, 'Hippy killer to turn on ex-lover', *Sunday Times*, 4 May 2014.
2 Growth Mindset Podcast, 'What on earth is a rainbow gathering and why you need to go', 9 July 2018.
3 S Eggington, 'How do I come to terms with this?', *Sunday Times*, 6 October 2013.
4 Nombembe, 'Hippy killer to turn on ex-lover'.
5 Ibid.
6 C Ludick and J Kinnear, 'Murder accused's troubled life', *Weekend Argus*, 3 October 2015.
7 C Rice, 'Maspero guilty of killing girlfriend's mom', *IOL*, 7 October 2015. Available at www.iol.co.za/news/maspero-guilty-of-killing-girlfriends-mom-1926397, accessed on 29 April 2019.
8 Ibid.
9 C Vermaak, 'Youth describes murdering ex's mom', *Knysna-Plett Herald*, 8 October 2015. Available at www.knysnaplettherald.com/news/News/General/148909/Youth-describes-murdering-exs-mother, accessed on 2 May 2019.
10 Ibid.
11 Ibid.

12 Ibid.
13 J Hichens, 'R.I.P. Rosemary Theron, found murdered', *News24*, 8 October 2013. Available at www.news24.com/xArchive/Voices/rip-rosemary-theron-found-murdered-20180719, accessed on 29 April 2019.
14 Ibid.
15 M Hampton, 'Murder of ex-Knysna mom, Rosemary Theron, shocks and saddens Knysna', *MyNews24*, 3 October 2013. Available at www.news24.com/MyNews24/Murder-of-ex-Knysna-Mom-Rosemary-Theron-Shocks-and-Saddens-Knysna-20131003, accessed on 29 April 2019.
16 N Prince, 'Grief and relief as mom's body found', *Cape Argus*, 30 September 2013.
17 N Prince, 'Mom murder: Accused's family want answers', *Cape Argus*, 20 November 2013.
18 J Kinnear and W Martin, 'Memorial for slain mother', *Weekend Argus*, 12 October 2013.
19 C Ludick, 'Beach memorial for Rosemary Theron', *Knysna-Plett Herald*, 9 October 2013.
20 K Solomons, 'Phoenix's life of abuse', *Weekend Argus*, 3 May 2013.
21 N Prince, 'Theron murder: Teen sent to Valkenberg', *Cape Argus*, 9 June 2014.
22 Kyle Maspero's plea agreement statement, as detailed in the *Knysna-Plett Herald*, 8 October 2015. Available at www.knysnaplettherald.com/news/News/General/148909/Youth-describes-murdering-exs-mother, accessed on 2 May 2019.
23 Rice, C, 'Maspero sentenced to 13 years in jail', *IOL*, 9 December 2015. Available at www.iol.co.za/news/maspero-sentenced-to-13-years-in-jail-1957781, accessed on 29 April 2019.
24 Ibid.
25 Rice, C, 'Theron family angered by Maspero sentence', *IOL*, 9 December 2015. Available at www.iol.co.za/news/theron-family-angered-by-maspero-sentence-1957908, accessed on 25 May 2019.

CHAPTER 10   INSIGHTS

1. United Nations Office on Drugs and Crime, 'Global Study on Homicide 2013: Trends, context, data'. Available at www.unodc.org/documents/data-and-analysis/statistics/GSH2013/2014_GLOBAL_HOMICIDE_BOOK_web.pdf, accessed on 30 April 2019.
2. C Mims, 'Testosterone's bad rep', *Scientific American*, 1 August 2012.
3. All quotations from Giada del Fabbro are from an interview conducted with her by the author.
4. M Pistorius, *Fatal Females: Women Who Kill*, Penguin Random House South Africa, 2004, p 1. All quotations from Micki Pistorius are from this book.
5. Ibid.
6. Ibid, p 2.
7. Ibid.
8. A Africa, 'Women offenders' narratives of violent crime', unpublished PhD thesis, Department of Psychology, University of Cape Town, September 2011, p 12.
9. Pistorius, *Fatal Females*, p 10.
10. M Harrison, 'Female serial killers in the United States: Means, motives, and makings', *The Journal of Forensic Psychiatry & Psychology*, vol 26, no 3 (February 2015), pp 383–406.
11. B Parker, 'Seven deadly sins: Developing a qualitative understanding of homicide offender motive', unpublished PhD thesis, School of Justice, Faculty of Law, Queensland University of Technology, 2017.
12. See, for example, G Simon, 'Is psychopathy genetic?', blog post, 24 August 2012, Available at www.drgeorgesimon.com/is-psychopathy-genetic/, accessed on 6 May 2019.
13. School of Medicine and Public Health, University of Wisconsin-Madison, 'Psychopaths' brains show differences in structure and function', media release, 11 July 2017. Available at www.med.wisc.edu/news-and-events/2011/november/psychopaths-brains-differences-structure-function/, accessed on 6 May 2019.
14. Ibid.

15 Ibid.

16 R Felson, 'Anger, aggression, and violence in love triangles', *Violence and Victims*, vol 12, no 4 (1997), pp 345–362.

17 Pistorius, *Fatal Females*, p 74.

18 Ibid.

19 Ibid.

20 Ibid.

21 Ibid.

22 Ibid.

23 S Bonn, 'Why spree killers are not serial killers', *Psychology Today*, 21 July 2014.

24 Ibid.

25 Pistorius, *Fatal Females*, pp 270–275.

26 S-A Maritz, 'Women who kill: A psycho-legal literature review', unpublished MA thesis, Department of Psychology, Rand Afrikaans University, October 2003, pp 38–39.

27 Ibid.

28 Ibid.

29 J Johnston, 'Five myths about female serial killers', *Psychology Today*, 8 March 2018.

30 J Johnston, 'The psychology of murder for hire', *Psychology Today*, 23 March 2016.

31 Ibid.

32 D Wilson and M Rahman, 'Becoming a hitman', *The Howard Journal of Criminal Justice*, vol 54, no 3 (2015), pp 250–264

33 Africa, 'Women offenders' narratives of violent crime', p 1.

34 Staff Reporter, 'Najwa fit to stand trial, court finds', *Mail & Guardian*, 17 August 2007.

35 All quotations from Dr Gerard Labuschagne are from an interview conducted with him by the author.

36 T Farber, N Davids and A Hyman, 'What turns a husband into a killer', *Sunday Times*, 11 March 2018.

37 All quotations from Kelly Phelps are taken from an interview conducted with her by the author.
38 Sapa, 'Occult killer shows no remorse', *Daily News*, 21 November 2011.
39 Staff Reporter, 'Skinning murder unique, expert testifies', *News24*, 22 November 2011.
40 H Schechter, *Deviant: The Shocking True Story of Ed Gein, the Original 'Psycho'*, Gallery Books, 1998.
41 J Johnston, 'Matricide by teen girls', *Psychology Today*, 16 July 2012.
42 Ibid.
43 Ibid.
44 Ibid.

SOURCES

CHAPTER 1   DAISY DE MELKER

Afshari, R. 'The chronicle of arsenic poisoning in the 19th century'. *Asia Pacific Journal of Medical Toxicology*, vol 5, no 2 (Spring 2016), pp 36–41.

Beukes, L. *Maverick: Extraordinary Women from South Africa's Past*. Penguin Random House South Africa, 2005.

'Constitution Hill – The Women's Jail'. Official website of Constitution Hill, 2019. Available at www.constitutionhill.org.za/sites/site-womens-jail. Accessed on 3 May 2019.

'Daisy de Melker – Johannesburg's black widow'. Gauteng Tourism Authority official website, 2019. Available at www.gauteng.net/pages/daisy_de_melker. Accessed on 3 May 2019.

'Daisy de Melker, South African serial killer – 1932'. Blog post, The Unknown History of Misandry, 22 September 2011. Available at unknownmisandry.blogspot.com/search?q=daisy+de+melker. Accessed on 3 May 2019.

'Daisy Louisa Hancorn Smith'. British 1820 Settlers to South Africa, online resource, no date. Available at www.1820settlers.com/genealogy/getperson.php?personID=I67399&tree=master. Accessed on 3 May 2019.

'Fanny Augusta Mathilda Hancorn-Smith'. Geni online genealogy resource, 23 May 2018. Available at www.geni.com/people/Fanny-Hancorn-Smith/6000000009331802065. Accessed on 19 April 2019.

Farber, T. 'Daisy de Melker gave "care" of a special kind'. *Sunday Times*, 30 July 2017.

Grogan, B. 'Perceptions of Daisy de Melker: Representations of a sensational trial'. *Journal of Southern African Studies,* vol 42, no 6 (November 2016), pp 1125–1142.

Maritz, S-A. 'Women who kill: A psycho-legal literature review'. Unpublished MA thesis, Department of Psychology, Rand Afrikaans University, October 2003.

Marsh, R. 'South Africa's most famous poisoner'. Famous South African Crimes, 2003. Available at www.africacrime-mystery.co.za/books/fsac/chp6.htm. Accessed on 19 April 2019.

Pistorius, M. *Fatal Females: Women Who Kill*. Penguin Books, 2004.

Seal, L. *Women, Murder and Femininity: Gender Representations of Women Who Kill*. Palgrave Macmillan, 2010

Snow, J. 'Poisoning by arsenic'. *The Lancet*, 20 January 1838.

Tomlins, MZ. 'Daisy de Melker: South Africa's first serial killer'. *Crime Magazine* (online), 2 December 2007.

Wade, M. 'Myth, truth and the South African reality in the fiction of Sarah Gertrude Millin'. *Journal of Southern African Studies*, vol 1, no 1 (1974), pp 91–108.

Whitbourne, S. 'Can we identify psychopathy in a young child?'. *Psychology Today*, 26 November 2016.

CHAPTER 2   MARLENE LEHNBERG

Africa, A. 'Women offenders' narratives of violent crime'. Unpublished PhD thesis, Department of Psychology, University of Cape Town, September 2011.

Farber, T. 'Why women kill'. *Sunday Times*, 30 July 2017.

'In the shadow of the noose: The Scissors Murder'. *Flatnote Magazine*, 21 December 2015. Available at flatnote.co.za/scissors-murder/. Accessed on 19 April 2019.

Maritz, S-A. 'Women who kill: A psycho-legal literature review'. Unpublished MA thesis, Department of Psychology, Rand Afrikaans University, October 2003.

Marsh, R. 'The "Scissors Murder"'. *Famous South African Crimes*, 2009. Available at www.africacrime-mystery.co.za/books/fsac/chp18.htm. Aaccessed on 19 April 2019.

Pistorius, M. *Fatal Females: Women Who Kill*. Penguin Books, 2004.

CHAPTER 3   CHARMAINE PHILLIPS

Africa, A. 'Women offenders' narratives of violent crime'. Unpublished PhD thesis, Department of Psychology, University of Cape Town, September 2011.

Ancer, J. 'A bonny day for Charmaine Phillips'. *IOL*, 8 August 2004. Available at www.iol.co.za/news/south-africa/a-bonny-day-for-charmaine-phillips-219135. Accessed on 19 April 2019.

Ancer, J. 'Trendy salon employs ex-con'. *IOL*, 21 August 2004. Available at www.iol.co.za/news/south-africa/trendy-salon-employs-ex-con-charmaine-220043. Accessed on 19 April 2019.

Bridgland, F. 'Paintings are the path to killer's 20-year rehabilitation'. *The Scotsman*, 23 August 2004.

Ellis, E. 'Bloody trail of couple who put death on road'. *Cape Argus*, 5 August 2004.

Holtzhauzen, E. 'In court I understood why he killed for her'. *Sunday Times Lifestyle*, 15 August 2004.

Hosken, G. 'Brother of victim angry over killer's release'. *IOL*, 21 August 2004. Available at www.iol.co.za/news/south-africa/brother-of-victim-angry-over-killers-release-220044. Accessed on 19 April 2019.

Maritz, S-A. 'Women who kill: A psycho-legal literature review'.

Unpublished MA thesis, Department of Psychology, Rand Afrikaans University, October 2003.

Pistorius, M. *Fatal Females: Women Who Kill*. Penguin Books, 2004.

Staff Reporter. '"Bonnie" a free woman'. *News24*, 20 August 2004. Available at www.news24.com/SouthAfrica/News/Bonnie-a-free-woman-20040820. Accessed on 3 May 2019.

Staff Reporter. 'Charmaine Phillips's love-child laid to rest'. *IOL*, 25 March 2006. Available at www.iol.co.za/news/south-africa/charmaine-phillipss-love-child-laid-to-rest-270678. Accessed on 19 April 2019.

Staff Reporter. 'Partner in crime's date with death'. *Sunday Times Lifestyle*, 15 August 2004.

CHAPTER 4   JOEY HAARHOFF

Farber, T. 'The life of Mark Scott-Crossley'. *Sowetan*, 23 December 2016.

Keeton, C. 'I'm a missing Gert van Rooyen girl'. *Sunday Times*, 27 January 2019.

Magnus, L. 'Happy sparks hope'. *News24*, 23 May 2003.

Pillay, K. 'Fiona Harvey woman is an imposter'. *The Witness*, 11 February 2019.

SABC Digital News. 'Daughter of notorious Haarhoff speaks'. *Fokus*, 8 July 2016. Available at www.youtube.com/watch?v=AUKkS-Kdv6M. Accessed on 25 April 2019.

SABC Digital News. 'The search for Gert van Rooyen's victims'. *Fokus*, 18 June 2017. Available at www.youtube.com/watch?v=L5fqNr9sdbM&t=913s. Accessed on 25 April 2019.

Smillie, S. 'They have to be somewhere: Fresh bid to find Gert van Rooyen's victims'. *Saturday Star*, 12 January 2019.

Stephenson, B. 'Psychic leads hunt for 6 girls missing for 30 years'. *The Citizen*, 24 June 2017.

Uitenhage Forum. 'One who got away tells of her kidnap by Van Rooyen'. Blog post, 23 November 2009. Available at uitenhage.org.za/2009/11/one-who-got-away-tells-of-her-kidnap-by-van-rooyen/. Accessed on 25 April 2019.

Van de Spuy, C and A van der Westhuyzen. *Battered, Abused, Shamed: Joey Haarhoff Was My Mother*. Lapa Publishers. 2016.

Waterworth, T. 'Could the sands be holding Gert van Rooyen's secrets?'. *IOL*, 17 June 2017. www.iol.co.za/news/could-the-sands-be-holding-gertvanrooyens-secrets-9827931. Accessed on 3 May 2019.

Wicks, J. 'A close encounter with killer'. *The Witness*, 19 December 2014. Available at www.news24.com/Archives/Witness/A-close-encounter-with-killer-20150430. Accessed on 3 May 2019.

Wicks, J. 'Bodies of suspected serial killer's victims still missing'. *Sunday Times*, 18 June 2017.

Wicks, J. 'Fiona: the search continues'. *The Witness*, 18 December 2014. Available at www.news24.com/Archives/Witness/Fiona-the-search-continues-20150430. Accessed on 3 May 2019.

Wicks, J. 'Police dig up beach looking for serial killer's victims'. *TimesLive*, 14 June 2007. Available at www.timeslive.co.za/news/2017-06-14-police-dig-up-beach-looking-for-serial-killers-victims/. Accessed on 3 May 2019.

Wicks, J. 'Sniffer dogs sent in at Van Rooyen beach excavation site'. *TimesLive*, 15 June 2007. Available at www.timeslive.co.za/news/2017-06-15-sniffer-dogs-sent-in-at-van-rooyen-beach-excavation-site/. Accessed on 3 May 2019.

CHAPTER 5 DINA RODRIGUES

Caelers, D and J Steele. 'I'm praying for you – Dina'. *IOL*, 1 February 2006. Available at www.iol.co.za/news/south-africa/im-praying-for-you-dina-265151. Accessed on 3 May 2019.

Davids, N and B Makwabe. 'Moment of truth for baby killer Rodrigues'. *Sunday Times*, 3 June 2007.

Farber, T. 'The white lady of the necrothon'. *Mail & Guardian*, 10 May 2005.

High Court of South Africa (Western Cape High Court). *Mfazwe and Others* v *State* (A562/07) [2009] ZAWCHC 160; 2010 (1) SACR 504 (WCC) (29 October 2009). Available at www.saflii.org/za/cases/ZAWCHC/2009/160.html. Accessed on 25 April 2019.

Makwabe, B. 'Squalid lives of men hired to kill Jordan'. *Sunday Times*, 13 May 2007.

Maughan, K. 'My little baby sister's no killer'. *IOL*, 1 July 2005. Available at www.iol.co.za/news/south-africa/my-little-sisters-no-baby-killer-245263. Accessed on 3 May 2019.

Maughan, K. 'I believed we were a match made in heaven'. *IOL*, 8 May 2007. Available at www.iol.co.za/news/south-africa/i-believed-we-were-a-match-made-in-heaven-351917. Accessed on 3 May 2019.

Maughan, K. 'Book sheds light on baby Jordan'. *IOL*, 1 December 2007. Available at www.iol.co.za/news/south-africa/book-sheds-light-on-baby-jordan-380971. Accessed on 3 May 2019.

Roelf, W. 'Jordan-Leigh Norton: Anatomy of a murder'. *Mail & Guardian*, 2 February 2006.

Schroeder, F. 'Dina: Why I killed baby Jordan'. *IOL*, 17 August 2013. Available at www.iol.co.za/news/dina-why-i-killed-baby-jordan-1563905. Accessed on 3 May 2019.

CHAPTER 6   NAJWA PETERSEN

BBC News. 'SA celebrity murdered in robbery', 17 December 2006. Available at news.bbc.co.uk/2/hi/africa/6188061.stm. Accessed on 25 April 2019.

Breytenbach, K. 'Najwa's diamond scams'. *IOL*, 29 July 2008. Available at www.iol.co.za/news/south-africa/najwas-diamond-scams-410124. Accessed on 3 May 2019.

Davids, N. 'Taliep Petersen: Tale of two wives'. *Sunday Times*, 24 June 2007.

Eggington, S. 'Back on stage in spirit with slain dad Taliep'. *Sunday Times*, 1 December 2013.

Ferreira, A. 'Engaging co-operative – Petersen will stand trial'. *Sunday Times*, 1 September 2009.

High Court of South Africa (Cape of Good Hope Division). *State* v *Petersen and Others* (02/08) [2008] ZAWCHC 64 (1 December 2008).

Available at www.saflii.org/za/cases/ZAWCHC/2008/64.html. Accessed on 25 April 2019.

Staff Reporter. 'All I could see was blood'. *News24*, 5 May 2008. Available at www.news24.com/SouthAfrica/News/All-I-could-see-was-blood-20080505. Accessed on 3 May 2019.

Staff Reporter. 'Taliep's daughter takes stand in Najwa trial'. *Mail & Guardian*, 5 May 2008.

Voice of the Cape. 'My father's murder is an everyday struggle'. 17 December 2016.

CHAPTER 7   CELIWE MBOKAZI

Barron, C. 'Franz Richter: Pioneer of game tourism in SA'. *Sunday Times*, 2 December 2007.

Fraser, B. 'Family nightmare is finally over'. *Sowetan*, 16 March 2010.

Hawkey, K. 'Cleaning lady link to R1m fund'. *Reef Metro*, 27 January 2008.

South Gauteng High Court. *State* v *Chirwa and Others* (SS118/2008) [2010] ZAGPJHC 168 (5 March 2010). Available at www.saflii.org/za/cases/ZAGPJHC/2010/168.html, accessed on 29 April 2019.

CHAPTER 8   CHANÉ VAN HEERDEN

Attwood, V. 'Under the skin of a killer'. *Sunday Tribune*, 27 November 2011.

Mahlangu, I. 'Loving pair held over grim killing'. *Sunday Times*, 10 April 2011.

Naik, S. 'Serial killer jailed for at least 20 years'. *Saturday Star*, 26 November 2011.

Sapa. 'Occult killer shows no remorse'. *Daily News*, 21 November 2011.

Sapa. 'Woman skinned occult victim'. *IOL*, 22 November 2011. Available at www.iol.co.za/news/woman-skinned-occult-victim-1183921. Accessed on 29 April 2019.

Simasiku, M. 'State v Chane van Heerden and Maartens van der Merwe: The Welkom cult murder'. *Khasho*, November/December 2011.

Available at www.npa.gov.za/sites/default/files/newsletters/Khasho-November-December-2011.pdf. Accessed on 29 April 2019.

Staff Reporter. 'Cemetery killer: We did it together'. *News24*, 30 October 2012. Available at www.news24.com/southafrica/news/cemetery-killer-we-did-it-together-20121030, accessed on 29 April 2019.

Staff Reporter. 'Murderer to appear in 20 years'. *The Citizen*, 28 November 2011.

Van der Merwe, J. *Grave Murder: The Story Behind the Brutal Welkom Killing*, Penguin Random House South Africa, 2015.

CHAPTER 9   PHOENIX RACING CLOUD THERON

Eggington, S. 'How do I come to terms with this?'. *Sunday Times*, 6 October 2013.

Growth Mindset Podcast. 'What on earth is a rainbow gathering and why you need to go', 9 July 2018.

Hampton, M. 'Murder of ex-Knysna mom, Rosemary Theron, shocks and saddens Knysna'. *MyNews24*, 3 October 2013. Available at www.news24.com/MyNews24/Murder-of-ex-Knysna-Mom-Rosemary-Theron-Shocks-and-Saddens-Knysna-20131003. Accessed on 29 April 2019.

Hichens, J. 'R.I.P. Rosemary Theron, found murdered'. *News24*, 8 October 2013. Available at www.news24.com/xArchive/Voices/rip-rosemary-theron-found-murdered-20180719. Accessed on 29 April 2019.

Kinnear, J and W Martin. 'Memorial for slain mother'. *Weekend Argus*, 12 October 2013.

Ludick, C. 'Beach memorial for Rosemary Theron'. *Knysna-Plett Herald*, 9 October 2013.

Ludick, C and J Kinnear. 'Murder accused's troubled life'. *Weekend Argus*, 3 October 2015.

Nombembe, P. 'Hippy killer to turn on ex-lover'. *Sunday Times*, 4 May 2014.

Prince, N. 'Grief and relief as mom's body found'. *Cape Argus*, 30 September 2013.

Prince, N. 'Mom murder: accused's family want answers'. *Cape Argus*, 20 November 2013.

Prince, N. 'Theron murder: teen sent to Valkenberg'. *Cape Argus*, 9 June 2014.

Rice, C. 'Maspero guilty of killing girlfriend's mom'. *IOL*, 7 October 2015. Available at www.iol.co.za/news/maspero-guilty-of-killing-girlfriends-mom-1926397. Accessed on 29 April 2019.

Rice, C. 'Maspero sentenced to 13 years in jail'. *IOL*, 9 December 2015. Available at www.iol.co.za/news/maspero-sentenced-to-13-years-in-jail-1957781. Accessed on 29 April 2019.

Solomons, K. 'Phoenix's life of abuse'. *Weekend Argus*, 3 May 2013.

Vermaak, C. 'Youth describes murdering ex's mom'. *Knysna-Plett Herald*, 8 October 2015. Available at www.knysnaplettherald.com/news/News/General/148909/Youth-describes-murdering-exs-mother. Accessed on 2 May 2019. (Note: contains Kyle Maspero's plea agreement statement.)

H Shechter, *Deviant: The Shocking True Story of Ed Gein, the Original 'Psycho'*, Gallery Books, 1998.

CHAPTER 10   INSIGHTS

Africa, A. 'Women offenders' narratives of violent crime'. Unpublished PhD thesis, Department of Psychology, University of Cape Town, September 2011

Bonn, S. 'Why spree killers are not serial killers'. *Psychology Today*, 21 July 2014.

Farber, T, N Davids and A Hyman. 'What turns a husband into a killer'. *Sunday Times*, 11 March 2018.

Felson, R. 'Anger, aggression, and violence in love triangles'. *Violence and Victims*, vol 12, no 4 (1997), pp 345–362.

Harrison, M. 'Female serial killers in the United States: means, motives, and makings'. *The Journal of Forensic Psychiatry & Psychology*, vol 26, no 3 (February 2015), pp 383–406.

Johnston, J. 'Five myths about female serial killers'. *Psychology Today*, 8 March 2018.

Johnston, J. 'Matricide by teen girls'. *Psychology Today*, 16 July 2012.

Johnston, J. 'The psychology of murder for hire'. *Psychology Today*, 23 March 2016.

Maritz, S-A. 'Women who kill: A psycho-legal literature review'. Unpublished MA thesis, Department of Psychology, Rand Afrikaans University, October 2003.

Mims, C. Testosterone's bad rep'. *Scientific American*, 1 August 2012.

Parker, B. 'Seven deadly sins: Developing a qualitative understanding of homicide offender motive'. Unpublished PhD thesis, School of Justice, Faculty of Law, Queensland University of Technology, 2017.

Pistorius, M. *Fatal Females: Women Who Kill*. Penguin Books, 2004.

Sapa. 'Occult killer shows no remorse'. *Daily News*, 21 November 2011.

H Schechter. *Deviant: The Shocking True Story of Ed Gein, the Original 'Psycho'*. Gallery Books, 1998.

School of Medicine and Public Health, University of Wisconsin-Madison. 'Psychopaths' brains show differences in structure and function'. Media release, 11 July 2017. Available at www.med.wisc.edu/news-and-events/2011/november/psychopaths-brains-differences-structure-function/. Accessed on 6 May 2019.

Simon, G. 'Is psychopathy genetic?' Blog post, 24 August 2012, Available at www.drgeorgesimon.com/is-psychopathy-genetic/. Accessed on 6 May 2019.

Staff Reporter. 'Najwa fit to stand trial, court finds'. *Mail & Guardian*, 17 August 2007.

Staff Reporter. 'Skinning murder unique, expert testifies'. *News24*, 22 November 2011.

United Nations Office on Drugs and Crime. 'Global Study on Homicide 2013: Trends, context, data'. Available at www.unodc.org/documents/data-and-analysis/statistics/GSH2013/2014_GLOBAL_HOMICIDE_BOOK_web.pdf. Accessed on 30 April 2019.

Wilson, D and M Rahman. 'Becoming a hitman'. *The Howard Journal of Criminal Justice*, vol 54, no 3 (2015), pp 250–264.

INTERVIEWS
Gerard Labuschagne
Giada del Fabbro
Kelly Phelps

www.ingramcontent.com/pod-product-compliance
Lightning Source LLC
Chambersburg PA
CBHW071000160426
43193CB00012B/1856